Bargaining for Reality

For Michael,
with best
wishes, Larry

Lawrence Rosen

Bargaining for Reality
The Construction of
Social Relations in a
Muslim Community

The University of Chicago Press
Chicago and London

LAWRENCE ROSEN is professor of anthropology at Princeton University.

The University of Chicago Press, Chicago 60637
The University of Chicago Press, Ltd., London
© 1984 by The University of Chicago
All rights reserved. Published 1984
Printed in the United States of America

93 92 91 90 89 88 87 86 85 84   54321

Library of Congress Cataloging in Publication Data
Rosen, Lawrence, 1941–
    Bargaining for reality.

    Bibliography: p.
    Includes index.
    1. Sefrou (Morocco)—Social life and customs.
I. Title.
DT329.S44R67   1984   306′.0964′3   84-2501
ISBN 0-226-72609-6
ISBN 0-226-72611-8 (pbk.)

For my parents
George Rosen and Hannah Persky Rosen

Contents

Preface

This study of the social life of the Moroccan city of Sefrou and its region focuses on the ways a set of cultural concepts is drawn on in negotiating interpersonal relations. It attempts to pursue the proposition that the people of this community create their social reality by constantly bargaining over and through the terms that compose it. It is a process and a world of enormous subtlety and vitality, and my own view of that world is based, among other factors, on a number of experiences and associations.

My fieldwork in Morocco was carried out during three separate periods: for twenty months from January 1966 to August 1967, during three months of the summer of 1969, and for the four months of June through September 1978. During each period I lived in different parts of the city of Sefrou while making frequent trips to a cluster of Arabic- and Berber-speaking settlements in the nearby countryside. I had studied colloquial Moroccan Arabic for three months before going to Morocco, and after my arrival in Sefrou I continued work on the language with several local teachers. Except for rare instances when government officials chose to use French, my research was conducted entirely in colloquial Moroccan Arabic (*dārija*).

It was with great effort and imagination that many Moroccans sought to make their language and culture comprehensible to me. Mustafa Benyaklef, then a graduate student in Chicago and now the director of the Institut National de Statistique et Economie Appliquée, was my first language teacher, and the grace and energy with which he introduced me to the language and customs of Morocco set a tone of generosity and conviviality that has stayed with me over the years. In Sefrou I continued to study the language with local teachers and began my anthropological inquiries. I paid the informants with whom I worked regularly. They, like everyone I encountered, understood

very clearly what it meant to study the customs of other people since knowledge of others' ways is a vital element in the store of information they seek in
their own lives. I can only say that the friendships I developed went far beyond the instruction they gave me.

The matter of identifying my informants by name, however, creates a slight
problem. I asked every informant I worked with if I could use his or her name,
and without exception they agreed. Many people were surprised that I would
consider not using their names: the idea of anonymity or a pseudonym seemed
to call into question the credibility of anything I might attribute to them.
Indeed, they would often ask me to pull out my notebook and make certain I
recorded something accurately if the matter came up during a casual moment.
On certain occasions people would specifically ask me not to mark something
down and I respected their wishes. Notwithstanding the permission they gave
me, I feel it would be inappropriate to identify informants by name: there
were undoubtedly moments when, had the issue arisen, they might have indicated a desire to remain anonymous, and there are places in this study where
they might feel their privacy affected by reference to statements made about
them by others. I have, therefore, chosen not to identify any of my informants
by name and have, on occasion, altered minor facts in order to preserve this
anonymity. In doing so I hope they will understand that hiding their names is
intended as a mark of my respect, my gratitude, and my affection.

Sefrou is only a small part of Morocco, much less of the Arab world, and,
like any anthropologist, my analysis is at once restricted to this single place
yet intended to cast light on a far broader realm. Often I will refer to Arabs,
the Near East, or the Islamic religion in very general terms. Perhaps the reader
would be well-advised to treat these comments like those of a modern Parson
Thwackum and to remember that when I mention the Middle East I mean the
country of Morocco, and not only the country of Morocco but the region of
Sefrou, and not only the region of Sefrou but those people who were patient
enough to tolerate my inquiries. Like Fielding's parson, however, I believe
that through the focus of this one place much can be seen; but unlike his, I
hope my claims will appear neither dogmatic nor overblown.

If there are people in Sefrou who must remain unnamed there are teachers
and colleagues whose help I am pleased to acknowledge. In the mid-1960s a
number of young American scholars in various disciplines began to work in
Morocco. We were then, as we have been over the years, the beneficiaries
of the knowledge and advice of our predecessors in the field. In particular,
Ernest Gellner and David Hart have given unstintingly of their experience and
ideas, and I am much indebted to them. Among my fellow Moroccanists I
have gained much from my discussions with Kenneth Brown, Edmund Burke
III, Vincent Crapanzano, Abdullah Hammoudi, Ross Dunn, Daisy Dwyer,
Dale Eickelman, Paul Rabinow, Amal Rassam, and John Waterbury. Maurice
Flory and the staff of the library at the Centre de Recherches et d'Etudes sur

les Sociétés Méditerranéenes at the Université de Aix-Marseilles, the staff at the Centre des Hautes Etudes sur L'Afrique et l'Asie Moderne in Paris, and the archivists at the Alliance Israélite Universelle were most helpful with my research. In Morocco I am particularly grateful to the Ministry of Interior, the Ministry of Justice, and the municipal, rural, and court officials of Sefrou for their hospitality and assistance. At Princeton University I have had the help of many colleagues: Roy Mottahedeh and A. L. Udovitch have been especially helpful over the years in sharing with me their insights into the history and culture of the Middle East. In the preparation of the manuscript I have also benefited from the skill and patience of Pauline Caulk and Anne Benson.

Financial support for my research was supplied over the years by the National Institutes of Health, the University of Illinois, and the American Council of Learned Societies, while support for the preparation of the manuscript came from a John Simon Guggenheim Foundation Fellowship and the John D. and Catherine T. MacArthur Foundation Award. A portion of the manuscript was completed in the idyllic surroundings of the Rockefeller Foundation Study Center at Bellagio, Italy. To each of these foundations, to their directors and staff, I can only express my sincerest gratitude.

Three people must receive special thanks. My wife, Mary Beth Rose, not only shared with me the field experience of 1978 but has, through her understanding of literature and cultural styles, contributed more to the development of this manuscript than I can ever properly acknowledge. Without her innate anthropological sensibility, her patience, and her strength, my own understanding of Morocco and its people would have been much diminished.

I learned how to be an anthropologist as much from Hildred Geertz as from anyone else. Her work in Sefrou, where we overlapped several months at the beginning of my research, demonstrated to me a style of inquiry and an appreciation for oral and documentary evidence that has served as a model ever since. Her critical sense and her lively intelligence have made her a cherished colleague and friend.

It is to Clifford Geertz that I owe my greatest debt. It was he who invited me to work with him in Sefrou and it is he from whom I have gained so much of my orientation in the discipline. We were only in the field for a few months at the same time but his gentle direction, his egalitarianism, and his open-mindedness were the perfect stimulus to one just learning the ropes. In the years since he has never failed to share his insights into many subjects, and I am eternally in his debt for opening to me the fascinating worlds of Sefrou and his own mind.

In an earlier publication, *Meaning and Order in Moroccan Society,* Clifford Geertz, Hildred Geertz, and I recorded a number of our findings about the Sefrou region. Readers of the present work should perhaps bear in mind that it was our intention in co-authoring that book to make available a wider range of data than monographs such as this can adequately communicate. Specific reference will be made in the present study to information contained in that joint effort, but many of the interpretations presented here will find further factual support in the essays contained in the earlier work. Some parts of the present volume have also appeared in my previous publications, specifically those listed in the reference list under my name as 1968a, 1970, 1972a, 1972b, 1973, 1978, 1979, 1980–81, and 1985. Excerpts from these articles are reprinted here by agreement with the original publishers.

The system used here for transcribing Arabic words follows that adopted in the co-authored volume mentioned above. Briefly, the transcription, with certain minor alterations made for colloquial Moroccan Arabic pronunciation, is the one utilized by Hans Wehr in his *Dictionary of Modern Written Arabic:* the use of a short *e* to indicate that the vowel in Moroccan Arabic is even shorter than in modern literary Arabic, the omission of those emphatic vowels that do not appear in Moroccan Arabic, and the transcription of definite articles as *l-, š-, b-l, d-, j-, r-,* and *ṭ-*. On its initial appearance in the text each Arabic word will be transcribed with full diacritics according to this system. Thereafter, it will appear in a form more readily accessible to English-speakers or in a mode of transcription more commonly employed in the literature. Thus *mrabíṭ* will become marabout and *šīk* will become sheikh. Generally speaking, *ḵ* will become kh, *š* will become sh, *ḡ* will become gh, and *ḥ* will become h. In the index the formal spelling will be utilized and the page on which the fullest definition of the term appears will be highlighted. By this system it is hoped that Arabic scholars will have no difficulty identifying words and comparing them to the entries in the Wehr dictionary, *The Encyclopaedia of Islam* or other standard reference works, while the ordinary reader will not be distracted from the central issues with which we will be concerned.

One

Bargaining for Reality

The Nature of the Problem

When I arrived in the small Moroccan city of Sefrou in the mid-1960s it was only natural that, as an anthropologist interested in the social organization of a traditional Muslim city and its hinterland, I looked for the social groups to which people belonged and the categories and principles by which these families, tribes, quarters, and brotherhoods were ordered. In a very short time, however, it became apparent that the presumed subjects of my study, social groups, were far less corporeal and durable than current ethnography and theory had suggested. Whether it was a tribal fraction described by informants as linked to others by a specified principle yet almost never operating according to it or an extended family said to possess corporate characteristics yet fraught with contrary personal arrangements, the simplest inquiry into actual relationships and events was sufficient to dissolve my presumed units of analysis into atomized and seemingly disconnected parts. It was not that people failed to acknowledge perduring ties with others, but that their actions could not be contained by a set of limitations associated with familial or tribal affiliation. It was not that people failed to evince a definite set of ideas about the nature of humanity and their ties to each other, but that the concepts themselves, far from being closed and ready for application, were no more severely constricted than the arrangements people created through them. Everywhere I looked I was struck by the extent to which social life and the ideas that informed it possessed an open, malleable quality that took shape only as these concepts and relationships became attached to and identified with the lives of individual men and women. Clearly, I thought, a credible account of Sefrou would require both a point of entry and an analytic framework that would not do violence to this highly individuated, capacious enactment of social relations and the concrete yet open-ended set of concepts through which the people of Sefrou create a meaningful world.

No single theory of social organization or descriptive analogy seemed entirely appropriate. Depending on the theorist, societies have been said to possess a "structure" that resides in the rules by which groups are composed and directed, to be governed by the formulas that unite disparate elements of individual and collective endeavor, to be reducible to the statistical frequency with which particular patterns of behavior occur, or to be characterized by the range of beliefs, ideas, and values enclosed in a word, an artifact, or a style and joined together by a common logic or design. Yet as much as each approach cast valuable light on the connections that bind the parts of a culture to one another, the choice of an entrée, a conceptual framework for understanding this particular society, remained elusive. For just as corporate social groups, observed closely, dissipated under the daily implementation of individual choice and open manipulation, so too the words Moroccans used to describe and enact their relationships—from specific kin terms to notions of "obligation," "right," and "group feeling"—were subject to multifarious meanings and attachments. What seemed initially to be a problem of incomplete fluency that could be solved by collecting enough information about all possible groupings, modes of social manipulation, or comprehensible linguistic usages came instead to appear attributable to a flawed perspective. Just as it may be error in science to attempt simultaneously to plot the position of an object and to measure its velocity, so too it began to seem mistaken, in the realm of Sefrou social life, to try to capture from a single perspective the ongoing creation of social relations and the patterns that could be observed at any given moment. What was needed, rather, was an orientation and a chosen set of cultural attributes that would allow me to move back and forth between form and process, concept and enactment, individual effort and collective attachment in such a way as to capture the living quality of my subject. In constructing an appropriate perspective, several features of Moroccan life could not help but impress themselves on me.

Students of the Middle East have long noted the personalistic nature of Arab thought and culture. Whether in the Islamic religion where each individual approaches God directly, or in the stories, poems, and songs where individual word and deed are central, the unifying point for the disparate elements of life resides in the single person. Similarly, in politics or social relationships, culturally ascribed qualities were seldom referred to in the abstract, unconnected from a particular person; rather they came to mean something, to count for something, to *be* something only as they formed part of an amalgam that rested in and characterized the relationships of a named individual. This style of individuals set in a distinct, yet loosely structured framework, of the individual as the fundamental unit of social relations and cultural logic, and of the broad design informing the particular rather than the other way around, seemed to clarify what might otherwise appear to be a society and a mode of thought of almost atomistic design.

I also began to see that integral to the unification of the social and conceptual domains of Sefrou life was the role played by language in the formation of social relations. There is, of course, nothing mysterious about the central role of speech in Middle Eastern societies, notwithstanding certain myths that surround the Arabic language: that the lexicon of Arabic—from the subtlety of its political distinctions to its prodigious enumeration of the camel's delights—renders it beyond the grasp of those who do not entwine their lives with it, that every speaker of the tongue is either a renowned orator or a poet manqué, that the structure of the language is consonant with the true workings of the Arab mind, or that only the form of Arabic used in one's own natal region conforms to that spoken by the Prophet Muhammad. Yet even these exaggerations underscore the importance Arabs attach to the implementation of their language. As I watched the people of Sefrou maneuver within the range of terms and meanings available for the characterization of their relationships, I saw that linguistic usages were not simply labels attached to an available array of social positions and roles but were integral to the very creation of those ties. Every linguistic practice was redolent of a theory of language as a vehicle of social creativity. To watch two Moroccans expend a great deal of time groping for a way of characterizing the relationship they would form or acknowledge was to see that utterances may be forms of action and not merely labels or reflections of some underlying reality; to hear people argue over the meaning a term will have for their particular situation was to comprehend that the use of a word or a sentence tells more about its meaning than grammar or syntax alone can convey; to note how men and women might vary the applicability of recognized concepts was to observe in its natural setting that language may be constitutive of the very reality it seeks to describe.

Indeed, there were two particular qualities of language as used in Sefrou that were especially noteworthy. Many of the terms used by the people of Sefrou to categorize their relations with each other were, by their very nature, open-ended—capable of being extended and manipulated in a number of different, even contradictory, ways. A concept like "cousin" or "tribal fraction" could, therefore, apply narrowly or broadly, or be used to encompass or orient a diverse range of meanings. Indeed, these meanings were not fixed and limited by a settled repertoire but could be worked and reworked as situation and circumstance demanded. Friedrich Waismann had referred to this flexibility as the "open texture" of a term, a quality that allows concepts to be extended in directions that are not set in advance and that can never be reduced to a closed or simple definition (Waismann 1960). But where all languages may possess an element of open texture, in Sefrou this quality appeared to form a central feature of those terms for relationship that are far more restrictive and determinate in other cultures. And where many linguists and anthropologists have noted the existence of "loosely structured" social relations or the open texture of key concepts, few have pursued the implications of this finding for an understanding of the distinctive quality of a culture, preferring instead to return to the familiar terrain of resultant groups, rules of recruitment, or the internal logic of cultural abstractions. The more I was confronted by the astonishing malleability of social relations and the supple yet distinct shape of their conceptual surround, the more I appreciated the need to take seriously the idea that the open-ended quality of Moroccan concepts was integral to the shape of Moroccan social relations.

But there was also a second, deeper quality that suggested itself, a quality that seemed central to the design and enactment of the everyday life of a community in which the use of language was vital to the construction of social ties. For although the concepts that serve to shape relationships in Sefrou appeared open textured, they also appeared to acquire meaning not as the result of mechanical application but as the result of a distinct process of negotiation. It was not only that individuals drew on the relations and concepts available to them or even that they could on occasion dicker with one another over their mutual obligations. Rather, the process of bargaining out the terms of their relations, the definition of their situation, and the implications of their attachment were at the heart of the way such ties were conceived and formed. The terms of relationship acquired meaning only as the bargains struck in and through them took shape. Reality for the Moroccan is the distribution of ties that he or she possesses to others. And that reality is achieved through a process of negotiating the meaning of the terms and relationships of which it is composed.

The image of bargaining is, of course, a familiar one for the Arab world. From the haggling that takes place in the market to the mediation of tribal or familial disputes, bargaining appears as a theme of broad application. To say that language is a critical instrument for negotiating interpersonal ties and that, more to the point, this negotiability is inscribed in the nature and use of Moroccan Arabic does not mean that only from this vantage can Sefrou society be understood. However, by following through with some rigor the implications of this theme, it may be possible to cast additional light on our understanding of this energetic and elusive social form.

Ideally, every anthropologist or linguist would hope to follow, through documentary if not firsthand experience, the shifts and variations that occur in the language and relationships that interest him. However, the lives of the Sefrou people have been available to me only for a limited number of years, and I cannot hope in such a compass to capture all of its mutations or transformations. Through their enacted concepts—through the semantic range of their terms and the array of their constructed ties—the image of a society presents itself to the investigator's eye. In taking such a cross section of time and society, what is revealed, as one commentator has noted, is a surface that appears static only at the macroscopic level: observed closely, arrayed before our view and challenging our imagination is a "surface seething with life and movement" (Izutsu 1964, 38). It is to an understanding of this life, this movement, this constant quest for a reality of their own making—so vivid to our experience, so alluring to our comprehension—that the present study of the people who live in the Sefrou region is directed.

Sefrou: The Cultural and Social Landscape

The city of Sefrou is located some fifteen miles south of Fez, at the base of the foothills leading into the Middle Atlas Mountains. Viewed from the surrounding hills, the sharply bounded periphery of irrigated gardens and the whitewashed city they enfold might seem to form an isolated entity set off, whether as refuge or precipitate, from the arid countryside beyond. Indeed, nature and culture may here seem to have conspired to fashion an environment of unavoidable contrast and constraint: the oasis, its gardens irrigated by the waters that bubble up from the foot of the mountains to form a river that cuts through the heart of the old city, set against the slopes and pastures of the surrounding plains and hills dependent, as they are, on an irregular fall of rain; the institutions and amenities of urban life—the mosques, baths, cafés, markets, schools, and offices—set off from the rural hamlet, the isolated mud hut, the transhumant's black goat-hair tent. Such contrasts, though marked, may, however, be misleading, not only in terms of the basic ecology of the region but for an understanding of Sefrou as a historical and social environment. For if it is true, as anthropologists have come to argue, that the physical qualities of a place set neither limits to its human use nor predetermine the lives lived in it; if indeed a human landscape is shot through with the ways in which its inhabitants, by the application of their concepts and their organization, have constructed a vision of their setting and its coherence; and if, in this particular case, a common if varied culture binds the entire region—city and country— into a variegated whole, then it is indispensable to see how the distinctions drawn by the people of the Sefrou area are integral to the emplacement on, the adaptation to, and indeed the very definition and comprehension of their land.[1]

Approached from this perspective the people of Sefrou convey above all a sense of their landscape as a supremely lived-in space: a region in which every garden is named, every site known for the people it nurtures or whose presence gave it note; a territory of shifting boundaries and perduring claims that

1. For a detailed analysis of the ecology of the Sefrou region, see Rosen 1979:1–68, 113–22, and the works cited therein.

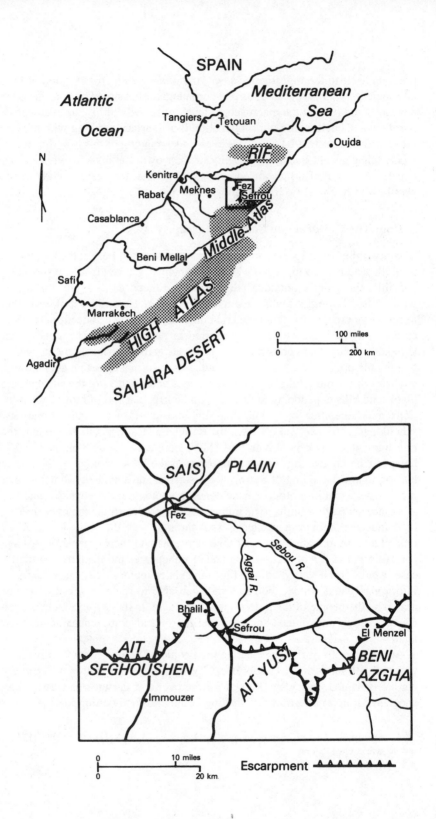

transfigure the flow of water into personalized entitlements and collective plots into an equivocal map of shifting affiliations; an expanse of exquisitely differentiated parts—from the branch of a single olive tree, its bounty accorded by the terms of an ancient religious trust, to a vast tract of land shamelessly seized with a bribe—each portion described by the bonds people form in relation to it; a labyrinth of sanctuaries and meeting places, pathways and fora through which individuals move with greater or lesser knowledge to greater or lesser effect. For these Moroccans nature does not stand apart from humanity—an object of conquest or mystical unification—nor even as a stage upon which the force of history reveals itself as supernatural design or material command. Rather, the domain of the Sefrou people presents itself as a series of located encounters, an arena where the possibilities inherent in human relationships, shaped by the career of a people, acquire a local habitation and a name.

Three themes stand out in particular when one discusses with Sefrawis their territory and the ways in which they and their predecessors have related to it, themes to which outside observers have attached more technical terms and interpretations. First, Sefrou is, at base, a single region, not a land in which city and country stand in irreconcilable contradistinction. When people speak of *bled Sefrou*—the term bled meaning ''country,'' ''territory,'' and ''land,'' but here approximating most closely our own idea of a ''region''—they are not merely employing a classificatory concept of abstract proportions: they are conveying a concrete image of the whole Sefrou area as an integrated zone. Indeed, since, as we shall see later, territory is deeply intertwined with social identity, bled is not just a physical territory, however regionalized, but a terrain of interaction, a domain of complex and crosscutting social relationships. At the same time, and in no way contradictorily, the Sefrou people see within this region a host of differentiable segments, each with its own environmental and social features. In the parlance of ecologists, it is a territory of numerous microenvironments—where rain may fall on one hillside and not the next, where the soil will sustain bountiful crops in one part of a valley and be wholly unyielding to a similar crop a short distance beyond. Groups placed in each of these zones are deeply influenced by their terrain and affect its use and character in turn. That these mini-ecologies are a factor in the physical and social lives of the people of the region calls for accurate and up-to-date knowledge of many such areas if one is to operate attentively in the world.

If unity and diversity are two of the characterizing features of the region, uncertainty is clearly a third. It is an uncertainty born, like the other features, of an interaction of culture and place: rainfall is highly irregular, but so is the success of various crops (and not as a factor in a simple chain of cause and effect). People's dealings with each other are uncertain, and there is, therefore, great need to find out all one can to secure oneself as best as possible.

Relations are not determined and precisely sanctioned by ascribed status or kinship, therefore one must constantly construct an image of oneself and a web of relationships appropriate to the indeterminate world of human ties. And over (or under) all of this uncertainty resides a sense—indeed a fear—of chaos (*fitna,* in Arabic), a belief that the orderliness of the world is contingent on many factors and that the tendency, or at least the strong possibility, exists that this uncertain physical and social environment might well give way to utter disorder. The world being such, and people being what they are, steps must be taken to secure oneself and one's dependents against such eventualities. It is, then, from the perspective of these themes—regional unity, localized diversity, and premonitory chaos—that one can begin to see the history and the human geography of Sefrou as interrelated aspects of the region's culture and ecology.

The city of Sefrou probably dates from the ninth century when Moulay Idriss II, the founder of Fez and an important propagator of Islam, enlarged and enhanced a small settlement of great antiquity.[2] Although Sefrou and the surrounding countryside possessed from this early period features that may be discerned in present times—a significant Jewish population, a predominantly Arabic-speaking urban population, and a Berber-speaking hinterland—it was not until the latter part of the seventeenth century that the region began to take on a still-recognizable shape. The Berber dynasties of the eleventh to fifteenth centuries—the Almoravids, the Almohades, and the Merinids—had left their mark not only in the great monuments of Moorish Spain and the capitol cities of Morocco, but in the pattern of a central government, or *makzen,* which was itself an imperfect extension of the power of dominant families and which sought to capitalize on religious zeal and military prowess to enforce, with uneven effect yet symbolic coherence, a vague sense of territorial unity and common identity. Encountering European force and subject to internal disorganization, each dynasty ebbed back to its Moroccan strongholds and declined. The European powers in turn probed outward; their presence along the Atlantic coast of Africa in the mid-fifteenth century coincided with a major political and religious crisis inside Morocco. The crisis was, in essence, a struggle for the bases of political legitimacy, made noteworthy by the proliferation of numerous holy men, called marabouts (Arabic, *mrābṭin*—from a root meaning "attachment" or "bond"), who were said to possess spiritual powers, reinforced, in many instances, by claims to descent from the Prophet Muhammad. When in 1668 the Alawite dynasty began the reign that continues to the present day, they were able to support their position by unifying a set of cultural themes that remain central to Moroccan political life: the amalgamation, within a single individual, of genealogical attachment to the Proph-

---

2. Discussions of the history of the Sefrou region can be found in Geertz, Geertz, and Rosen 1979, Rosen 1968b, and in the references cited in each.

et and the energetic force of a powerful man moving through his realm to forge alliances and constrain obedience by means that were as recognizably human as they were purportedly blessed.

By the mid-seventeenth century Sefrou had come to look much as it was to remain until the French established their Protectorate in 1912. As a transit point in the caravan trade leading from the Sahara to Fez, Sefrou was both a way station along a major axis of the nation's economy and a useful depot or sanctuary for those in opposition to the central regime. As a result of drought and political rivalry in the Sahara, Berber tribesmen bound in a loose confederation pushed their way up and over the Middle Atlas Mountains in the seventeenth century and quickly established settlements in the hills and valleys surrounding Sefrou.[3] The predominant tribe of the Sefrou region, known as the Ait Yusi, was, like most of the mountain groups of Morocco, never fully subjugated to central control; the tribe's fissiparous attachments, its symbiosis with the city and the peddlers who traversed its domains, and its constant regrouping around powerful or charismatic local figures proceeded along culturally consistent lines, even as it embraced moments and regions of relative insecurity.

By the late nineteenth century, on the eve of the Protectorate, the city of Sefrou gave the appearance of a small fortified town situated between mountain and plain, Berber and Arab, politically subservient and persistently recalcitrant. The city, its crenelated walls reinforced in the mid-nineteenth century, was physically subdivided within by a series of massive gates, which, like the main entryways, were closed at night to frustrate potential wrongdoers. Given a total urban population of three or four thousand persons, each quarter of the city would have included roughly a hundred families, many of whom were related by blood or marriage. Neither an entire quarter (*ḥuma*) nor a portion of a single street (*derb*), however, formed a corporate unit whose members, recruited on the basis of residence or kinship, were obliged to undertake a variety of activities in common. Indeed, each residential area included people of quite varied economic standing and personal attachment. An extended kin group, many of whose members might live in proximity to one another, generally included individuals of widely varying financial stature, and the blank facades and grillwork-covered windows that faced out to the narrow, winding streets of any district were as likely to enclose a rich man's home as the single room of a poor neighbor. Security of income, property, and, at times, of one's person being perceived as contingent and uncertain, individuals sought aid from their unrelated neighbors as much as from their kinsmen and allies. Indeed, the Arabic term for neighbor, *jār* (plural, *jīrān*), which conveyed the idea of a ''protected person'' to the early Arabians, im-

3. See generally Lesne 1959 on tribal movements in the Middle Atlas Mountains during this period.

plied for the Sefrawis as well the sense that neighbors were often the most reliable people with whom to share one's safety and one's familial privacy.[4] A city of agriculturalists, craftsmen, and traders, Sefrou was, in the last quarter of the nineteenth century, a central market for the entire region and, like much of Morocco, an area in which the struggle between local power and an ineffective sultanate was helping to shape the context for European domination.

One of the striking features of Moroccan political life in the pre-Protectorate period is that the process and style of the sultan and his government were repeated in microcosm over much of the countryside, including areas that were not subject to regular government control. No better example exists than that of Sefrou at the end of the nineteenth century when the region was controlled by Caid Omar al-Yusi. Omar constructed his power by a combination of strategic alliances, brute force, and the manipulation of the symbols associated with successful governance. Building on the ties his father had established before he was killed by members of a rival fraction, Omar's own power became both a prop and a threat to the central government. Effectively controlling most of the wool and hides that passed from the mountains through Sefrou to Fez and the Moroccan north and granted formal control of the city of Sefrou by a sultan eager to secure Sefrou from the rebellion in the north of the famous pretender Buḥamara, Caid Omar proceeded to steal garden land, falsify deeds, and murder even the most respected elders of the community in order to further consolidate his power.

Although himself unlearned, Omar sought to surround himself with those who were both learned in the law and willing to ignore some of his violations of that law. No doubt he felt that he was abiding by the intent of the law even when he was violating its letter by imprisoning or murdering those who did not recognize his supreme authority. No doubt, too, he felt the tension between his own Berber, Bedouin values and his desire to take on the characteristics of an educated urban Arab. Omar, like so many Moroccan big men, seems to have embodied in far beyond average proportions just those characteristics of piety and lawlessness, rigidity and impulsiveness, brutality and banality that were found writ small in practically every man who made up the milieu from which he was derived.

In time Omar's own ambitions led to protests by the citizenry and a period of enforced presence at the sultan's court. Returned to power in the early years of the century, he was himself assassinated in 1904; afterwards there followed a period of looting and disorder that the monarchy, now financially and militarily pressed by the European powers, was unable to check. The career of a "little sultan" like Caid Omar is revealing in that it embraced, in heightened form, features that were evident in the formation of personal net-

---

4. On the concept of *jār* in early Arabia, see W. Robertson Smith 1903, 49–53.

works ranging from those of the lowliest practitioner of the everyday to the sultan himself. Each attachment, each personal quality, each basis for affiliation became a resource to be utilized in fabricating a set of allies and dependents. The resources useful to the formation of such associations being diverse, the alliances that were formed were brittle and ephemeral and were only as strong as the individual who stood at their center. Individuals tried to cumulate within themselves a broad range of desired traits and ties and sought to indicate to others that they possessed the features of reliability and power that would themselves attract dependents and allies. Whether it was in the claim of spiritual power devolving from a saint or the Prophet Muhammad, or the qualities of a mediator or learned man that others came to acknowledge, the sheer personalism of social ties at all levels of society remained central. No social category—whether descendants of the Prophet (*šurfā*) or learned men (*'ulamā*)—formed tightly organized corporate groups, and thus the lines of power and influence were as diverse as the resources and resourcefulness of their purveyors. Lacking a central bureaucratic structure, the government depended for its effectiveness on the alliances of the sultan, who moved around the countryside servicing his claims to legitimacy and tribute. By the early part of the twentieth century, however, European intrusion had not only weakened the power of such traditional leaders but led to its replacement by direct colonial control.

The effects of forty-four years of French colonization were diverse and pervasive. The strategy of the French regime was, as Janet Abu-Lughod says, "to retain the form of the traditional system while emptying it of its powers" (Abu-Lughod 1980, 174). The marketplace, courts, and administration of the city were under the careful control of native appointees and French military commanders until the early 1930s when the latter were replaced by French civil servants. Pursuing their policy of divide and conquer, the French established new rural markets and administrative districts in the countryside. Owing to the long-term fluidity of Berber fractional association and to the fact that loyalties were felt more or less intensely only on the level of the localized tribal fraction and granted to higher orders of affiliation only on limited, ad hoc bases, those new administrative and economic divisions served both to weaken the bases of former social ties and to encourage the nodal points around which new associations were formed. The Moroccan genius for structural adaptability, particularly above the fractional level, tended to spare the people from the more debilitating social repercussions associated with many colonial administrations. The economic and demographic repercussions of French colonialism, however, were somewhat more severe.

In the countryside French controls on pasturing rights had substantial effects on the semisedentary herders. In the pre-Protectorate period the Ait Yusi, like the other Middle Atlas tribes, had to move their herds in winter from the high forest pastures to the lower plateaus of the northwestern escarpment. Some groups had their own winter pastures, but most tribal fractions had to arrange some sort of agreement or engage in some form of combat with the residents of the low-lying pasture lands. Tenuous equilibrium was generally established throughout the whole chain of Berber tribes in the region, an equilibrium that might be based on reciprocal summer-pasture rights in the highlands, payment for pasturing rights, symbolic skirmishes by the lowlanders who thereby emphasized their summer rights to a given pasture before yielding to the winter rights of the descending mountaineers, or yearly unrestrained warfare ending in lopsided victory or the mediation of a holy man.[5] In a system of this sort any pressures brought to bear on accessibility to the lowland pastures in the area south of Meknes had significant repercussions all the way up the chain of interlocking transhumants to the highest slopes of the mountains. The Moroccan tribes occupying the lowlands were aware of the leverage this control of the lowland pastures carried and were sometimes able to use it to their advantage. The Berber fractions of the high mountains were generally more warlike than their lowland brethren, if for no other reason than because they could not survive comfortably without being able to force their way into the winter pastures at the times when cold and snow spelled almost certain death for their major source of livelihood, their flocks. This does not mean that simple control of the lowlands was tantamount to having a stranglehold on the highlanders: isolated valleys, relative underpopulation, timing of sales, and, later, the purchasing of fodder could vitiate this type of broadly political control in the pre-Protectorate period. But alterations in accessibility to such warm pastures could and did put a great strain on the whole socioecological adaptation the highlanders had made to the land, the climate, the flocks, and their neighbors. Thus, in the early years of struggle against the new French Protectorate, the Zaen tribe, under the forceful leadership of the great Moha ou Hamu, denied the Beni Mguild access, even with pay, to their pastures in an attempt to get the latter to carry the brunt of the battle against the French. Unable to get into their winter pastures, the Beni Mguild backed up toward the Timhadite area, to which the Ait Yusi mountaineers generally brought their flocks. Demographic pressures (of flocks as well as people) not unlike those that had gradually forced these same Berber tribes to move up to the mountains from the pre-Saharan zone in the sixteenth to eighteenth centuries, cut down the alternatives formerly available to the herdsmen and made their situation quite difficult.

In the 1920s and 1930s the pressures on the mountain herders were intensified by the influx of colonial farmers. Establishing themselves in the foothills north of Sefrou and the plain south of Meknes, the *colons* not only cut off access to many of the winter pastures but forced the sedentary grain

---

5. For detailed descriptions of transhumance in the Middle Atlas and regions to the south, see Vinogradov 1974a, Chiapuris 1979, and Hart 1981.

growers to move to more marginal lands. The Water and Forestry Service also severely restricted pasturing in the woodlands as overgrazing threatened erosion and flooding. The repercussions of these actions were predictable: in the early 1930s, for instance, the Ait Arfa were refused entry to the colon-crowded plain and were thus unable to take in the flocks of the Ait Yusi of Guigou. The latter in turn were unable to give way to the people of Marmusha who were also restricted from moving into the colon-occupied territory to the north of Sefrou. Widely fluctuating rainfalls and severe winter snows that cost up to half of the flocks contributed their share to undermining the collective pasture ties and fractional solidarities that characterized the earlier period. Communal lands were divided into private sectors both as a means of assuring oneself some pasture or farm land and because of the pressures of the colonists eager to purchase the land with an air of legality. For the agriculturalist, bad weather (particularly in the 1940s), fragmentation of land holdings owing to population pressures and inheritance patterns, and the fact that hard wheat crops raised on marginal land at high cost could neither be marketed abroad to gain capital nor harvested in sufficient quantities locally to allow for a proper measure of nutrition or security contributed to the significant but not total weakening of the social and economic bases of rural life.[6]

In the city of Sefrou, during this period, the situation was somewhat more mixed. Garden produce, including strawberries, could now be marketed more easily owing to the availability of roads and trucks, but overproduction in the national and international market, fragmentation of land, and the fact that population pressures made some garden land more valuable as building sites than as agricultural areas tended to limit the growth of the city's farming community. French economic input aided the Jews of the city for a time, but as early as the 1930s and 1940s a number of Jews began moving to the coastal cities where the industrial, commercial, and marketing centers were located. Between 1913 and 1952 the increase in Sefrou's population can be accounted for primarily by the natural growth of the population of the city itself: the French took great pains to keep rural people from pouring into the city, but the depredations of local officials and fluctuations in agricultural output often sent people fleeing to urban areas. By their control of land use and building permits, the French encouraged the construction alongside the old city of a separate Ville Nouvelle, complete with French-occupied villas, gardens, recreational facilities, and a modern street of shops, cafés, and administrative buildings. Like other cities of colonial Morocco, Sefrou was divided into three broad sectors: the old walled city (*medina*) occupied by older urban families and, increasingly, urban migrants; the "new medina" quarters—Muslim-oc-

6. On the control of land in the colonial period, see generally Laroui 1977 and Stewart 1964. On urban land development, see Abu-Lughod 1980, 174–95. On contemporary land-holding patterns in the oasis of Sefrou, see Benhalima 1977b:82–100, 193–98; Chaoui 1978, 35.

cupied districts that developed beyond the old city, consisting of new native-style homes and populated initially by somewhat more affluent urbanites and newcomers; and the French Ville Nouvelle, set apart from the other quarters and effectively segregated from them.

The French Protectorate came to an end in 1956, and with independence came significant alterations in the population and social composition of the Sefrou region. Not only has the overall size of the population increased dramatically but there has been substantial migration from the countryside to the city. From a population of roughly seventeen thousand in 1956, the city of Sefrou grew to more than twenty-one thousand in 1960, twenty-eight thousand in 1971, and well over forty thousand by the early 1980s. Sefrou has long been the focus of rural migration, for all or part of the year, as a result of political, economic, or ecological disruption, but what was once an intermittent or episodic flow has become a steady stream. In 1960, 56.2 percent of the Muslims living in the city had been born there; in 1971, that figure had de-

Table 1.1
Population of the City of Sefrou

Year	Muslims	Jews	Europeans	Total Moroccans	Total
1883	2,000	1,000	—	3,000	3,000
1903	3,000	3,000	—	6,000	6,000
1913	—	—	—	6,400	6,400
1917	4,150	2,950	—	7,100	7,100
1926	4,894	3,444	140	8,338	8,478
1931	5,635	4,046	218	9,681	9,899
1936	7,288	4,346	246	11,634	11,880
1941	9,095	5,474	339	14,569	14,908
1947	11,342	5,757	495	17,099	17,594
1951–52	11,520	4,360	710	15,880	16,590
1960	17,583	3,041	337	20,624	20,961
1971	28,312	222	73	28,534	28,607

Sources: Figures for each year are derived from the following sources. *1883*: Foucauld 1888, 38; *1903*: Aubin 1908, 396; *1913*: Caix 1913, 180; *1917*: Périgny 1917, 256; *1941*: Institut des Hautes Etudes Marocaines 1945, 256; *1947*: Chouraqui 1950, 33. The figures for 1926, 1931, 1936, 1951–52, 1960, and 1971 come from the official census for each of those years. Precise figures for the census of the early 1980s are not yet available. Benhalima (1977b, 4) reports that the population was estimated at 45,000 in 1976; in 1978, the administrator of the Sefrou region told me the population of the city was nearly 50,000. There is every reason to believe that for the decade of the 1970s, the growth of the city's population exceeded the national growth rate of 32 percent. The Jewish population of the city was estimated at 199 in 1972 by Stillman (1973): in the late 1970s there were only a few families remaining in the city and none in the surrounding countryside. A detailed statistical analysis of the 1960 census, based on a 100-percent sample of the original census documents, will be found in H. Geertz 1979b. An analysis of the 1971 census data is available in Benhalima 1977a, 1977b; Chaoui 1978. For an argument that the 1971 census underestimated the population of Morocco by 5 to 10 percent, see Mounir 1971.

clined to 52.8 percent.[7] Of all those people living in Sefrou in 1971 who had migrated from the countryside, two-thirds had done so within the preceding decade. More than half are Berber-speakers from the Middle Atlas Mountains, but an increasing proportion come from the foothills and highlands of the Rif Mountains to the north (Benhalima 1977b, 57–63; see also H. Geertz 1979b, 401–9). Many of the migrants, especially the poorest among them, have moved into the medina, the old walled section of the city, raising the proportion of the medina's population who are rural born from 40 percent in 1960 to 60 percent in 1971.[8] Houses, many of which had been subdivided by heirs and tenants in the postwar years, now became even further fragmented. For example, in the old Jewish quarter, the mellah, which was still 84-percent Jewish in 1960 but without any Jews a decade later, poor rural immigrants further subdivided the multi-storied houses of the quarter, lifting the population density from 1,155 to 1,833 people/hectare in less than ten years (Benhalima 1977b, 187).[9]

The migration to the city is ascribable both to economic factors pushing people out of the countryside and equally powerful attractions drawing them to Sefrou. The economic decline occasioned by the departure of the French (and, in the eyes of many Sefrawis, the gradual withdrawal of the area's Jewish merchants) combined with the increase in population and greater freedom of movement to bring many people into the city. As the population has grown, the proportion of young people and their importance to the city has grown. Well over half the population is now under the age of twenty.[10] So many of these young people have been brought to the city by rural parents eager for them to have the advantage of urban schooling that Sefrou has, in the words of one commentator, become a veritable "education factory" (Benhalima 1977b, 143).[11] This emphasis on education is not only a man-

7. For the 1960 figure, see H. Geertz 1979b, 403; for 1971, see Royaume du Maroc 1977.

8. For 1960, see H. Geertz 1979b, 459; for 1971, Benhalima 1977b, 187. The proportion of the total population of the city living in the medina stayed roughly the same (28.8 percent compared with 32.9 percent) from 1960 to 1971.

9. The percentage of Jews in the mellah in 1960 is from H. Geertz 1979b, 452. The total population of the mellah rose from 6,909 to 8,567 in the decade of the 1960s. See H. Geertz 1979b, 459; Benhalima 1977b, 187.

10. According to the official census of 1971, 46 percent (N = 13,621) of all males in the city and 42 percent (N = 14,032) of the females were under fifteen years of age. Comparable figures in the rural areas were: 48-percent males (N = 38,476) and 46-percent females (N = 36,432). Sixty-three percent of all males and 60 percent of all females in the administrative district (*cercle*) encompassing city and countryside were under the age of twenty-five (Royaume du Maroc 1977, 39–42).

11. According to Benhalima (1977b, 145), the number of students in the Sefrou schools totaled 10,078 in 1975–76, the primary-school population of 5,840 representing a 25-percent increase over the 1970 figure.

ifestation of the generally high value Moroccans place on the acquisition of useful knowledge, it is also a contemporary version of that same quest for education by poor people that led to such a high proportion of them in earlier times among the students of the Quranic centers of Fez and Marrakech.[12] The present quest for education is, like that of an earlier age, closely related to the shift in economic opportunity and social status. Almost all parents now want their sons (and sometimes even their daughters) to become civil servants because such jobs offer the security of a regular salary—the French term *mandat,* with its implication of a steady monetary payment, having become an accepted item in the modern Moroccan lexicon—and constitute a point of personal connection to others in power. The national government, faced with an oversupply of unemployable degree recipients, has frequently shifted the requirements for acquisition of the baccalaureate diploma, thus increasing the insecurity and value attached to this degree. Nevertheless parents are willing to make great sacrifices and disrupt their living arrangements to further the chances for success by their offspring.

Indeed, like many other cities in Morocco, Sefrou has become increasingly a city of salaried workers.[13] The number of artisans has declined to less than one in eight employed persons while the bureaucratic and commercial sectors (18 percent and 27.9 percent respectively) have grown at the expense of the agricultural (11.1 percent) (Benhalima 1977b, 75; see also 1977a).[14] Unemployment hovers around the 20- to 25-percent mark although a much larger proportion is clearly underemployed. Moreover, all statistical indications confirm the casual observation that the discrepancy between rich and poor has widened in recent years.[15] City and country, bound together as a single political and economic entity, jointly experience, and indeed contribute to, these shifts of occupation and wealth, even though the localized impact varies significantly. Thus it is increasingly common to find rural dwellers who live part of the time in the city or who maintain a strong interest in a parcel of rural property, or urban dwellers whose administrative or commercial dealings bring them into deepened contact with countrymen and recent immigrants. With more direct transportation to rural markets and more massive contact by

12. One is reminded of the Moroccan saying: "Without the sons of the poor, scholarship would die." It should also be noted that with the increase in the student population, there has not only been a concomitant rise in the number of teachers, but that these teachers have come to form a potent force on the local political scene. See below, p. 116, n. 50.

13. In 1971, 44.7 percent of all employed persons in Sefrou were salaried, 26.9 percent in the private sector and 17.8 percent in the public (Benhalima 1977b, 79).

14. For national figures see Abu-Lughod 1980, 246.

15. Physicians at the local hospital thus reported in 1978 that they were seeing far more cases of malnutrition-related ailments than they had seen in previous years. See also disease statistics in Benhalima 1977b, 141. On the different levels of household expenditures of bureaucrats and others, see Royaume du Maroc 1973, 29–30.

country dwellers with the city, there has been a tendency for the hinterland to seem more like the city even as the city—its infrastructure in disrepair, its outskirts marked by unregulated squatter settlements—appears increasingly ruralized.

Only a little over half a century before fieldwork for this study began, there was not a single paved road in Morocco. Informants who were in their early seventies when I began fieldwork could easily recall the days of their youth when caravans passed on their way to the Sahara, when Berber tribesmen cut the road and charged tolls to "protect" travellers, and when the heads of political foes and convicted criminals were impaled on the city walls. The changes wrought by the relatively brief but intensive period of foreign colonization and entry into the world of modern nation-states have been enormous. Yet the detailed reconstruction of social alignments and cultural concepts on which they have been based display a remarkable continuity during the course of an otherwise tumultuous century. Throughout, the individual, as a freely contracting party arranging ties in accordance with acknowledged standards for interpreting the meaning and import of another's actions, has remained central to the Moroccan style of social organization. No doubt families and tribal fractions have become less crucial bases for the formation of personal alliances, and no doubt a decline in the sanctioning force of crosscutting ties has coincided with greater skepticism in some guiding concepts and nostalgia for past forms of disorder over current ones. Nevertheless, the very personalism and the inherent negotiability of these individual-centered networks of affiliation remain a constant theme in the life of the Sefrou people. In the years covered by this study—in that time slice "seething with life and movement" to which our attention will be directed—the world of the Sefrou people—the landscape of their ideas no less than the landscape of their acts—presents itself as a universe of orderly manipulation and open-ended regularity. It is to the parameters and implications of this constructed world that we must turn our attention.

Two

The Construction of Social Identity

For the people of Sefrou predominant attention is directed toward the acquisition of knowledge about other people—who they are, where they come from, what attachments they possess, how they are used to dealing with others. However much they may seek to secure the privacy of their thoughts or the seclusion of their homes, Moroccans constantly seek information that bears on the public acts of others. This is not a quest for the stuff of idle gossip or perfervid curiosity. In a society in which ties of kinship and residence, economic category and religious attachment do not by themselves dictate the entire range or course of actual relationships, knowledge about those with whom one may interact, by choice or by necessity, becomes vital for control over one's own associations and dependencies.

As in any such informational quest, what constitutes worthwhile data and how it shall be evaluated is given broad definition by a set of cultural constructs, a series of linguistically or symbolically encapsulated guides that demarcate the valuable and delineate the useful. In Morocco this set of cultural constructs includes concepts that for purposes of organization can be grouped into three distinct clusters: the attribution and assessment of characteristics associated with one's social-group attachments; the articulation of basic human nature and its impact on establishing standards for the evaluation of different types of people; and the discernment of another's intentions based on the consequences of his or her actions. The features drawn from each of these conceptual domains are, moreover, brought together by means of a particular form of cultural logic and find their meaning, their life, their impact in the world as they come to characterize individuals and their bonds with others. In a world where people's words and deeds create the reality of their ties to others, it is to the creation of their social identity that primary attention must be paid.

Attributing Traits and Ties

To Moroccans the issue of how a person is known is, in no small part, a summary of the qualities and attachments others need to know about if they are to negotiate obligations with that individual. But unlike some societies where rank is central and name or title designates one's place, however contested, within a hierarchy of ordered social categories, or other societies in which people harbor their appraisal of others in attributions that are not meant to be carried, as it were, on one's sleeve, in Morocco one finds a host of distinct concepts that organize the public expression of another's traits and ties. As they set about the construction of an identity—whether their own or another's—the people of Sefrou recognize that no single feature—of nature or background, temper or physique—can stand for the whole person. It is the sum that counts: it is the multiplicity of features and contexts, situations and aspects that one displays and encounters by which each individual will be known. Yet like John Ruskin, Moroccans clearly believe that "there is a science of aspects, as well as of things," and it is in the encompassing format of identifying terms that the sense of an individual's attributes and affiliations are given public shape.

Among the most significant of the symbolic forms used to specify the aspects of one's identity is that which, as Clifford Geertz has so clearly demonstrated, is embraced in the linguistic form known in Arabic as the *nisba* (C. Geertz 1976; 1979, 140–50).[1] The root of the term nisba (*n-s-b*) yields a variety of words centered around the verbs "to link," "to bring into relation," "to trace one's ancestry." Among its many ramifications are words that translate as "lineage," "relativity," "proportionate," and "apt." Nisba itself means "attribution," "ascription," and "relationship," and as a linguistic form it thus encapsulates a particular attachment or quality by which its bearer may, in part, be known. In Moroccan Arabic almost any attribute or relationship may be given a nisba form by the simple addition of an *i* or *iy* suffix to the characteristic in question. This characteristic may be a place of origin or residence, a family name, an occupational or ethnic category, a physical peculiarity, or childhood trait. Thus, one may speak of an individual who comes from Sefrou as a *Sefrawi,* a Beni Mtir tribesman as a *Mtiri,* a bowlegged man as *qawasi,* or derive from the word *yahūd* (the Jews as a people) the nisba for a single Jew, *yahūdī.* Moreover, each nisba may act

---

1. See also Berque 1974, 129. On the implication of biological heredity in the concept of nisba in an earlier period, see Mottahedeh 1980, 98–99.

simultaneously as a descriptor and a name, such that one may both refer to another by a given nisba and attach it to that person—or oneself—as part of the individual's appellation. Since nisbas may be drawn from such diverse realms as occupation, religious confrerie, and family line, no less than geographical or ethnic attachment, the series of names applicable to any individual may be numerous and varied.[2]

As Geertz is quick to point out, the intriguing aspect of this nisba system is not simply that it stamps on each individual a series of names that call forth various ascriptive sources or even that these attributes are formed by the characterization of an individual by the particular contexts in which he or she is associated with others of a similar sort. Rather, since the very contexts in which a person operates are themselves relative—that is, subject to varying interpretations and manipulation—the sheer relativity of such names is itself made subject to a further relativizing process. Thus, a man from Sefrou would only be called a Sefrawi when away from the city, be known as a member of a given tribal fraction when such a distinction is asserted as relevant, or be called by any of a host of identifiers—*Begrawi* (member of the family of that name), *nejjāri* (carpenter), *Derqawi* (adherent of the Derqawa religious brotherhood), etc.—in contexts where further distinction is appropriate. Each nisba by itself places an individual in a given social framework; each instance in which it is invoked serves to characterize the situation of its use. Each nisba and each context of its usage have within them the power to signal one's place on the social map and to define the very context of one's encounter. Individuals may try to characterize themselves by a certain nisba or have one thrust upon them; they may be known intimately through a regional or familial nisba by people who do not have a clear idea of their given names. A person may be so variously called that when it is necessary to establish a legal identity or entitlement, that person must bring forth witnesses who will swear that it is indeed all the same individual who is so variously and confusingly known. What matters, as Geertz says, is that it is through this pervasive social contextualization—this "promiscuous tumbling in public settings of varieties of men kept carefully segregated in private ones"—that the framework for individual action is given recognizable symbolic embodiment (C. Geertz 1976).

No single nisba, nor, indeed, any elaborate collection of them, can fully and certainly characterize a person. Each does, however, provide, in the eye

2. A person's nisba is only one of many names he or she may possess. Personal names such as Muhammad or one of its derivatives are relatively few in number, greater specificity being added by the designation "son of" or "daughter of" so-and-so. Earlier in the century it was not uncommon for the women of Sefrou to take personal names that were the feminine form of their father's name or for an aged widow to use the feminine form of her dead husband's name. See Biarnay 1924, 17.

of the beholder, that additional element of information, that element of basic and relational knowledge that helps to clarify another's preexisting ties and the place an individual may occupy within the range of one's own potential network. It is precisely because the nisba system, like so many other aspects of Moroccan language and life, draws meaning from context yet remains open to alternative implications that it can operate as both a vehicle and product of social identity. In order to see more precisely what kind of information is conveyed by the knowledge embraced in a nisba and what Moroccans do with such information, it may help to consider in detail one aspect of this system of social identity and through it some more general features of Arabic language use.

Nisbas may as we mentioned refer to particular places with which a person is associated. This notion of place, which is very important to the way Moroccans identify others and create a baseline for relationship, is itself embraced in the Arabic word *aṣel*. In its most basic application asel means "origin," "root," and "source." But it also carries a series of further implications and uses that are intimately connected to the way in which Arabic terms are themselves constructed. Since many of the concepts with which we will be dealing depend for part of their semantic range on this linguistic structure, it is worth noting at this point some basic features of Arabic, in both its literary and colloquial forms.

The ramifications of a concept like asel find expression in the very structure of the Arabic language. The fundamental unit on which Arabic is constructed is a group of consonants, usually three in number, more rarely two or four. Within this "consonantal shell" vowels may shift or prefixes and infixes attach themselves, each shift or addition striking a new meaning off the fundamental core of consonants.[3] One can, therefore, take a single verb root and, by tracing it through a variety of inflections and transmutations, capture the semantic realm of which the root is both source and result.

An example to which we will have recourse later will help illustrate how this system of root and modification works. The root ʿ-*r-f* (the first consonant being one of those Arabic gutterals quite unlike anything in English) has the following verb derivations:[4]

(I)	ʿraf	to know, recognize, perceive
(II)	ʿaraf	to announce, inform; introduce; explain
(V)	tʿaraf	to become acquainted, disclose one's identity; trace, discover, uncover
(VI)	tʿāraf	to get to known one another
(VIII)	ʿtāraf	to confess, admit, acknowledge

---

3. The phrase "consonontal shell" comes from E. Wilson's (1956, 393–94) discussion of Hebrew—a similarly constructed language.

4. The Roman numeral represents the verb form as conventionally numbered by Arabists.

(X)   sta'rf   to discern, recognize

From this same root are also derived:

'arf	fragrance, perfume, aroma
'urf	beneficence, kindness; custom, traditional; customary law
'arīf	expert, specialist; teacher
'arrāf	diviner, fortune-teller
'arafāt	the mountain near Mecca, important in the Pilgrimage, where according to legend Adam and Eve, separated after the expulsion, met and recognized one another (ta'ārafa)
ma'rifa	knowledge, learning; experience, realization
ta'rīf	announcement, communication
ma'rūf	well-known; conventional; kindness; equitableness, fairness
muta'āraf	common, usual; hackneyed, banal

There is, of course, a certain logic to this, as to any, set of derivations, a rationale that binds them together in a single semantic realm. But it is a logic far more dependent on history, poetic insight, perduring idiosyncrasy, and collective perception than grammatical or structural necessity. Sometimes the logic is intriguing; sometimes amusing. Is it a comment on their character—or a subtle insight into life on the barren steppes—that the root from which the word "Bedouin" is derived also yields "to be obvious," "to seem good," "caprice," "ill-humor," "whim," and "desert"? Is it only in the Arab world that one might comprehend a set of associations that combines

---

Although lacking fixed meanings, one can generally ascribe the following meaning to each form:

Form I: basic form (x)
Form II: to cause to be or to make (x)
Form III: to cause or make (x)
Form IV: to cause to be or do (x)
Form V: to be or to become (x)
Form VI: to do (x) naturally
Form VII: to have (x) be done
Form VIII: to do (x) to oneself
Form IX: to be or become a given color; to have a defect associated with (x)
Form X: to force oneself to (x)

Thus if we think of the basic form $c - r - f$ as meaning "to know," then Form VI, to know in a natural way, has been used to mean "getting to know one another," and Form VIII, to know oneself, becomes the form meaning "to confess or admit."

Not all verbs have all forms. Indeed, one might think of the system of verb forms as a kind of verbal periodic chart which for certain verbs is empty in a given cell but which could, in theory, be filled in by verbal creativity. The Arabization of Western scientific terms and the neologisms of poets and philosophers are often based on the suffusion of new meaning into the derivations of verbal roots. On such verbal constructions in Moroccan Arabic, see Abdel-Masih 1970, 121 and Harrell 1962.

"to shackle," "bind," "fetter," "chain," "captivate," and "fascinate" with "family," "kinsfolk," and "relatives"? And who can disagree with Jonathan Raban when, upon learning that the literary Arabic word for "child" comes from a root (*t-f-l*) that yields: "to intrude," "disturb," "impose (upon)"; "to sponge," "live at other people's expense"; "to arrive uninvited or at an inconvenient time"; "to be a sycophant or parasite," he should comment that "no richer or more skeptical definition of childhood has, as far as I know, ever been made" (Raban 1979, 22).

It is, however, incorrect to see in these shadings either "a labyrinth of false meanings" or an instrument that mutes needed distinctions between the real and imagined.[5] Admittedly, we cannot show with precision that any given term calls forth in the Arabic-speaker's mind the set of associations one will find in a dictionary of Arabic roots. It is also true that "the bulk of the modern Arabic verbal lexicon consists not of formal derivations of totally new words, but of semantically extended preexisting ones" (Stetkevych 1970, 38). And it is probably no less true that the daunting size of the Arabic lexicon is further inflated by the antiquarian practices of those who compile some Arabic dictionaries (Lewis 1980, 43).[6] Nevertheless, the range of meanings that cohere around these roots affords both those who study and those who use them an entrée into the realms of meaning through which experience is given voice and voice association.

The term asel partakes of this elaboration process. In addition to "origin" and "root," its derived forms include "to found or establish," "lineage," "descent," "nobility of descent," "real estate," "strength of character," "authentic," "proper," and "indigenous." What binds these elements together is the belief that a very considerable part of an individual's character is constituted by the social milieu from which he draws his nurture. To Moroccans, geographical regions are inhabited spaces, realms within which communities organize themselves to wrest a living and forge a degree of security. The identity of people and place becomes close, therefore, but not as a result of any simple theory of geographical determinism. True, Moroccans may say that the English are aloof because their land is cold or the Africans display lassitude because of the humidity of tropical climes. But their main focus is on the identity of persons in situ because the site itself is a social context through which an individual becomes used to ways of creating a lived-in space. To be attached to a place is, therefore, not only to have a point of origin—it is to have those social roots, those human attachments, that are distinctive to the kind of social person one is.

This quality of social rootedness is further embraced in a term that has great

---

5. The labyrinth phrase is from Raban 1979, 22; the absurd argument that Arabic is associated with the native speaker's inability to discern the real will be found in Patai 1976, 41–72.

6. This characterization would not, however, be applicable to the Wehr dictionary.

currency and importance for Moroccans, the word *mul* (pl. *mwalin*). Although it is usually rendered in Western languages as "owner," the semantic implications are more subtle. When one speaks of someone as the mul of a piece of property, of a wife as the mul of one's household, of a practitioner as the mul of his craft or commodity, of the rich as "mul-s of their times" (*mwalin z-zman*), or (in an ultimate yet strikingly characteristic way) of Allah as "my mul," the idea that is implied is not simply one of control, of the power to alienate: it is to imply that the thing and the person are characterized by one another, that property is a social framework and social character contextualized nurturance. To speak of a group of people as *mwalin l-bled*, "the mul-s of a place," is, therefore, to convey that it is they who by their association with one another in that place, by being so deeply rooted, so clearly tied to that place, have given to it its distinctively human character and derived from their association in that place their own distinguishing qualities. To speak of a person's asel, of the place where one's people are the mwalin, is not to express any mystical union of the individual and the environment: it is to place a person in a world that is quintessentially peopled.

We are now in a position to suggest, in part, what it is that makes the knowledge of "origins," captured and adduced in the form of a nisba, so valuable. For to know another's origins, in this broadly geo-social sense, is to know what kinds of personal characteristics a person does or is most likely to display or acquire, what kinds of ties he or she may already possess, according to what customs one is most used to forming relationships with others, and—perhaps most importantly—what bases exist for the establishment of a personal bond between another and oneself. When, therefore, in response to the everready question *menayn asl-u* ("Where is his 'origin?' "), the nisba identifying a person conveys a place, a tribe, an ethnic group, or a family line—that information itself begins to clarify some of the contexts through which the other, and potentially oneself, can be conjoined and known.

Consider, for example, that aspect of the knowledge conveyed by a nisba of origins that bears on the kinds of traits and ties another may possess. Moroccans are extremely sensitive to regional customs and what they perceive to be, if not with total uniformity or clear articulation, differences of temperament and character depending on the place and people associated with one's nurturance. There is a saying: "Each absence increases prestige" (*kull l-ḡiba katzid l-hība*), because as a person travels he becomes increasingly familiar with the qualities and customs of people in surrounding areas—he sees the same people in more varied contexts, he sees people interacting with whom he or someone he knows may have contact—in short, he acquires information that he may use to form his own network. (The masculine pronoun is used advisedly here since women are largely restrained from such movement. As another proverb says, "There is no good in a woman who roams about and no good in a man who does not.") The information may be sufficient to make distinctions only at a rather broad level: he may learn that countrymen from different areas may be recognized by their garments (Bhalil men fold the hem of their jellabas under, Ait Yusi Berbers tuck the hem over); that many people from the Sahara claim descent from the Prophet through the Drissi line and are flattered by the use of titles indicative of such descent; that a rural man is less likely to be concerned about hiding the women of his household than are some urban men. At other times the knowledge of another's customs and connections may be extremely detailed: it may become known that the villagers of Sidi Youssef, as part of their disputed claim to descent from a minor local saint, are eager to serve as go-betweens since this is a quality associated with saintly descent; that members of the rural Haynajen fraction have numerous marital and economic ties with the old families of the Qla'a quarter and that if one wishes to have dealings with such a Qlawi it may be wise to arrange it through one of the Haynajen; or that people from the village of Bhalil, being relatively poor, use lower bridewealth payments and have, in the past, even agreed to keep such payments fixed at a common level for all. The list is endless, exquisite, imprecise, frightfully exact, and—perhaps most important—differentially shared. For it is this knowledge of others' ways and connections that can be vital to predicting how they are most likely to act in a variety of situations, and therefore what kinds of relationships are most advantageous with them. Whether it is a case, as we shall see in some detail later, of arranging a marriage, a political alliance, an economic network, or acting as a knowledgeable go-between facilitating such arrangements for others, it is this knowledge of others that is the indispensable resource, the stock in trade, to be garnered, compounded, expended, and displayed.

Information acquired by knowledge of another's asel is particularly valuable to the extent that it denotes a whole set of features that cluster around it. If, for example, a particular family is known to be of long duration in an area, if many of its members are generally affiliated with a particular occupation, religious brotherhood, or level of income, then knowledge of one feature may suggest a far broader set of implications. Thus older residents of Sefrou know full well that the Bouabids were farriers and blacksmiths who came "originally" from the Jabala region to the north, lived in the quarter of Chebbak, belonged to the Derqawa brotherhood, and attended the Semarine Mosque. Or that the Ben Khadira family converted from Judaism to Islam centuries ago, that most of them are farmers, and that they intermarry a good deal with two other well-known families in the city. However, the particular way in which knowledge of another's asel implies a set of associated features may have begun to shift in recent decades. We can see this process at work if we look a bit more closely at the question of ethnic-group identity.

Earlier it was noted that Moroccans distinguish between Berbers and Arabs and that, as both analytic and indigenous categories, these distinctions make sense predominantly as linguistic categories since the customs and practices of each overlap and intertwine greatly. In the Sefrou area, therefore, "Berbers" may simply be regarded as those who speak one of the four main dialects of Berber found in Morocco whether or not they also speak Arabic. In fact, throughout the Sefrou region most of the Berber men, even those living in remote areas, and a large proportion of Berber women, especially those living in or near the city, also speak Arabic quite well. In the city proper about one out of every eight people spoke some Berber in 1960; since more than half of the city is presently composed of rural immigrants, this figure may now exceed 30 percent. However, with the help of census data from 1960 and 1971, it is possible to formulate a more precise statistical profile of the ethnic and social-group composition of the city.[7] While the data are suggestive of certain propensities, they demonstrate that the Berber-Arab distinction does not simply correlate with a series of social indicators.

Thus in 1960, although nearly all (93 percent) of the Berbers in Sefrou were born in the countryside, two-thirds had already been living in the city for five or more years. In succeeding decades the pace of immigration has grown rapidly: by 1971, two-thirds of all immigrants, Arab and Berber, living in Sefrou had come in the past decade. Since a quarter of these immigrants came from the territory of the Ait Yusi and another 18 percent from the Rif and pre-Rif (Jabala) regions to the north, Sefrou has undoubtedly acquired a population at least one-third Berber. Berbers are not, however, separately grouped in any particular parts of the city; like rural-born Arabs they live predominantly in the medina and new-medina quarters and are broadly scattered throughout these neighborhoods. Current data on literacy and occupation are not available. However, we do know that in 1960 Berber men of rural origins tended to hold jobs that paid as well as those occupied by Arab men born in the city itself; although they tended to rent entire houses more often (55 percent) than Sefrou-born Arabs (38 percent) and tended toward greater unemployment (35 percent as opposed to 19 percent for Sefrou-born Arabs), in both cases the figures for rural-born Berbers and rural-born Arabs were quite similar. Although rural-born Arab and Berber men were more illiterate (70 and 72 percent respectively) than Sefrou-born Arab men (46 percent), their children are proportionately well represented in the school population, many rural families making substantial efforts to find places in the city's schools for their children. In short, for most aspects of economic status, residential placement, and level of education, the Berber-Arab distinction is not very significant, the predominant axis being rural-urban. To identify someone as being of Berber

7. The 1960 census data is from H. Geertz 1979b; the 1971 data from Benhalima 1977b. In some instances the 1960 data in Geertz disagrees with data for the same census in Benhalima or with the official census. Although these discrepancies never exceed 5 percent in either direction, I have chosen to rely on Geertz's figures since they are based on computations from the original census documents. For national comparisons on the figures cited here, see Noin 1970.

or Arab origins by no means affords ready access to an exclusive set of characteristics and affiliations. Similarly, it can be shown that other social categories—especially urban versus rural—are not set groupings that move across the field of social life as fixed and solidary units (see Rosen 1979, 93–96).

Just as it is possible to draw up a statistical profile of the social groups comprising the population of Sefrou, so, too, the Sefrawis themselves assume that certain features tend to cluster together. Although the ordinary man may not be able to attach numbers to the frequency with which people born in Fez practice the cloth trade, or members of the Meghrawa family inhabit the Zemghila quarter, or rural-born Arabs frequent gatherings of the Aisawa religious brotherhood, he will undoubtedly assume that certain features tend to be correlated. In the past this association of features may have been broadly recognized: to know a man's origins, then, may have given a quick insight into his likely occupation, income level, religious attachments, etc. To know one feature was to know the probability of many of the others. In more recent times, as the sheer number of people, especially migrants, has increased and new categories have opened up, this correlation may be less tightly integrated. Greater effort now must be expended on the search for information or greater reliance must be placed on social origins or other indicators—not as shorthand expressions of a series of features that tend to clump together but as stereotypes that restrict further inquiry and limit knowledge. We will return to this question of stereotypes shortly.

If knowledge of asel suggests a range of social, political, and economic affiliations, it is also true that this concept is used to convey ideas about a person's motivations and overall worth. To many Sefrou people—especially older, more traditional men and women—the notion of asel serves as a shorthand not merely for that particular source of nurturance of which the other partakes but of that "strength of character" and "steadfastness," that "purity" and "authenticity" conveyed by the term itself.[8] To say of another ʿandu aṣel (he has asel) means that he is so well rooted in the sources that have nurtured him that he will probably act in recognizably acceptable ways. Conversely, someone who acts improperly must by definition be without adequate roots, without at least an attachment to basic principles and affiliations that would place bounds on his behavior. Commenting on a European living in Sefrou, a storekeeper once said of the man, "He is without asel because he brings women to the apartment he rents in the house of another": no one, he said, who "has asel," who has a sense of place and an appreciation of the consequences that flow from being connected to others, would act in such a

---

8. On the contemporary use of *aṣāla* as the focus for discussions among Arab intellectuals about the need to reconfirm what is "authentic" in their culture, see Berque 1978, 7 and the criticism of his viewpoint in Khatibi 1976, 2172–73.

fashion. Another man—a retired court official—discussed the connection between propriety and origins by citing several commonly used proverbs:

> In the past (he said) you always knew a man's "origins." We always
> asked about it in court. There is a saying: "Only a mule denies his
> origins" (*ma-inkr aṣlu ḡir l-bḡāl*), because his father is a donkey and his
> mother is a horse and you never know what he will do. "If you know a
> man's dress [i.e., origins], don't bother about his nakedness." Earlier
> on, you could always look at a man's origins and tell if he was lying.
> You knew his people, his customs, his nature (*ṭabīʿa*). But nowadays
> even those with asel lie.

Moroccans, therefore, often assume a set of entailments that flow from
knowledge of origins. A person's "roots," the place where his people are
mwalin of the area, the "patrimony" that is or once was his allows an entry
point into a whole range of features which finds practical application in forming networks and assessing others.

That Moroccans find in another's "origins" a starting point for assessment
comes out with further clarity when one observes the order in which an appraisal of another is made. The following example will help to illustrate this
point:

> My wife and I were speaking with Y., a man in his early forties who
> teaches in the girls' grammar school in Sefrou. A native of Fez, he re-
> ceived a traditional education at the mosque university there, the
> Qarawiyin. As a student he also headed a group of amateur actors who
> performed many European plays in translation, including those of Shake-
> speare. When he learned that my wife was writing her dissertation about
> Beaumont and Fletcher, the playwrights who dominated the theatre after
> Shakespeare's death, Y. said that if you want to see in what way their
> work was significant in its own right you must look at four things.
> "First," he said, "you must ask who they were. What was their 'origin'
> (asel)? Who were their families and what did they do? Were they from
> the city or countryside? Were they learned (*qāriʾ*) or not? Second, you
> have to look at the reason (*sabab*) they were writing: Was it for money or
> were they trying to attain something higher? Third, you have to see if
> they were political (*siyāsī*) or not: Were they writing plays and sketches
> to make a political point? And fourth, you have to look at the times and
> the relations of England with other countries: Were there wars or was
> everyone just resting? You have to know all these things in order to
> understand what they were saying. It is hard, that study" he concluded,
> "very hard."

Although the topic of this conversation may have been unusual, the order in
which the assessment of the men involved was made is typical of Moroccan
social perception. Whereas Westerners would not initially assume that the
most important thing to know about the meaning of an artist's work is his or

her origins, this information is precisely what our friend chose to stress. Like his fellow Moroccans he gave predominant stress, first, to origins and then to other features. "If a person's origin is unknown to you, look at his doing," says the Moroccan proverb—but always try to discern origins first. As we shall see later, this emphasis on asel as implying action, and action (rather than intention) implying worth is a distinctive aspect of Moroccan social perception.

If one's identity is composed, in part, of one's "origins," it is also important to note that this identity is not immutable. Indeed, it is contingent on situation and context and is, to a certain extent, subject to negotiation. In the countryside, for example, it is generally true that a person will be identified by the people among whom he or she lives. To reside in a given area means that one has access to the common properties there as well as a correlative duty to defend them. The more one owns property in the area, the firmer the identification. Thus a man who comes as a refugee from another area or who marries into a group pledging his own labor to his father-in-law in place of a significant bridewealth payment will be regarded as less than a full "citizen" of the group and will be identified less fully with it.[9] Whether he comes from outside or within he will have to make a clear choice of identity in various situations. If there is a dispute—whether relatively peaceful, calling for financial assistance or legal co-surety, or (as in the past) as part of a blood feud, calling for collective security and group liability for bloodmoney payments— a man may ultimately be required to declare his identity. Even this identity, however, may be situational. One man I know, who married in from another region, normally identified himself as a descendant of the Prophet in the Drissi line and claimed to be related to the acknowledged group of Drissi living near the Berber fraction into which he had married. However, he did not hesitate to claim he was completely unrelated to the latter group whenever a dispute broke out involving them. Whole tribes or fractions may also manipulate their identities as situation and credibility permit.[10] Thus it is quite common for people to alter their claimed or attributed "origins" so that the consequences normally attached to that identity may be available to them.

Indeed there is even an element of negotiability involved. I do not mean that a person may try to take on a nisba that seems inappropriate—that one may claim to be descended from a minor saint of a distant area when that claim is undocumented, or that away from a given place one may fancy oneself with a name of fine proportions. Rather, I mean that there is genuine open-endedness to the applicability of alternative names as one tries to call forth the contextual implications that may be borne by the name. Thus a Sefrou man living in another area may try to set the implications of his attachments and

9. On the status of such an outsider (amḥuz) see Hart 1976.
10. See, for example, the case study in Rosen 1979, 53–57.

customs by using the nisba *Sefrawi* because he hopes to portray himself as coming from a true city and not a small town. Or the official in charge of registering names on the civil-status lists (necessary for obtaining passports and other legal documents) may refuse to allow people to choose names he feels are inappropriate to their "real" origins. If, for Moroccans, it is contextual man who forges ties with others, contexts, like the ties themselves, are subject to manipulation.

In the terms that mark an individual, then, we find some of the most characteristic features of Moroccan social organization. A common set of rules for attribution, themselves inherently open-ended and subject to considerable limitation within a definite framework, shapes the repertoire individuals may draw on in forging interpersonal ties. By being able to place another in a host of contexts, one learns vital information about others' networks and sets the stage for further developing one's own. But social identity—the repertoire of nisbas, the manipulation of affiliations, the assumptions of varied ethnic or regional origins—are only one element in the mix. Before we can see in more detail how the knowledge and attributes described here bear on the broader questions of Moroccan cultural logic and network formation, we must look at two other aspects of social identity: the perception of human nature and the comprehension of the workings of another's mind.

The Nature of Human Nature

It was the great fourteenth-century North African historian Ibn Khaldun, blending his own ideas with those of Aristotle and Plato, who argued that cultural life is not separate from but an integral aspect of a person's very nature. Set in a natural environment that nurtures individual qualities of character and temperament, and channels collective relationships and institutions, human beings are both the products and the fabricators of their own natures. Born with the desire to gratify bodily needs as well as the urge to achieve calmness, hope, confidence, superiority in conflict, emulation, and affiliation with others, individuals draw upon their reasoning powers to apprehend the order in which cause and effect are related and to learn, through their own actions, how best to establish relations with others. Just as the repetition of physical tasks leads to the formation of habits capable of satisfying one's desires, so too, the forms of action our reason leads us to perform become, through habit, stabilized in the arts, customs, and conventions that are themselves a property of human nature. Since attachments to others do not occur fortuitously, it is possible, Ibn Khaldun argued, to observe the patterns through which, as a product of reason and desire, cultural habits are formed and to develop these observations into a rational science of culture (see Mahdi 1957, 171–87).

Doubtless there are few people in the Sefrou region who have read much of

Ibn Khaldun's writing and only a modest number who could give precise directions to the street the French named after him in the Ville Nouvelle. But his description of the constitution and importance of human nature as embracing reason and passion, custom and character, convention and creation strikes a chord that reverberates throughout North African social life and history. For Moroccans, assessments based on the concepts embraced under the rubric of human nature are essential to the order of everyday life, and no one, whether professional student of culture or practitioner of normal existence, can fail to draw on concepts familiar to Ibn Khaldun in the cumulative process of weighing one's own actions and another's possibilities. In turning to the concept of human nature, therefore, one adds, as do the Moroccans, to that store of knowledge which may subsequently be ordered into useful relationships.

As in any society there are in Sefrou certain individuals who are more capable than others of articulating their views about the nature of humanity and its various subdivisions. I was fortunate in having as one of my language teachers and initial informants a man, referred to here as Si Abdallah, who was particularly good at organizing his ideas and communicating them to a foreigner. From one of our earliest interviews Abdallah set forth a paradigm that must be regarded as central to the Moroccans' conception of the nature of human beings.

"There are," said Abdallah, "three fundamental elements of which human nature is composed: *rūḥ, nafs,* and *ʿaqel.* Ruh refers to one's soul. It is that portion of one's nature that will continue to exist after one's death. It comes from God and will return to God. No one can understand God. If we did know our souls, we would lock them up in our bodies and never die.

"Now there are some," Abdallah continued, "who say that one's nafs and one's soul are really the same thing. But this is only partly true. Like the soul, nafs is life itself, hence all living creatures—angels, men, animals, and the *jnūn* [the invisible creatures of the netherworld]—all possess nafs. Nafs is really all the thoughts and attitudes we have that lead us to do bad things. Well, actually, it doesn't always lead to bad things, but it can. It is all the things we share in common with the animals, all the passions and lusts. Sometimes these desires are necessary for doing good things, but then only if they are guided by reason.

"And that is what ʿaqel means: reason, rationality, the ability to use our heads in order to keep our passions from getting hold of us and controlling us. God gave Adam reason so he would know good from bad. God gave man the freedom to act as he pleases, but he also gave us reason so we would not be completely at the mercy of our nafs. By studying the Quran and by following the advice of good teachers and good leaders we can develop our reasoning abilities so that we can use our passions as we want instead of being led around by them.

"So nafs," he continued, "really has two sides to it: We need desire, for example, in order to have children, but if it is not controlled by reason we would just be like animals. We need to think about ourselves in order to get money and provide for our families, but if we don't control it with our reason we would just be greedy. We say that when a man 'has nafs' he has 'self-respect,' but if he is 'in love with his nafs' he is just an 'egotist.' What you call psychology we call ʿilm n-nafs, 'the study of nafs.' Reason gives us the flexibility to handle our nafs and all the bad things it might lead us to do. Just as God put joints in our body so that we would be flexible enough to cope with a variety of physical situations, so too He gave us ʿaqel so we might also have flexibility of mind and know good from bad, right from wrong.''

I then asked Abdallah whether nafs and ʿaqel were the same in all kinds of people—in children as opposed to adults, for example, or in women as opposed to men.

''Yes,'' he replied, ''because we are all human beings we all have nafs and ʿaqel, but not all in the same amount or pattern. It is all a question of proportions. When children are born they are all nafs and only a little bit ʿaqel. Their minds are totally blank and their senses work like a camera taking a picture of this, an impression of that. Unlike the animals, though, we have the potential for developing our ʿaqel to a very high degree, but first, as the Commentaries say, our minds are like empty pieces of paper on which our fathers write. Only learning and discipline will develop a child's ʿaqel until he is old enough to control his own nafs. That is why you frequently have to punish a child even if he may not have done something bad, because unless you do his passions will later be his master.''

''And what about women?'' I asked.

''Ah,'' he said with a smile, ''women are quite another matter. You see, women too have ʿaqel, but in their case it can't develop as much as in men. It's just in their nature. Women have very great sexual desires and that's why a man is always necessary to control them, to keep them from creating all sorts of disorder, to keep them from leading men astray. Why else do we call women ḥbel šaiṭān, 'the rope of Satan'?[11] That is why women must be cloaked when in public, live in houses with small windows placed so that others cannot see in, and married off before they can give their fathers any

---

11. In a personal communication, Kenneth Brown notes that the term ḥbel šaiṭān also has a second meaning. In addition to ''rope'' or ''towline,'' ḥbel can refer to the string of beads that the members of a religious brotherhood use in the recitation of their prayers. The implication, then, is that women are associated with the ''brotherhood of the Devil'' and that close attachment to them is tantamount to paying homage to their spiritual leader, Satan himself. Or, it might be interpreted as meaning that women are in the hands of the Devil like prayer beads in the hands of the faithful. Vinogradov (1974b, 196) also notes: ''It is no accident that women are referred to in Morocco as Habl el-Shitan, the Rope of Satan. For in addition to being Satan's towline, they are also capable of tying a man up, rbt, thqef a cultural euphemism for saying that he is rendered 'impotent.' ''

trouble. It's like the saying goes: 'A woman by herself is like a Turkish bath without water,' because she is always hot and without a man she has no way to slake the fire.''

Abdallah's utilization of the nafs-ʿaqel paradigm, though colored by his own style and analogies, is clearly within the mainstream of Muslim conceptions of human nature.[12] The Quran distinguishes among three characteristics in the composition of human nafs: the portion of the nafs that, by virtue of simple faith in Allah, remains at all times tranquil (*muṭma'inna*); the portion that censors or upbraids a person for improper actions (*lawwāma*); and the portion that commands an individual toward the performance of lustful, generally evil, deeds (*ammāra*) (Calverley 1943, 254; Tritton 1971, 491).[13] Human intellect (ʿaqel) shapes these forces, giving them a valued direction and quality. To many classical commentors, human intellect differs more in degree than in kind from that of Allah: human reason is to God's as light is to the sun (see Tritton 1971, 494). It is one's duty to seek knowledge.[14] By following the teachings of the Prophet and wise leaders, individuals train their reasoning powers to guide them in the pursuit of knowledge, both spiritual and practical, by which they can be directed to everlasting reward. By nature, though, each person is forgetful, a quality inscribed in the very term for human beings, *al-insān*—''the forgetful ones.'' That is why it is so important to garner knowledge through constant repetition: children learn best by rote memorization and adults retain the preeminence of reason over passion by repetitive ritual acts because repetition creates habit, and habit creates predictable acts within a community of believers. The ideal, therefore, is not the fashioning of one's soul, though mystics may seek to mold themselves to the characteristics they believe Allah to possess. Rather, for the ordinary person the ideal is to acquire such knowledge of this world and Holy Writ, and to channel one's passions in the process in such a fashion, as to conform to the will of God and the duties assigned humanity.

In ordinary discourse, the concept of nafs is, therefore, deeply intertwined with the notion of the person, for what is distinctive to an individual is, in

---

12. For a similar account, see Bowles 1963. For additional views of North African men toward women, see Al Amin 1968 and Boudjedra 1969. For an analysis of the nafs-ʿaqel paradigm in an Indonesian setting see Siegel 1969.

13. The lustful aspect of human nature is often equated in the Quran and popular discourse with *ḥawwā*, the Arabic name for the first woman, Eve. *Nafisa* is a woman's name, that of both a patron saint of Cairo and the name chosen by the Egyptian novelist Mahfouz for the sexually demanding woman in one of his best-known works (see Somekh 1973, 80 and 83). On the change in meaning of nafs from the pre-Islamic ''vegetative'' soul to the Quranic concept of a ''thinking'' soul, see Chelhod 1955, 106–15. On the role of Nafs, ruh, and ʿaqel in sleep and death, mysticism, theology, and classical narratives, see respectively, J. Smith 1979; Michon 1973, 220–28; Gardet 1967, 241–47; and Goitein 1977, 10.

14. See Grunebaum 1953, 234 for traditions of the Prophet on this topic.

part, the concatenation of knowledgeability and passions by which one is characterized. Moreover, the concept of nafs is entwined with a person's own self-regard. In classical Arabic "to pay deference to or esteem one's nafs" (*iḥtirām an-nafs*) or, in the simpler colloquial, "to have nafs" ('*and n-nafs*) is properly equated with the notion of self-respect. But where, to many Americans, self-respect may imply not just regard for one's social position or duties but willingness to take responsibility for the choice of standards on which to model one's actions and values, in Islam self-respect arises from the process of acknowledging the sole God-given standard that defines proper conduct and developing those habits by which one may bring oneself into accord with what is innate in each person and indispensable to the community. "Study (knowledge) adds to human nafs" (*l-qraya katzid n-nafs d-ben ādam*), said one informant, not because it suppresses undesirable urges but because it conduces the soul to be socially useful.

If possession of nafs is, therefore, tantamount to a tranquil regard of one's innate worth, "to lack nafs" is to be indecisive, slipshod, cowardly, impotent. The implications of sexuality and maturity are clear. Although people in Sefrou, unlike those in parts of Algeria, do not use the word nafs to refer to female genitals and ruh to penis, the implication that men and women are to be assessed in terms of their basic sexual drives is clear.[15] Notwithstanding some folk beliefs that men and women contribute equally to the formation of a child, the nature of the sexes is made comprehensible to Moroccans in terms of the distinctions contained in the nafs-'aqel model. Thus it is worth returning to the example of male-female relations in order to see how this model, which is applicable to other domains of interpersonal assessment as well, is linked to the social order.

In many respects the men and women of Sefrou, like those of other areas in Morocco, live in separate worlds, their relationships more intensely cultivated within distinct realms of activity than in direct interchange with each other. But just as those two worlds meet and diverge at numerous points, and just as their conceptions of each other touch common themes in their different orientations, so, too, does each rely on principles of relatedness that share certain features.

It is often remarked that women's lives are largely restricted to the private realm of household, family, and kin group while men lead public lives in the workplace, the market, and the sphere of political relations. Women, as we shall see, are viewed by men as naturally weak and unreliable, and the differentiation of spheres is directly related to this view. As noted by Amal Rassam Vinogradov: "The inherent limitations in the character of women confine them in the sphere of 'nature,' whereas men are capable of operating in the sphere of 'culture.' These two worlds of 'nature' and 'culture' correlate with

15. On the Algerian usage, see Bourdieu 1977, 139.

the private and public sectors of social life. A woman, therefore, is relegated to the 'natural' and private world of child-rearing and general domesticity, while a man's life unfolds in the 'cultural' or public world of politics, trade, and religion" (Vinogradov 1974b, 193).

From the studies of Moroccan women conducted by Vinogradov, Maher, H. Geertz, and others, a picture of the separate social lives of women emerges with great consistency.[16] Although young girls may attend Quranic schools with boys, and some few—mainly in the larger cities—continue their segregated education beyond, once most Arab girls reach puberty they are kept very close to, if not actually confined within, the precincts of their homes. The household itself is often occupied by an extended family, with different nuclear families occupying separate rooms around a common courtyard. Although men and women of the extended family mix a good deal within the house complex, it is not uncommon, particularly among larger and wealthier groups, for men to eat and sleep in separate quarters from the women. Conversation between men and women within the house is common, but the topics and styles of communication differ in mixed and segregated company.

Once she is married, a woman's role changes significantly. In most cases a newly married couple resides in the home of the husband's parents. As a wife, a woman may be subjected to substantial confinement within the house. Occasional visits to friends or relatives may be made in the company of other women of the house, although poorer women may do their own marketing. The young wife is, however, largely dominated by her mother-in-law. The latter, jealously guarding her role as manager of the household and common kitchen, asserts her control over the internal workings of the home in many ways. She will often claim the right to teach the new wife how to cook—even though the girl is perfectly competent in this respect—and she guards the young woman's seclusion at home and veiled appearances outside with great care. The young wife is drawn into the constant talk by the women of the household concerning their lives, their relationships with the men, and the faults each of the women sees in the others. Quarrels are frequent and often spill over into public view, with neighbors and relatives called upon to notice, to support, or to mediate. Men are often caught up in the tensions that arise between their wives and mothers: a man who shows too much love for his wife will be thought by his mother to be in need of a magical remedy, which may be added surreptitiously to his food (see Vinogradov 1973; Maher 1974, 100–103); a father whose wife and daughter-in-law are at odds will be badgered by each for favors or find his pronouncements purposely undermined as each of the disputants seeks to establish her own position.

In most instances, however, men seek to interpose themselves between the

16. Vinogradov 1973, 1974b; Maher 1974, 1978; H. Geertz 1979a, 315–79; D. Dwyer 1978; Mernissi 1975.

women as infrequently as possible. As young boys they spent much of their time in the company of women—witnessing their internal differences, being used by the women as vehicles for communication and spying between households, and observing the rituals and erotic dances engaged in by the women during festive periods of visiting. As they grow into young manhood their relationship to parents and different categories of women is an anomalous one. Sons should not engage their fathers in any discussion relating to sex, and since their decorum in front of their fathers should continue throughout life to be circumspect and reserved, it is not uncommon to see a grown man extinguish his cigarette or rise to leave the rough-talking environment of the café when his father enters. His tie to his mother, if less clearly regulated by etiquette, is no less intense. It is she who may be instrumental in viewing prospective brides, and it is she who may intercede with his father for favors. At the same time, she is a woman, a creature of less responsibility and self-regulation, and hence an individual to be honored as much in her person as she may be the object of anger for her weakness and petty manipulations.

The separation of the domains of men and women is deeply affected by their differential access to resources and the general insecurity of married life. As Maher notes, Moroccan women are largely excluded from earning wages, and what properties they do possess tend to be dominated by their husbands or agnatic kin (Maher 1974, 121–31). To achieve some minimal security and companionship, they are forced to depend on other women. Their ties with one another, however, are necessarily strained. On the one hand, they depend on one another for mutual support and the sharing of everyday tasks; on the other hand, they are often in direct competition with one another for scarce resources and for influence over the men. Alliances are constantly shifted as individual women seek both security and relative advantage, and the full range of social ties is constantly employed and rearranged in the process.

The economic insecurity of women is intensified by the frequency of divorce. In any given year, between one-third and one-half as many divorces as marriages are recorded in Morocco. The proportions vary from city to countryside and from one region of the country to another, and there is reason to believe that many marriages and divorces are never registered. Although polygamy is lawful though rare, serial monogamy is very common. Thus, in his study of a shantytown of Casablanca in the late 1940s, Adam found that the average number of marriages was 2.4 for men and 1.7 for women and that 6.8 percent of the men had married more than five times (Adam 1949–50). Contemporary figures for the Sefrou region remain broadly comparable. As we shall see in greater detail later, although men possess the legal power to divorce their wives arbitrarily, wives, often with the aid of their male kinsmen, may be able to arrange their social ties in such a way as to blunt the husbands' legal powers. The sheer dependency of women and their quest for security through the manipulation of familial relationships is, however, explained by men largely in terms of the idiom of nafs and 'aqel, the differences in sexual drives and rationality of men and women.

Recall, for example, Abdallah's comments about the nature of female sexuality. In his descriptions, and those of many other Sefrou-area men, endless examples were adduced to show how essential it is for men to control the sexual drives of women. Like many others, Abdallah assured me that the high incidence of adultery in Europe was due to the fact that uncircumcised husbands lack the strength to keep their women satisfied and that it was, therefore, only natural that these women would have to seek relations with a number of different men. The sexual potency of the Muslim man, I was nevertheless assured, was enough to handle several women at the same time, hence the feasibility of polygamy in their part of the world.

I remember, too, being shown a marriage manual by another of my informants. The book had been published in Egypt some fifteen years earlier and had obviously passed through a number of inquisitive hands since that time. It was a thick book, well laden with illustrations intended to depict certain points about the nature of women and the relations between the sexes. There were pictures of men smoking hashish and drinking liquor while haunting visions of the malformed offspring they would produce hovered in the background. There were pictures of middle-aged matrons who were constantly thinking about men's bodies, and more provocatively posed young ladies displaying the irrepressible sexuality of the female. There was even one drawing purportedly representing a woman who failed to respond to her husband altogether. This, I was told, was due to the fact that a woman's sexual desires are inversely proportional to those of her father, so that if a man was himself consumed by his passions, he would deprive his daughters of even that degree of passion desirable for a proper marriage and legitimate procreation.

The pattern, then, is reasonably clear and straightforward. For Abdallah, as for his male compatriots, women are seen as possessing extremely intense sexual desires which, untempered by an equally well-developed reasoning ability, are capable of wreaking havoc on the established social order. Men, in turn, are extremely vulnerable to this feminine sexual onslaught, simply because the best among them still possess passions of their own. To place a man and a woman together in any situation in which this quintessential force would have the opportunity to take its ''natural course'' is considered both socially foolish and morally suspect. This is not to say that women are regarded as wholly lacking in intelligence or wit; but in the absence of great ability to develop their reasoning powers through Quranic study and regular prayer, they are more likely to have their intellectual powers turned to the formulation of devious plots or the practice of various magical arts. Thus, for all the variation from person to person that exists for each of the above features, it is, I shall argue, through this overall image of the *natural* differences between the sexes that Moroccan men conceive of women. It is through this focus, this cultural screen, that Moroccan men comprehend their actual ties with women and define, in very concrete situations, the relevant features of those ties and the ways in which they ought to be handled (see Al Amin 1968, 38–39; Maher 1974, 84–85; Vinogradov 1974b, 193–96).

But what of the women's view of men? Do they too rely on an explanatory scheme which, perhaps with its own peculiar twist, defines the relation between the sexes in terms of an indigenous "natural science"? Since I was unable to carry out intensive interviews with many Moroccan women, the answer to this question must be based, in part, on somewhat more indirect and inferential data and in part on the findings of female anthropologists who have done careful studies of Moroccan women. From this evidence it may be argued that it is not primarily in terms of a set of concepts dealing with the nature of the sexes as such that women seek to understand their relations with men. Rather, the women focus on the specifically *social* as opposed to *natural* relations between the sexes, and therefore their conceptual orientation is substantially different from that of the men. This argument requires some elaboration.

We have already seen that from the men's point of view the relationship with any particular woman, regardless of her role or status position, is not really a relationship of equals. In a sense, it is not even a relationship of two kinds of the same creature, for the nature of woman is regarded as unalterably different from that of man. Whether as cause or effect, there are a number of sociological repercussions attendant on this assertion. One of them is the fact that, broadly speaking, provided women do not overstep the bounds of public decency and do not create unmanageable strains within the household, they are generally left to handle their own affairs and to pursue their own social lives in reasonable separation from those of men. In Sefrou, as in most parts of Morocco, this means that women spend most of their time in the company of other women preparing meals, caring for children, celebrating various festivities, and establishing an internal pecking order through gossiping about others, berating the dependent members of their households, forging cooperative attachments, and exercising their relative powers and influence over men.

If the worlds of men and women are largely separate, it is nonetheless quite obvious that the two frequently impinge on each other directly. In the distribution of household resources, for example, or in the quest for a relative's mediating influence, there are many social situations in which particular men and women must contend with the simple fact of each other's existence. Thus, in addition to ordering their own internal social hierarchy—and perhaps because of it—the women themselves must often bring whatever influence or power they possess to bear on those decisions that will directly affect the character and composition of their own social world. This is not the place to discuss the legal arrangements that may exist between a husband and wife: the financial burden a man might have to bear in case of divorce, or the partial safeguards a wife might possess by virtue of the terms of her marital contract or legal standing. Nor can we adequately relate the innumerable ways in which a Moroccan woman, lacking other resources, might make the life of her husband or certain other men one that is dominated by nagging and bickering, recrimination and argument with other close relatives. The point to be stressed here is that insofar as questions arise for Moroccan women that bear directly on their own rather separate social world, primary attention is given by them to the various social relationships involved and to the ways in which these relationships can be manipulated to one's own particular advantage. Women may, on occasion, refer to men as intrinsically worthless or childish, but they are more likely to give greatest emphasis to the ways in which men can be ignored, outflanked, or outwitted by the arrangement of various social pressures within the household or family.[17]

This is not to say that men are totally unaware or unconcerned with the actual relations that exist between themselves and their women or that the women, on their side, may not refer to the relations between the sexes in terms of certain assumptions about basic human nature. Instead, it is to say that each possesses a different primary conceptual orientation, a different set of guiding ideas through which particular situations are defined and particular beliefs maintained. It is no simple perpetuation of the bias of Moroccan men, therefore, to argue that, by and large, women who are confronted with problems that involve men focus most of their attention on manipulating social relations in the family rather than on interpreting such relations in terms of a clearly defined stereotype of essential human nature. Being less capable than men of imposing decisions from on high, Moroccan women simply must work with the primary resource available to them—the relations among members of the family—in order to influence situations and decisions to their own benefit.

This orientation becomes most clear when the question arises as to the choice of mates for one's sons and daughters. From the women's point of view, a marriage changes not only the relationships of the dependent involved but the composition—and perhaps the internal order and hierarchy—of the women's social world. Particularly in the case of a son's marriage, each of the women will be affected by the arrival of a new bride in the house (assuming patrilocal residence) and the creation of new ties with the women of the bride's own family. Similarly, the marriage of a daughter establishes new social ties for all the women concerned as well as for the girl herself. Whether a particular marriage is in some degree endogamous or involves a family of outsiders, a whole new element is injected into the women's world by the

17. On men as *bāṭil* ("worthless," "vain," "absurd") and childish, see Vinogradov 1974b, 196.

formation of a marital bond. One can, therefore, study a series of marital negotiations and consequences with an eye to the structural arrangements that occur in the wake of such an event (see, for example, H. Geertz 1979a, 363–77). On the other hand, one can study the same situations from a primarily cultural perspective in which closest consideration is given to the various ideas that the participants themselves employ in defining and guiding their own actions.

It is from this latter perspective that we shall look at a specific marriage negotiation that occurred in Sefrou and on its basis seek answers to the following questions: What really happens when the separate conceptual schemes of men and women—one stressing the perception of human nature, the other the structure of actual relationships—come into direct contact, and indeed conflict, with each other? What forces are at work in the definition and resolution of such a situation, and how do they relate to the conceptions held by the parties involved? The specific incident around which the answers to these questions will be built concerns a conversation I overheard during one of my return visits to Sefrou.

I had been staying in Sefrou at the home of Haj Muhammad, a wonderful old man whose dignified carriage and rich raconteurial skills blended magnificently with his little-boy smiles and the insouciant tilt he gave to the favorite old *tarbush* on his head. One morning shortly after my arrival, the Haj suggested we go visit a friend of his. We wound our way down the hill from the Haj's house, past the crenelated walls of the Old City, to the door of the house of Si Abdelqader. A young girl opened the door, ushered us into the guest room, noted that her father had already left on his regular trip to the countryside, and fetched a pot of tea before hurrying off to tell her mother that there were guests in the house. A moment later Si Abdelqader's wife entered the room and greeted us. She was a stout woman, well into her middle years, and the Haj was such an old and dear friend of the family that there was no discomfort whatsoever in the quiet, intense conversation that ensued. I had visited in Si Abdelqader's home a few years earlier and was aware that several of his daughters were of marriageable age. It took me some time, however, to fit together enough pieces of the conversation between Si Abdelqader's wife and the Haj to realize that a marriage had been arranged for one of these daughters and that while the girl had no objection to an arranged marriage as such, she was adamantly opposed to this particular union since the man in question lived in a city that would place the girl far away from her own family and friends. As I later recollected, a portion of the conversation concerning the marriage went something like this:

Mother: Well, she comes to me and she cries and she says: ''Mother, I don't want to marry him. He lives far away and is always moving and I won't have anyone from my own family nearby.''

Haj: Why is she crying? Doesn't she have any sense (*'aqel*)? Doesn't her own family know what's best for her?

Mother: She goes to her sister and she says that in the house of this man she will have no one to talk to, none of her own relatives. And her sister comes to me and says that we won't be able to visit her in that man's house, and maybe if I were to talk to her father he would see how much his little baby is suffering.

Haj: Ach! That girl is crazy. Her head is spinning, that "daughter of sin" (*bint l-ḥarām*). She has no self-respect (*qlīl nafs-ha*). She has no respect for her father at all.

Mother: And then she says that she will wait until her brother comes home from Europe next month with his wife, that Frenchwoman. She says her brother's wife would never approve of such a marriage and that she, in turn, will get her husband to talk to Si Abdelqader and convince him that this is not a good marriage.

Haj: May Allah give her pain, that little bitch! She makes for such unrest! She is absolutely consumed with passions, like all girls. But we'll take care of everything.

Mother: Well, I don't know. Who knows what's what. I don't understand it. It's in God's hands.

Haj: Of course. And we'll fix everything as soon as Si Abdelqader gets back—and before his son comes home.

Mother: Well, it's up to God. I don't know.

Haj: It's all set. When Si Abdelqader returns we'll take the groom to my house, bring two notaries up from the court, make a *fātḥa* prayer, and register the marriage. That will finish the matter once and for all. That will cool your daughter off.

Mother: Well, sir, I don't know. Maybe that's the way it is. I just don't know. Everything is in the hands of Allah!

There are a number of points that can be drawn from a study of this particular case. Although characterized by certain unusual features (such as the fact that the brother of the potential bride is married to a foreigner and returns to Morocco only occasionally), it does indeed exemplify some of the more important mechanisms of Moroccan marital politics. In terms of contemporary Moroccan law it is illegal for a marriage to be recorded if the bride has not appeared before the notaries to give her personal consent—a fact of which almost all women are aware. But if the registration of such a marriage without the bride's knowledge is irregular, it is not at all unusual for the bride to be constrained to accede to the wishes of her marital guardian, whatever her own feelings about the union may be.

But in order to understand the full implications of the conversation between the Haj and Si Abdelqader's wife, it is necessary to go beyond the strictly legal or sociological aspects of the case. Indeed we can see in this example precisely that theoretical argument that lies at the very heart of this study. For it is possible to look at this conversation as an example of an encounter between a man and a woman, each of whom maintains a rather different view about the nature of the sexes and their respective social roles, and who, when they are brought into direct confrontation, must now engage in what might be called a process of "bargaining for reality." As developed by psychologist Thomas J. Scheff, this notion of reality bargaining refers to the process by which several actors, each of whom possesses a different view of what is really true about the situation in which all are involved, attempt to make his or her definition of the situation prevail (Scheff 1968). Because these individuals are engaged in a common activity demanding both definition and resolution, their concepts of reality are subject to negotiation, which in turn is significantly affected by the relative power possessed by each of the participants in this particular situation. Scheff thus refers to psychiatric interviews in which a therapist may impose his version of reality on a patient as the price for his personal and professional aid, or a lawyer may suggest to his client a version of what "really happened" that will absolve the client of any legal responsibility. If, as Scheff implies, reality is not an objective fact to be recognized but a definition to be bargained over, it is necessary to ask how we are to determine when such a situation exists and what role the different powers of men and women play in its application.

In the sense in which the term *reality* is used here, it refers to an experience of the world in which one lives rather than to that world as a set of physical constructs neutrally defined and existentially given. Moreover, as an experience of that world, reality, in this highly expressive sense, is, for any man or woman, best regarded as an ongoing experience, an activity, a continuing realization rather than a product, a fact, or a truth. But to say that it is created and lives in the "mind" rather than in "nature" is by no means to say that any given view of reality is without its own distinct regularities. Quite the contrary, an image of reality must conform with certain facts external to itself (the brute facts of sexual dimorphism, for example) and certain forms of internal consistency and coherence. And of at least equal importance is the fact that such a conception of reality must be sufficiently comprehensible to and consonant with the views of others as to permit, and indeed to vitalize, relations with those persons who form part of one's social and cultural environment.

In the case of the Moroccans' expressed views of the opposite sex, the canons of consistency and congruity are indeed discernible. In almost any situation in which the subject of women arises, one constantly hears men refer to the generic consitution of that gender: women, say men, do not possess "the wherewithal" to grasp fully the essential elements of pure religion; they are "naturally" prone to traffic with powerful forces of the netherworld; they are "by natural disposition" led to create problems in the family; and so on.

For men, the experience of women is so constantly mediated by a set of terms and referents concerning the nature of the sexes as to constitute persuasive evidence that the view of women as naturally different from men is indeed a fundamental feature of the men's orientation to the real world. And, although less direct evidence can be cited, a similar degree of consistency and pervasiveness appears to inform the women's own more "sociological" orientation to men. If the references by men to women or women to men were mere verbalizations, post hoc rationales or "as if" propositions, a much less uniform, pervasive, and regular set of expressions might be employed. Accordingly, it can be argued, at least as a working hypothesis, that the "natural" and "social" orientations of each of the sexes do indeed constitute fundamental conceptual orientations which define and make meaningful each group's perception of reality.

Inasmuch as the concepts involved are capable of being used to define different situations—and capable, too, of being manipulated in this way for quite varied purposes—we can, building on the ideas of Scheff and Gallie, refer to such concepts as "essentially negotiable" (Scheff 1968; Gallie 1968, 157–91).[18] That is, a certain degree of vagueness accompanies the use to which any of the terms referred to can be put: there is an element of uncertainty inherent in these terms, such that their application to any situation by one person may be contested by another. This uncertainty of application is so very much a part of the concept's own composition and the resolution of any dispute so dependent on the ways they can be employed as to grant the concepts themselves an aspect of essential negotiability.

In the specific case of Si Abdelqader's daughter, the concepts employed by the Haj and the girl's mother clearly display this quality of essential negotiability. Each understands the meaning the other associates with such words as *passion, sense, respect, suffering,* and the more complex terms referring to familial dissension and relatedness. The question is whether these terms really define the present situation. The Haj, of course, thinks that his own conceptions should apply. He argues that this is a straightforward example of female sensuality blinding a girl to her natural place within a set of socio-legal arrangements sanctioned by the traditions of religion, society, and ordinary common sense. For Si Abdelqader's wife the reality is quite different. She believes it is a question of the actual relations that exist, or would be brought into existence, by the formation of this particular union. And since each of the terms and concepts employed can apply to a variety of different situations— and since this vagueness, this differential utility, is an inherent characteristic of the careers of these terms—it can be argued that it is, in no small part, the essential negotiability of these terms that makes this discussion a true dialogue

18. For a fuller discussion of this concept, see chapter 4 of this volume.

whose outcome is not prejudged by the terms used or the conceptions expressed.

The essential negotiability of the concepts makes bargaining over the definition of the situation capable of being articulated. In order to establish that the present case really does involve such a reality negotiation, we must read the text of the conversation between the Haj and the girl's mother in the light of certain additional information. That Si Abdelqader's wife and the Haj were bargaining for reality is indicated by several supplemental facts. For one, it must be understood that the dispute referred to had been going on for some time before the morning of the reported conversation and that it continued for some time afterward. Si Abdelqader, as further questioning revealed, had arranged this marriage without thinking of all its possible implications. Under the right circumstances he might very well have agreed to break the engagement. However, instead of engaging him in a subtle dialogue mediated by respected friends and relatives, Si Abdelqader's daughters openly declared their opposition to the marriage and attempted to forestall its enactment by constantly harassing their father and upsetting the order of the household. Accordingly, Si Abdelqader began to feel that, in part, his general position as the head of the household was being challenged. Although his right to choose his daughters' mates was never directly questioned, he was aware, on the one hand, that to give in to his daughters' tactics might have endangered his ability to make decisions for the women of his household on a wide range of issues. On the other hand, Si Abdelqader was constantly reminded of the women's capacity to disrupt the order of the house, a situation he sought to prevent not only for the sake of familial tranquility, but because he sincerely wished to find a workable solution to the problem. Although he seemed willing to seek some other husband for his daughter, no proper rationale or set of mediating persons had as yet come forward to save both Si Abdelqader's face and his regard for his daughter's happiness.

As a respected friend of the family the Haj was ideally placed to seek an appropriate solution. As a traditionalist, he could be counted on to express the male view of natural superiority. As a realist who had experienced many unsettling disputes within his own family, he could be relied on to listen to the mother's views and discern their strength and import. The sheer fact that the two came together for this conversation is of no small importance. They were indeed prepared to listen, to argue, and to negotiate their different views of the situation.

The actual course of their discussion further justifies the characterization of their engagement as a process of reality bargaining. Throughout, each of the parties not only implied a particular course of action that could be taken but argued for a way to define the very situation in which they were involved. In trying to establish that her conception of reality was the crucial one, the mother kept referring to the actual relationships of the people involved. The Haj, in turn, saw the matter from the perspective of essential human nature and the implied need for men to act with reference to that fact above all others. The mother in particular seemed to be trying to suggest a basis for resolving the conflict if only the Haj would accept that this was a case of placing one's regard for the social well-being of one's dependent women over simple assertions of male dominance. The Haj, in turn, was suggesting the terms in which the mother ought to explain the situation to her daughter, thus acknowledging the issues of paternal decision making. Each played the role assigned members of their sex with classic precision: the Haj acted the part of the forceful male while the mother played the role of the dependent and submissive woman. Many of the harsh things said by the Haj ("May Allah give her pain, that little bitch!") are not only common to the Haj's rather robust style but are also far less severe Arabic idioms than my literal translations may suggest. Similarly, the mother showed no surprise when the Haj indicated the men's intention simply to marry the girl off regardless of the women's desires. Whether she regarded it as a bluff or a show of expectable male authoritarianism is unclear, but her response, from the look on her face to the gestures of her hand, was one of feminine confusion and uncertainty. Her overt assertions of divine omnipotence and personal obtuseness, however, were not simple assertions of weakness and fatalism. Quite the contrary, it may be argued that by her expression and her utterance ("It's in the hands of Allah!"), she was, in fact, implying that the men might think they had a grasp of the situation but that control over the matter was not theirs alone. Nor does this comment mean that the situation is in the hands of God. For just as the Haj could acknowledge the total power of Allah and proceed to indicate what the men were going to do about the situation, so too the mother was able to imply that the women were also not without additional resources of their own. The reference to Allah, then, might be interpreted less as a literal statement of theology than as a cautionary phrase, a sort of conditional marker, an assertion that power is not always what or where it appears to be. The mother's statements in this regard also buy time, since the Haj might begin to wonder exactly what temporal possibilities, what potential actions by the women, are really implied in the utterance of this supernatural platitude. The mother's statements were, therefore, revealing for their broader connotations and were themselves a function of the relative powerlessness of either party to impose his or her own concept of reality in an arbitrary or unilateral fashion.

The conversation between the Haj and Si Abdelqader's wife is neither an unusual encounter nor one limited solely to marital situations. We shall see similar instances of reality bargaining in a variety of social and political contexts throughout this study. In each of these situations it is clear that the kinds of resources on which each of the participants can draw is crucial to the outcome of the negotiation. But power—in the sense of control of critical resources through which one's will can be imposed—is, as we shall see, terribly diffused in Moroccan society; it seldom cumulates in unambiguous fashion for most or all of the possible situations a person may encounter.

Moroccan women in general are, as I intimated earlier, not without certain powers in their own homes. An issue may, of course, be joined in such a way as to pose a direct challenge to a man, who then relies on all his legal and economic resources to enforce his own solution. In certain instances a woman may be able to prevent or frustrate such arbitrary action by the contractual and financial limits that have been built into her marriage. But it is much more often the case that women will—perhaps must—give primary consideration to the actual relations that exist among the various members of the women's own social network. The ability of the women to make the lives of all concerned quite miserable, the ability to publicize a family quarrel to the point of threatening a public scandal, and the ability to exact revenge at a later time are all forms of action that women can use to considerable effect. Each case is, in this respect, a special one; but in general it can be said that the capacity to make one's own view of a situation and its solution stick is, if not equally divided between the sexes, certainly not weighted in all cases to the side of the men. In the case of Si Abdelqader's daughter the principals remained at a stalemate for more than a year and a half. Finally, at the instigation not only of the Haj but of his own wife and daughter-in-law, Si Abdelqader's daughter was invited to the Haj's house where, during nearly a week of browbeating by the Haj and his womenfolk, the girl was "convinced" that the marriage was indispensable to the repair of her father's declining economic status, whatever its merits as a question of filial respect. The marriage was forthwith performed and, at last count, the young wife, now resident with her husband in another city, was the mother of two children, her father the indirect recipient of some of the largesse that befalls a Moroccan pursuing a successful career in the public sector, and the Haj and his strong-minded womenfolk the pleased performers in what they regard as a story with a happy ending.

In sum, it appears that the social separation of Moroccan men and women also corresponds to a certain conceptual differentiation. Like the dialects of a single language, though, these different sets of ideas and beliefs are not so distant from each other as to restrict communication altogether. The separation is nonetheless great enough so that even, for example, in a marriage characterized by sincere and deep affection, there is on the man's part an assumption that this is not really a relation of equals, just as on the women's side there is a constant emphasis on the malleability of internal family relationships. When conceptual disagreements do occur, the terms in which they are expressed allow for a significant degree of bargaining and an exercise of respective powers. Although it is indeed possible for Moroccan men to proclaim that their definition of a given situation is the valid one, women possess sufficient means for hedging against the sheer imposition of this male fiat to grant them the capability of disputing the interpretation to be applied in the first place. Despite the fact that the statements made may appear to be simple and unilateral declarations, such encounters as we have described here might better be seen as processes of bargaining over which person's view will indeed be used to define a particular circumstance. What is negotiable, then, is less one's view of reality as such than its scope, its impact, and its differential importance.

Concepts like nafs and 'aqel may serve, therefore, as evaluative concepts and as instruments of social negotiation. As such they are by no means limited to instances involving cross-sex relations or the rationale for particular modes of child rearing. When men deal with one another, the assessment of another's self-control and reason, his sense of propriety and predictable behavior are similarly embraced in the concepts of nafs and aqel. All men are equal, says the prophetic tradition, except in learning. And it is knowledge—practical and religious—that can, in part, account for respect, mobility, and differences, even within families, of status, wealth, and influence. A man who possesses habits that give regularity to his actions is one who is to be emulated and respected. Similarly, if you know a man to be from a given people or region and know the customs that they use to form interpersonal ties, you will know how to evaluate and conduce another's acts. Each element contributes to the overall, integrated view of another that can then be fixed within one's own scheme of knowledge and network of relationships. But before making an initial effort to show how all this information receives patterned implementation, we must add one other cluster of features that bears on the assessment of others, namely those concerning another's interior state—one's motives and intentions.

The Problem of Other Minds in Morocco

> *A man claimed to be a prophet. They asked him, "What are the proofs of your being a prophet?" He said, "I shall tell you what is in your mind." They asked him, "What is in our minds?" He said, "You are thinking that I am a liar and not a prophet."*
>
> From a fourteenth-century Arab jokebook[19]

When Max Weber chose as the central focus of his sociology the ways in which individuals attach meaning to others' actions and orient their own activities accordingly, he was not ascribing to human beings either the characteristics of cultural automata—programed to decipher one another's moves by the dictates of inviolable custom—or the insight of born mindreaders—capable of clairvoyant apprehension of another's purpose and direction. Rather, for Weber, the meaning we attribute to others' acts is socially situated, cultur-

---

19. Quoted from Al-Nuwayrī, *Nihāyat al-Arab* in Lewis 1974, 284.

ally constructed: we direct our own actions in terms of the information that history, situation, and interpretive concepts aid us to formulate and apply with the rough-and-ready quality attached to all our everyday engagements. Moreover, as a number of philosophers, literary critics, and social scientists have noted, the ways in which people ascribe interior states to others is itself a public process, one in which the linguistic terms used are broadly shared and understood and in which the premises and ends of such ascription possess culturally distinctive qualities.[20] Taken from this angle, intentions and motives are neither private nor independently causal: they are culturally characteristic ascriptions through which the situations in which people find themselves and the categories in which they place others whom they encounter can be made more or less comprehensible.

To shift the quest for motives and intentions from the private to the public, from the causal to the ascriptive, and from the realm of the positive to that of the interpretive is to open up a whole new world of issues and ideas. Many of these issues were raised most provocatively by C. Wright Mills in his early article "Situated Actions and Vocabularies of Motive." Mills argued that "rather than fixed elements 'in' an individual, motives are the terms with which interpretation of conduct by social actors proceeds" (Mills 1940, 904). Whenever we attribute motives to another, he said, we are really trying to define the situation in which we find ourselves. To speak of a situation as one involving "love" or "duty," "faith" or "policy," or (to recall our North African concerns) "obligation" or common "origins" is to anticipate certain consequences that may follow when an individual engages in the action associated with such a situation. Motives and intentions do not, therefore, exist in psychic isolation; they are ways we talk about the situations in which individuals' actions take place. The imputation of motives thus has both interpretive and instrumental aspects. If we locate the terms by which we attribute motives and intentions in their historical and institutional contexts, we can see how perceptions of others vary over time from one social group or class to another. By tracing the relation between vocabularies of motive and situated actions we may also understand how, by characterizing a situation in a particular way, we may create in the observer a set of expectations and hence an image of the actor's intent. Indeed, in its most instrumental form, we can appreciate that by the way we define a situation we may be able to induce others to develop precisely the interior state we wish them to possess. In Mills' own words:

Men discern situations with particular vocabularies, and it is in terms of

---

20. In addition to specific works cited below, see Blum and McHugh 1971; K. Burke 1945; Fish 1980, especially 268–92; C. Geertz 1973; Percy 1976, especially 64–82, 189–214, 265–76; and Taylor 1971.

some delimited vocabulary that they anticipate consequences of conduct. . . . In a societal situation, implicit in the names for consequences
is the social dimension of motives. . . . We influence a man by naming
his acts or imputing motives to them—or to "him". . . . The research
task is the locating of particular types of action within typal frames of
normative actions and socially situated clusters of motive. (Mills
1940:906, 908, 913)

To Mills, then, the way we speak about others' minds is really an attempt to
comprehend and direct another's actions. Mills himself was particularly concerned to see how this process of motive attribution helped to shape various
occupational and status groups in the United States. Our concern here is both
wider and more specific. For if it is true, as we have been arguing, that
Moroccans orient their actions largely in terms of their personally contracted
ties to others, it is important to understand whether and how they account for
another's acts in terms of motives and intentions. Toward this end we must
pursue three inquiries simultaneously. First, we need to understand the terms
that are used to characterize another's interior state and to see how these terms
are connected to the larger semantic realm that Moroccans draw upon to identify and assess others. Second, we must ask how the issue of intent manifests
itself in different institutional contexts—in religion, law, or the formation of
personal networks. And finally, we must try to see in what ways the issue of
other minds is connected to additional cultural assumptions in Moroccan life,
thus giving to the question of other minds a characteristically Moroccan
answer.

Our starting point must once again be a key term, in this case the Arabic
word *nīya*. The word itself is generally translated as "intent," "design,"
"purpose," "plan," "will," "volition," "inclination," or "desire." Niya
also means "naive," "simple," "artless," "guileless," and "sincere." To
act "with niya" is to act with loyalty and good faith; "to have niya" is to feel
confident, assured, one's belief undiluted.[21] Niya also has specific religious
significance. At the start of each of the five daily prayers—and, in some
traditions, before a variety of other ritual and legal acts—the believer declares
the niya, the statement of intent by which one signifies the meaning and purpose of this act. Niya, it is said, arises from the heart, the seat of intellect and
attention, and, when unaffected by other factors, possesses qualities of purity
and truth.[22] Although Islam has rightly been characterized as a religion of
orthopraxis more than orthodoxy—one that stresses the performance of requisite rituals over the grasp of refined doctrine—the formation of the proper
intent is indispensable to correct practice. But intent is not dissociated from

21. See Brunot 1952, 791–92. See also Bourdieu 1977, 173 and Maher 1978, 103–4 on the
relation of niya to peasant virtues in Algeria.
22. See Wensinck 1961, 449. The issue of truth and lying will be discussed at pp. 117 ff.

actions, and the key to understanding the Moroccan conception of other minds lies precisely in this link between mental state and overt act. To appreciate this connection it will help to look at some of the specific contexts—social, legal, and religious—in which the question of others' interior states arises.

In the course of ordinary conversations about other people it is unusual to hear a Moroccan man refer to what he imagines the other to be thinking or feeling. Even when the question of another's mind is posed directly, Moroccans will answer by addressing themselves to what a person did or said, rather than what he might have thought or felt. Descriptions of others' endeavors— whether posed as gossip, history, myth, or fiction—invariably concentrate on what is perceivable about another, rather than on what is imagined. This is not, however, to say that "intent," niya, is irrelevant. Instead, it is to assume that overt acts offer the surest clue to inner states and that these actions are themselves to be interpreted with reference to the characteristics of the actor and the situation in which he acts. This impression—gained by repeated observation of conversations about others—is confirmed by the remarks of numerous informants to my specific inquiries.

> Speaking with H., a shopkeeper who had moved to Sefrou about ten years earlier from the Beni Azgha territory where he grew up, I asked whether you can tell another man's niya and if so how. "You can only judge a man's niya from what you see," he replied. "Everything else is between him and God. If you know who he is and what he has done you will know what his niya was." Under further questioning he kept coming back to a person's characteristics: where he was from, what occupation he practices, whether man or woman, learned or unschooled. "But," I said, "people do not always do what they mean to do—they make mistakes and miscalculations." "Of course," he replied, "but some things are never mistakes (kaṭa'). 'Marriage and plowing are with niya' (žuaž b-nīya u l-ḥart b-nīya): you cannot later say you did not really mean to get married or to cultivate the land. These things come from your heart and you cannot later say 'I did not think I was getting married or digging up so-and-so's land.' If I know who a man is, who he knows, who he deals with I can tell why he does things and whether he is a man who has niya."

Comments of this sort are characteristic both in their emphasis and in their imprecision. Without trying to draw the line too sharply we can distinguish two kinds of explanations of others' behavior Moroccans generally employ: one that centers around the notion of intent (niya) and another that involves the notion of kaṭar—thought, choice, the exercise of free will, the taking of a risk. Niya, with its religious and moral overtones, implies a direct consonance between act and interior state. Those actions that are thought to reveal niya are primarily those that are directed to God—the niya for which is not subject to human discernment—and those that have significant repercussions on the orderliness of this world—for which consequence implies a requisite intent. It is these actions affecting the social order with which informants are most concerned. Earlier, we mentioned the notion of *fitna*—chaos, discord, civil strife—from a root meaning "to tempt," "seduce," "entice," or "enthrall."[23] Those acts—like marriage, physical assault, territorial encroachment, and the performance of religious duties—that could threaten the stability of society are not only surrounded by weighty human and supernatural sanction but are regarded as so directly arising out of one's niya that they must be what they seem to be. Deeds that touch on a person's loyalty and veracity and that maintain or threaten the social order are, informants imply, ones through which you can see directly into a person's intent. By assessing the nature and consequence of the act they attribute intent: by defining the situation they characterize the motivating force.

Explanations couched in terms of khatar are, roughly speaking, those concerning less weighty actions and for which society and the individual observer would appear to be given greater leeway for uncertainty. Two kinds of explanation, like those cited by Western philosophers and linguists, are prevalent in Morocco: 'in order to' explanations, signaled by the word *baš*, and 'because of' explanations, signaled by the phrase *'ala ḥaqq-aš.*[24] If the answer to the question Why did someone do something? is couched in terms of purpose ('in order to'), that purpose will itself usually be stated as a consequence in the world, not as an alteration in one's interior state. Similarly, 'because of' explanations of another's behavior usually have as their predicate an observable, not an inner state. Moreover, explanations of an 'in order to' or 'because of' form frequently are framed in terms of an individual's social identity. It is, as we saw in the negotiation between the old man and the prospective bride's mother, in terms of the nafs-'aqel paradigm that the old man explained the girl's behavior. It is in terms of Beaumont and Fletcher's origins, family, and occupation that the playwrights' meaning and motivations had been analyzed by our friend. For, as we have seen, to know as much as possible about a person's contexts and affiliations is to know how he or she is likely to act. And to know consequence is, from the Moroccan perspective, to know as much as one can or needs to know in order to assess another's inner state.

Two points thus emerge quite vividly. First, that for Moroccans a person's inner state is by no means irrelevant or wholly indiscernible. Overt acts correlate broadly with interior states. Where the act has serious religious and social

---

23. For a fuller discussion of this concept see Gardet 1967, 448–52.

24. On the distinction between 'because of' and 'in order to' explanations, see Schutz 1964, 3–19. For examples of this distinction and of the emphasis, in Moroccan narrative accounts, of consequence rather than inner state, see Bourgeois 1959–60, 2:80 and Boukous 1977, especially the texts at 169–85 and 207–25.

consequences, it is assumed that no one would engage in such actions without expecting such consequences to occur. Social identity matters for purposes of determining what kind of situation is involved in the first place. If a woman or an ignorant man wrongfully converts something of another's to his or her own use, it is regarded as having less serious social consequence than if a well-educated male member of an elite family does so, since the former are expected to be guided by the latter. Act and intent being mutually implied, once the act (and its concomitant repercussions) are settled, intent is directly inferable. The same is true even when one is simply trying to account for ordinary behavior, though here the need to agree on a definition of the situation may be less pressing and hence the moral/religious implications of the terms employed less weighty. The second point to emerge, however, is that the definition of the situation is critical to the attribution of intent or motive. Indeed, since Moroccans bargain a good deal over the definition of situations, they are necessarily bargaining over the explanations of actions as well. Thus the whole course of motive attribution and constraint are contingent on the outcome of contextual definition. Before elaborating these points, however, it may be useful to consider the development of intentionality in several other domains, namely those of law and religion.

The issue of intentionality may arise in a variety of legal contexts: in criminal law, the seriousness of the offense and the appropriate punishment for it may turn on the question of intent; in civil matters, intent may be central to determining the validity of a bequest or contract. Although specific aspects of an inquiry into intent vary from one legal issue to another, a glance at the example of homicide may help us to understand the general development of the concept of intentionality in Moroccan legal culture.[25]

In almost all parts of the Middle East and North Africa, in the years before Western influence became predominant, the appropriate recompense for the killing of another was the payment of bloodmoney (*diya*). Compensation was also the appropriate remedy for injury. The Quran distinguishes between killing with intent (*'amd*) and by mistake (*kaṭa'*), and the four main schools of Islamic law that developed in the early Islamic period made further refinements in this distinction (Quran 4:92 et. seq.; Schacht 1961a, 228–29). For Islamic jurists, therefore, the question of intent was very important: the amount of compensation due or the permissibility of retaliation (*qiṣāṣ*) was a function of whether the act was deemed intentional.[26] But for scholars and jurists alike, intent was not a question of the accused's state of mind as such. Rather, inner state was assumed from overt acts. The intention of killing was presumed whenever an illegal killing followed an act generally regarded as fatal in its result (Schacht 1961a, 288).[27] A great deal of casuistry developed

25. For an expanded version of these remarks, see Rosen 1985 and 1980–81.
26. See Schacht 1961c and Weir 1961. See also Juynboll 1961a; Schacht 1961b; 1961d, 526–27.
27. On intent as overt act in Islamic law, see generally Schacht 1964, 116–18.

over matters of external evidence, especially the nature of the weapon used: the fact, for example, that a deadly weapon was involved was sufficient to impute an intent to kill.[28] Even when an act was the result of a mistake—thinking the injured man was a wild animal, accidentally suffocating a bed partner by rolling over on him in the night—bloodmoney had to be paid by the offender or his kinsmen. Loubignac reports that among the Zaer tribe, for example, even if a harm was unintentional the perpetrator had to pay for the upkeep of the guests who visited the injured and for part of the injured man's support if his wounds were especially grave (Loubignac 1952:66–71, 273–75).

The emphasis, then, is squarely on the consequences of an act. External evidence, such as the kind of weapon used, is taken as an index of an interior state, an insight into what the person must have meant. By categorizing types of situations, jurists were saying something about a state of mind. The connecting point would appear to be the idea that no one who is not immature, insane, or spiritually possessed would engage in a particular kind of act without intending its usual consequences. Whatever the other advantages of, for example, bloodmoney payments—as a form of social insurance, as a limitation on the scope of violence, as a less harsh penalty when situation and intent were ambiguous—drawing a direct correlation between act and intent reaffirmed the link between private choice and public consequence. Intent, in Islamic law, was therefore neither irrelevant nor the subject of more direct religious or psychological inquiry: it was assumed to be a necessary and discernible element of a given act.

This emphasis on discerning intent through situated acts continues to manifest itself in Moroccan adjudication, notwithstanding the use, during the Protectorate and post-Protectorate periods, of European criminal codes. In interviews, judges repeatedly insist that they can tell what a man's intent is and whether he is lying simply by inquiring carefully into his background, relationships, and prior behavior. Similarly, when stories are told in Morocco—rather like those related in the *Thousand and One Nights*—of really clever judges, they often involve the judge disguising himself and entrapping the suspect into committing the same or a similar infraction as that of which he is accused. The clever judge is not, of course, determining whether the man did in fact do what he is accused of: he is seeing if he is a person who will ever do such a thing; he is making an investigation into the accused's character. "If a man is bad," one judge told me, "he cannot hide it. It will show up in the way he acts. If you ask a lot of questions, a man cannot keep his thoughts hidden: his intention (niya) will be obvious."

The belief that a man's inner state is relevant inasmuch as it is directly connected to who he is and what he does is not unrelated to the conception of

28. See Liebesny 1975, 230–32. On presumptions in the Malikite school of Islamic law, see Lapanne-Joinville 1957.

interiority as manifest in Islamic religious doctrine and practice. One of the traditions of the Prophet (*ḥadīt*) cited by educated and uneducated informants alike says, "Works are in their intention only" (*innama l-'amāl bi-l-nīya*).[29] A man's "works" are, as we have seen, not self-defining. As Stanley Cavell has said generally: "Apparently, *what* the 'case' in question is *forms part of the content of the moral argument itself.* Actions, unlike envelopes and goldfinches, do not come named for assessment, nor, like apples, ripe for grading" (quoted in Pitkin 1972, 166; italics in original). Islam itself provides some of the parameters of situational, and hence motivational, definition in the concept of moral gradations and the limits of human conduct.

The Quran, in an oft repeated phrase, speaks of "the limits of God": "These are the bounds prescribed by God, come not too near them" is a provision that follows many legal injunctions.[30] The requirements for adequate adherence to the faith are few, basically the famous "five pillars of Islam"—the profession of faith, prayer, charity, the month-long fast of Ramadan, and the Pilgrimage. Acts themselves are categorized along a continuum from obligatory (*farḍ*) to forbidden (*ḥaram*), with those characterized as recommended (*sunna, mandūb*), indifferent/permissible (*mubāh, ḥalal*), and reprehensible (*makrūh*) lying between. Except for those few practices established by the Quran as obligatory (e.g., the five pillars of faith themselves) or forbidden (e.g., eating pork, fornication), the characterization of acts and the assessment of consequences, although the subject of elaborate commentary by scholars, has not been an obsessive moral concern among ordinary believers. The intermediate categories of moral assessment thus allow a good deal of difference to exist within the "limits" of God. Once one oversteps these bounds, however, punishment, both temporal and supernatural, will follow. Yet—and this is the central point for our purposes—the role played by one's inner state in the moral quality of life is very much tied up with the results of one's acts.

In Islam, it is one's duty, through the use of reason, to understand and conform to the order established by God. Salvation lies not in the examination of individual conscience but in overt adherence to the law as conveyed through the illiterate Prophet and inscribed unalterably in the Quran. In the words of one analyst: "The individual was encouraged to perform, to the best of his ability, the duties assigned him by his religion or by custom, rather than to forge a subjective world for himself, based on his individual perceptions and needs" (Sandler 1976, 134).[31] It is a person's acts, not intentions, that may lead to social disorder, fitna. Although God may look to an individual's

---

29. This tradition is analyzed in Wensinck 1961, 449.

30. See for example, Quran 2:187 and 189. See generally Gardet 1967, 448–52.

31. See also the discussion of *amr* ("command," "intent") in early Arabic literature in Bravmann 1972, 39–63.

intentions on Judgement Day, it is more important that a person should have conformed his or her actions to the peaceful order of society. There is a tradition of the Prophet that says: "God loves those who hide their sins."[32] For if a person's actions have adverse social consequences, the welfare of the entire community of believers (*umma*) may be jeopardized. In law, the proof of such consequence may require the testimony of numerous witnesses. In the assessment of others it means that one looks to the effects of one's acts rather than to some hidden inner state. For Muslims, the concept of the self centers on those features and situated acts that bear on one's effect in the world.[33]

To put this matter in some perspective it is worth comparing the role of motive and intent in Islamic social perceptions with the development of these concepts in Europe.[34] Until the twelfth century the notion of intent played no clear role in European law and very little if any in social and religious life. An individual was judged by his or her strict adherence to rules, and since only God (or, perhaps, the devil) could know the mind of a person, ordeals were used to determine legal culpability and upright conduct the merit of one's social and religious life. By 1100, however, a major shift had begun to occur, one that is visible in the theology of men like Gregory of Tours and Bernard of Clairvaux, and in the laws of Henry II and Glanville's commentary. Concomitant with the development of logic, the emphasis on the emotional life, and the broader awareness of society as a moral unit, there developed an appreciation of the role of intentionality in personal salvation and ethical behavior. Intent became not only a subject of legal and moral concern: it was given separate and prior status as the vehicle through which one's soul was brought to full faith in God.

The contrast to Islam is striking. For the Christian West, intent became the primary concern, consequence a secondary factor. In Islam, intent and consequence were inseparable and knowledge of the latter gave one direct insight into the former. In Christianity the moral value of the true meaning of an individual's thoughts is critical; in Islam works may be in their intention, but it is precisely these works, this effect in the world, that will be judged against the standard of knowledge, propriety, and active engagement in the world God has created.

32. In the fuller version, this tradition states: "God will forgive the sins of every believer except when the sinner himself makes them known. God loves those of his servants that cover their sins" (cited and discussed in Juynboll 1961a, 15).

33. Schacht (1961d, 525) says: "The _sharīʿa_, as *forum externum*, regulates only the external relations of the subject to Allāh and his fellow-men and ignores his inner consciousness, his attitude to the *forum internum*. Even the *nīya* (intention) which is required, for example in many religious exercises, implies no impulse from the heart. Thus the _sharīʿa_ demands and is only concerned with the fulfillment of the prescribed duties." The lack of concern with a separate inner state in Morocco is also noted by Eickelman 1976, 134.

34. This comparison is elaborated in Rosen 1985.

The Moroccan pattern of person perception is fully consistent with this distinction. Since it is vital, in this highly personalistic society, to acquire knowledge of other persons and foresee to some extent the course of their individual relations with others, an assessment of another's motives and intent becomes conceivable. But such an assessment, though it may in some societies be framed as independently explanatory, is itself cast against a cultural background. As Gilbert Ryle put it:

> The curious conclusion results that though volitions were called in to explain our appraisals of actions, this explanation is just what they fail to provide. If we had no other antecedent grounds for applying appraisal-concepts to the actions of others, we should have no reasons at all for inferring from those actions to the volitions alleged to give rise to them. (Ryle 1949, 66).

In Morocco, background knowledge and knowledge of another's mind are intertwined. For intention, as we have seen, is assumed as a natural component of given acts; therefore it is to the discernment of situations that attention is addressed. The terminology of motives is, in actual discourse, little developed notwithstanding the otherwise vast vocabulary of Arabic. Rather it is the vocabulary of situations that takes its place. Kenneth Burke's assertion that "our words for motives are in reality words for situations" is not so much untrue for Moroccans as inexact because it places the emphasis the wrong way around (K. Burke 1965, 31). For them, the words that describe situations—which is to say, contextualized persons—imply attendant inner states. Great attention is paid to background (asel) and named attachments, to the intrinsic nature of different categories of humans and their perceived qualities, precisely because these are the contexts within which individuals engage one another and have an impact on the order of society. Moroccans solve the problem of other minds in a way that is, therefore, consistent with other elements of their culture: by searching for knowledge in the public sphere and bargaining with one another over the definition of the situation through which the other's intention is named and comprehended.

Knowledge and Cultural Logic

Knowledge, it may be argued, is seldom without its uses. Whether admired or disparaged, the object of concerted quest or idle assemblage, the information men and women acquire more often than not has its pragmatic qualities. What is knowable or worth knowing and how one can say he or she knows it are questions of eminently practical concern for which the received wisdom of the culture ordinarily offers a sufficient if inexact answer. Knowledge, far from being piled up haphazardly to be sorted out furiously or brooded over in workaday fashion, comes to us more or less organized, structured, arranged into meaningful clusters. Such knowledge as a person needs to operate in his or her world will, as Alfred Schutz noted, be at once incoherent, only partially clear, and not at all free from contradictions, but as a guide, a "tested system of recipes," a vehicle for disentangling the problematic it will display a distinctive kind of orderliness (Schutz 1964, 93–95).

For the people of Sefrou the concept of knowledge as something preeminently useful is an explicitly meaningful category. *Maʿrifa*, "knowledge," and its cognates enumerated earlier is a personal attribute of considerable importance throughout Islamic culture.[35] It has been said that for Muslims, knowledge of the present world and the hereafter lie along a single continuum in which death is but a natural marker along with many others. For Moroccans, the acquisition of religious and mundane knowledge are both "useful"—they contribute jointly to one's functioning according to one's will within a framework of divine construction and consent. Knowledge has a clear effect on social stature: Although Moroccans readily demonstrate their acceptance of the Islamic precept that a difference does not entail a distinction, they also exhibit appreciation of the Prophet's admonition that all men are equal except in learning. Knowledge of the Sacred Law stands at the pinnacle of traditional knowledge, but general literacy, expertise in a trade or craft, and awareness of the relationships and customs of others is one of the qualities that takes its ordered place within the scheme of attributes ascribed to individuals. Before turning in the next chapter to an analysis of the means by which individuals draw on these perceptions to arrange their ties with one another, it may prove valuable to suggest some of the ways in which the features of social identity we have been discussing are themselves patterned in relation to one another. In particular, we may briefly allude to three ordering principles: the hierarchy of social typifications, the code of cultural entailment, and the logic of social consequence.

In our discussion of the attribution of traits and ties, attention was given to the ways in which a person's origins, ethnicity, family, occupation and other social identifications contribute to that person's assessment by others. In a world of uncertain personal relationships—a world in which the threat of potential chaos is met, on the level of interpersonal ties, by the elaborate placement of another in his social contexts—the focus is at once on the typological features of an individual and the unique summation of these qualities in an individual personality. We can see the relation of these two levels of assessment if we frame the issue, as the sociologists of knowledge do, by asking what it is one really knows when one learns about the identify-

35.35. On the concept of knowledge in Morocco see Eickelman 1978 and C. Geertz 1979, 205–7. On knowledge in classical Islamic thought, see Rosenthal 1970; Grunebaum 1953, 230–41. For a theory and description of the Moroccan marketplace as an informational system, see C. Geertz 1979, 197–235.

ing features of another: What kind of information does an awareness of the identifying characteristics we have described give one, and how is this information internally arranged?

Clearly the most important information conveyed concerns the interpretation of another's past, present, and future actions. Knowledge of one's origins or ethnicity, for example, suggests the ties that someone with such a background is most likely to possess, the ways one is most used to forming relationships with others, and hence the common bases on which a personal, contractual tie may now be formed with this person. Ethnicity, occupation, family background, and so on do not, then, constitute all-embracing stereotypes which define the ways in which persons of different backgrounds must view and relate to one another in a wide range of circumstances. Rather, such identification gives one some of the basic information in terms of which particular kinds of personal relationships can be formed.

The components of one's identity are not, however, without their own internal organization. Like any informational system, features of identity carry a series of connections and implications about one another. Thus, as we have seen, knowledge that one is Berber or Arab, rural or urban, of one educational or occupational grouping or another carries information affecting other domains. Indeed, the link between the typifications we have been discussing may be formed into an informational hierarchy by a series of cultural implications which provide a code for the assessment of both character and action. It appears, for instance, that among the Sefrou people it is broadly assumed that women are more likely to be guided by passion and men by reason, that it is this natural disposition that structures one's knowledge of worldly and religious matters, that it is knowledge that distinguishes men from one another and sets one person's social stature above that of another, that stature is broadly related to the nature and extent of one's network of interpersonal ties, and that interrelationships of various kinds entail qualities of social responsibility and potential harm on which the evaluation of social and legal repercussions may be based. This code of cultural entailment may vary both regionally and temporally.[36] Indeed, as we have already noted, information about residence or family may previously have implied religious brotherhood or occupational attachments, where now the correlation of these elements, their overall integration, may be less tight. The result is a sort of entropy—entropy not in the sense of disorder but in the sense of uncertainty (see Bell 1966, 697). What has perhaps remained constant as the terms of cultural entailment have shifted over time is the emphasis on the use of such information to form personal,

36. The idea of a code of cultural entailment is discussed in Dominguez 1977. The term "entailment" is not used here in the formal logic sense of unambiguous necessity: it is used interchangeably here with, and bears greater technical similarity to, the concept of "implication" as developed, for example, in Hungerland 1960.

contractual bonds to others and the reduction in overall uncertainty of relationships that such a code provides its users.

Several aspects of this implicational system which will have particular relevance for our later discussions are worth underscoring. Identifying characteristics may be thought of not as intrinsic features that inhere in persons but as a series of contexts or frameworks through which individuals move and by means of which they become, as it were, socially visible. There is, as we shall see, a constant tension in Moroccan life between the private and public realms. The probing of relatives, neighbors, and acquaintances into the private realm is not, as in the post-Freudian West, an assault on the imperceptible but an attempt to extend the public categories of social placement to their farthest reach, to render comprehensible and useful all information that can be seized within the terms of nisba, nature, or overt act. The quest for information in social life, as in the marketplace, is both synoptic and precise—an effort to know who others are, what they do and what they might do, by charting their actions against the coordinates of an elaborate social map.

Central to this assessment process, as we have seen, is the result another's action has in the world. Indeed, this emphasis on impact contributes to the method by which others are perceived and judged. Following John Dewey we can think of it perhaps as a "logic of consequence" (Dewey 1924). Rather than focusing on what led up to a given act, Sefrou people concentrate on what happened as a result of an act—what difference it made in the world, especially its impact on networks of relationship. To possess certain ties is to imply the harm, and hence the level of responsibility, inherent in that tie. Legally and socially, therefore, Moroccans feel that it would be grossly unfair to hold men and women to the same standard of conduct, or to expect an unlettered man to achieve the same level of self-control as a learned man. Just as intent may be read out of overt acts, so, too, the consequences one's acts may have in the world may be read out of the other contexts that shape and reveal one's character. Neither Moroccan law nor Moroccan social perception gives predominant emphasis to abstract rights or standards. It is a contextualized individual whom they see, and it is through this individual's situated actions that place and attachment to one's own network of affiliations may be known and shaped. To see just how social relationships are forged and enacted, how the very definition of context becomes socially as well as culturally worked, we must look first at some of the specific contexts in which these ties of obligation are formed.

Three

The Formation of Personal Networks

The Concept of Ḥaqq

Linguists, philologists, antiquarians, and political strategists have long found in the language a people speaks an instrument for grasping the way such groups apprehend the world and orient themselves in it. Romantics have found in a nation's speech the soul of its people, historians their pedigree, politicians their racial destiny, and pietists their unique articulation of the ineffable. One need not, however, accept a belief either in the universality of human culture or the futility of translation to sense that there are indeed ideas, bound up in the words that give them voice, that are so characteristic of a people's views that understanding of their lives would be incomplete without a feel for what these very special words mean. Can one really capture the distinctiveness of their world without knowing what *agape* meant to the ancient Greeks, *kodesh* to the Hebrews, *gloire* to the French aristocracy, or *duty* to the Victorian Englishmen? For Moroccans there is a similarly noteworthy term, a word that encapsulates and recounts much of what is central to their perception—and our consequent interpretation—of the relationships that hold their world together. That word, in Arabic, is *ḥaqq*.

Haqq has a variety of interconnected meanings, among them "right," "duty," "truth," "reality," "title," "claim," and "obligation." *Al-Ḥaqq* is one of the ninety-nine names of God known to man. (The hundredth, it is said, is known but to the camel, hence his enigmatic smile!) In its most fundamental sense, haqq means "reality," but a reality that, because it centers on Allah and is suffused by Islamic doctrine, is not to be equated with Western conceptions of the real. In Islam, "Allah is real of himself and of necessity, while other beings depend for their reality on him" (Macdonald 1961a,126; see also Calverley 1965; Izutsu 1964,14). God is, as the root of the word haqq may imply, "fixed" and permanent. He is the source of those "creative commands" which bring the world to life.[1] In the Quran, therefore, haqq is usually opposed to *bāṭil*, "impermanence" and "nothingness," that which is "vain" and "futile." Yet from its earliest usages in the Islamic period, both as a name for Allah and as an ascribable quality, haqq conveyed not a sense of the static and self-absorbed but of the dynamic and interconnected. "Like God," writes Clifford Geertz, "haqq is a deeply moralized, active, demanding real, not a neutral ontological 'being' merely sitting there awaiting observation and reflection; a real of prophets not of philosophers" (C. Geertz, 1979,210).[2] In the Islamic scheme reality thus presents itself as a relational concept, a moral idea that imposes itself on the world as direction, instrument, and connector. Indeed, it is precisely this sense of duty and obligation that defines, from early Islamic times to the present, the essentially relational quality of the concept.

In pre-Islamic Arabia, it has been argued, haqq conveyed a sense of social duty, including that owed by the noble to the poor and needy members of one's tribe.[3] In the Quran, where the term appears in a variety of contexts, the idea of haqq as social obligation is continued and supplemented as pleasing to Allah. Fearful of the call to prophecy, Muhammad could be reassured by his wife Khadija who tells him that "God will never disgrace you; you do good to the kindred, bear the burden of the infirm, bestow alms on the poor, entertain the guest—and you help in cases of recurring obligation (*wa-tuʿīnu ʿalā nawāʾibi l-ḥaqqi*)."[4] This sense of obligation and its moral valence comes to the fore when the word is given application in any of a number of linguistic constructs. To say of another *ʿandu l-ḥaqq,* "the haqq is with him," means "he is right"; *fīh l-ḥaqq,* "the haqq is on him," means "he is wrong." *Makayn ḥaqq binathum,* "there is no haqq between them," means they have no ties, no debts, no relationship with each other, and since they owe one another nothing there is neither "truth" nor "justice" holding them together. A sharif (a descendant of the Prophet) may be described by a nonsharif with the phrase *ʿandu ḥaqq men Allah kbir,* "he has a great haqq from God," meaning that he possesses a large measure of the truth that resides in connection to the divine as well as a heightened obligational bond to the Almighty. To speak of haqq is, in short, to convey that sense of mutual obligation that binds men to

---

1. On the use of haqq as "creative command" see O'Shaughnessy 1971.
2. On the role of haqq as an active element in the Sacred Law, see Michon 1973, 251–52.
3. See Bravmann 1972, 252–53. Elements of this usage can still be found in Morocco and other parts of the Arab world. For an example drawn from literature, see Milson 1967, 86–87.
4. The translation and interpretation of this tradition are drawn from Kister 1965.

men, and man to God.[5] What is "true" or "real" is, in no small part, the web of indebtedness that links sentient beings to one another in a chain of obligations.

The model, the metaphor, indeed the very essence of most relationships in Islam is conceived as contractural. Drawing on the covenant between God and Abraham in ancient Judaism—and referring as well to the still more ancient compact with Adam—the Quran situates the element of contract at the heart of Allah's relation to the believer. By swearing loyalty to the Prophet, men swear their allegiance to Allah, and thereafter "whosoever breaks his oath breaks it only to his own hurt, and whosoever fulfills his covenant with God, on him will God bestow great reward" (Quran 48:10). Allah is, of course, free to do as He chooses, but He has voluntarily constrained Himself through His own word, and since Muhammad is the last of the prophets Allah will not change the terms of the contract conveyed through His messenger. "God never breaks His promise," says the Quran, "though most men do not know it" (Quran 30:5–6).

While God has set certain specific duties for His believers and inscribed these dicta in the Quran and Sacred Law, the range of man's free activity remains at once vast and closely linked to his covenant with God. Often in Morocco one hears the pivotal statement "God has given His trust to mankind" (Allah 'ata l-insan l-amana dyalu). The simplicity of this statement tends to belie its import. It is common to hear Moroccans say—as does the old man in the dispute over the young girl's marriage related earlier—that everything is in God's hands, and this is what we are going to do![6] The demands made by God are few and specific; being given God's trust means that anything set within the realm of man is meant by God to be handled by man. Men must still act in accord with the broad moral precepts established by God but need not have direct, exact, and constant reference to the supernatural for sanction, judgment, or intervention. It is in this light, too, that one can understand the Moroccan attitude toward fate.

Fate (maktab or maktūb—that which is "written," "recorded," "foreordained") or, more precisely, an attitude of fatalism, may be divided analytically into at least two distinct forms. Both begin with the same premise,

---

5. Thus many oaths and solemn promises begin with the word haqq as their utterers seek to attach their words to that which is real and fixed and true. See Westermarck 1926, 1: 493–505, 564–69.

6. See above, p. 41. One is also reminded in this context of the tradition that relates how a Bedouin once rode up to the Prophet's tent on his camel. Upon being greeted and asked the reason for his visit by the Prophet, the Bedouin said that he had come to hear the new prophecy at first hand. "Come down from your camel and enter my tent," said the Prophet, "and we shall speak of these matters." "But if I come down," replied the Bedouin, "I am afraid my camel will run away. What should I do? Should I trust to Allah or should I tie my camel down?" And the Prophet answered: "Trust to Allah. And tie your camel down!"

namely, that only God determines and knows what the future holds. One reaction to this unknown is to throw up one's hands, asserting that all human actions are useless in the face of the predetermined. Alternatively, one can take the attitude that since man cannot know where danger may come from, the sensible thing to do is to take precautions to meet it on all possible fronts. The result is to consider all contingencies and hedge against all possibilities. It is the latter attitude that is manifest in the actions of most of the Sefrou people. Faced with an economic and political environment of substantial uncertainty and a physical environment characterized by considerable, though seldom debilitating, fluctuations of climate, gardeners will plant their plots with several crops simultaneously, farmers will balance the purchase of a parcel of dry land with an irrigated site, alliances will be formed with members of several different tribes or fractions, and a father may take care to place one son in a dominant political party and another with the opposition. In each of these instances the need to know the alternatives available and to distribute one's risk within and beyond the bonds of kinship, residence, and occupation is seen as preeminent.

Moreover, the contractual element in man's relation to the divine manifests itself, in popular Islam, in certain attempts to constrain supernatural favor by fulfilling one's own part of the bargain, if not, indeed, over-fulfilling it in an effort to conduce a desired return. Numerous rituals bear witness to this contractual ingredient. Faced with a crisis, the community may organize a collective prayer known as a *laṭif*, from a root meaning "to be kind," "friendly," "affectionate"; "to mitigate" or "be polite." The object of the prayer may be the cessation of an earthquake or epidemic, the termination of a flood or famine. Latifs were also held during the struggle for national independence to counter such French policies as the Berber Dahir ("decree") of 1930 which sought to remove the Berbers from Islamic-law jurisdiction, a move seen by most Muslims as a veiled attempt by the French to convert and assimilate the Berbers.[7] The latif is held in a mosque or at the graveyard prayer site used for major religious festivals. Repeated chanting of the words *ya laṭif* or Quranic passages is sometimes followed, at the open-air site, by a communal meal. The belief that God will invariably respond to such a prayer was explained by one man in the following way:

> "God," he said, "will never turn away those who beg from him."
> When I suggested that God certainly must have the power to refuse such
> a request, he used the following analogy: If a beggar comes to the door of
> your house and knocks on it and you find a poor, hungry, destitute man,
> can you possibly refuse him when he puts his hand out to you for charity?
> On the street perhaps you could refuse him, but when he comes to the

7. See, e.g., the description of the ceremonies held in Salé in K. Brown 1976, 198–202.

very door of your home you know that his need is great and to refuse him would be "forbidden" (ḥaram). So, too, when we make a latif; it is like a beggar coming to one's door—one cannot possibly refuse him. If you ask God for something in all good faith (b-niya), God has said he definitely will grant your request.[8]

The broadly covenantal quality of the latif is made more explicit and instrumental in what is generally regarded as one of the most serious forms of the latif, the prayer for rain, ṣla l-istisqa'.[9] The form of this latif is quite distinctive because the prayer is not only, as in other prayers, led by one man, but the prayer centers directly on his relation to Allah. The man chosen must, informants insist, be so good a person, so honest and scrupulous in his religious duties that Allah will not fail to reward him. Together with the citizens of the town he goes out beyond the city, and at the chosen site, barefoot and bareheaded, he and the congregation chant the latif prayers and then shift their jelabbas—the loose, shirtlike garment worn over one's clothes—so as to be wearing them backwards, symbolizing the power of God to turn things from bad to good.[10] Moreover, it is believed that the pious man who makes the request for God's benevolence on behalf of the community should die soon after, in expectation of which he will have bathed and dressed himself in his funeral shroud. On January 4, 1967, during my first field trip to Sefrou, an

8. Similarly, many people in Sefrou believe that the reason some forms of abstinence (zuhed)—such as eating simply and giving the surplus to the poor—will result in benefits in the world to come is not because man can force Allah to do his bidding but because Allah has already committed himself to this course if man only fulfills his part of the bargain. This attitude contrasts sharply with the uncertain returns for those acts that are not part of the divine covenant.

9. See K. Brown 1976, 91. On the attitude of schoolchildren to these rain prayers, see Bourgeois 1959–60, 1: 88–91.

10. If drought persisted, representatives of the Muslim community would also ask the Jews to hold a special prayer at the cave sanctuary which, like many such religious sites in Morocco, was shared by Muslims and Jews. When the prayer was completed, Jewish informants said, the Muslims would greet the returning Jews with a great show of appreciation, clapping and dancing all around. Contrast this description with that of an eighteenth-century traveller: "The Moors have an opinion familiar to that of the Christians, that—'The kingdom of heaven suffereth violence, and the violent take it by force.' They think importunity will oblige God to grant their requests. In the time of heavy rains the children all day run about the streets, and bawl for fair weather; and, in the time of drought, for rain, making a hideous noise. They sometimes continue this practice for more than a week. Should God not listen to the children, they are joined by the Saints and Talbes [Quaranic scholars], who proceed altogether into the fields and call for rain. If this still prove ineffectual, they go barefoot in a body, and meanly cloathed, to pray at the tombs of their Saints for rain, to which pious practice the Emperor himself occasionally conforms. Should all these efforts fail, they at last drive the Jews out of the town, and forbid them to return without rain—'For,' say they, 'though God will not grant rain to our prayers, he will to those of the Jews, to rid himself of their importunity, and the stinking odour of their breath and feet.' (Chenier 1788, 345–46)" For further discussion of Muslim-Jewish relationships in such instances, see below pp. 148–63.

istisqa ceremony was held to break a severe drought.[11] The comments of one of the residents of the area at that time were characteristic of those commonly heard.

> Omar, an important member of his rural Berber fraction, told me that last year, during a less severe drought, a latif was held by many rural people at the shrine of Sidi Lahsen Lyusi, the main saint of the Ait Yusi tribe. "What happened?" I asked. "It rained," he said. "What do you mean it rained?" I said. "Most of the crop failed last year: that's why things are so serious now." "But it rained this fall," he answered. "You mean the rain that fell this fall was from the latif last May?" I inquired. "Of course," he replied. I then suggested that rain does not always follow a latif or an istisqa. "On the contrary," he insisted, "whenever people make a latif rain falls. God absolutely must respond to a latif. However," he said leaning toward me and lowering his voice, "people nowadays are no good. They use a latif when they should not— they do not realize its power, the fact that it can result in a flood. That is why the rain last fall reached flood proportions and washed away the El Menzel bridge. This year," he concluded grimly, "we must say the prayer because we need a whole lot of rain."

Two points emerge from the latif-istisqa rituals. First, the ritual is clearly based on the idea of a covenant in which humanity need but do what is assigned it in order to insure the promised reward of God. To fail to believe in the direct connection of these events, notwithstanding lapse of time or extent of reward, would be to call into question the nature of such covenants that run through much of Islamic belief and commonsense relationships in the society. And secondly, as the istisqa reveals with especial clarity, the relation to the supernatural is, notwithstanding certain collective elements, a highly personalistic one, a relation in which one person approaches God and seeks to invoke the compact to which he subscribes by his "submission" (the literal meaning of *islām*) to Allah. The compact binds each believer and is seen by each as a very personal relationship.

---

11. The choice of a man to make this important prayer was the subject of considerable speculation. Most of the people with whom I spoke and who were close to the mayor, the rural administrator, and the court officials who participated in the decision thought the nod would go to the prayer leader of the Semarine Mosque, an old man noted for his piety. In fact, the man chosen was a much younger man who delivers the sermon in the "mother mosque" of the city and is a teacher in the local *collège*. The latter also holds a high degree from the mosque-university in Fez, was a patriot sent to jail by the French during the struggle for independence, and was still very active in the Istiqlal political party. According to the assistant administrator, the older man had actually become quite senile, stopping on occasion during his prayers and acting like a child. Others saw the choice in more political terms. To the conservative men in the religious law court, where I was working at the time, the choice of the younger man was referred to as *diplomati, protocol,* and *zigzag*—three of the few French words these officials ever use. Like others of his predecessors named by informants, the man chosen survived his offering of the prayer.

These same features come through in a second broad category of supernaturally related contracts of obligation, those covered by the term ʿār. The
root from which ʿar is formed, ʿ-y-r, means to "wander" or "stray," and
many of its derivations—"measure," "reproach," "vagrant," "vices,"
"menstruation," "caravan," "wild ass"—appear to be linked by the central
idea of an action or an entity that roves or meanders yet may evoke or be
subject to some standard or regularity. ʿAr is thus commonly rendered as
"shame" or "dishonor" inasmuch as such actions have the quality of stray-
ing across acceptable and predictable lines of social behavior and must, therefore, be brought into accord with some standard or measure. In its strictest
form and as a particular institution of social life in the Sefrou region, however, ʿar refers to a practice by which one can constrain the actions of another by
calling forth the sanctioning power of God. Therefore, in the early years of
this century Westermarck glossed the term as "conditional curse," a rendi-
tion that continues to capture a vital aspect of the ʿar as an institution (Westermarck 1926,1:518,569).[12] Commonly the ʿar is initiated by thrusting upon
another person, or even a saint, an animal sacrifice or piece of one's garment,
uttering the words ha l-ʿar ʿalik, "here is the ʿar on you", and then indicating
what it is one seeks in return. Because the act carries with it the threat of
supernatural sanction if the desired response is not forthcoming, the ʿar has
traditionally been regarded as appropriate only where the outcome of ordinary
reciprocity is somewhat problematic. An outsider seeking refuge or use of an
unused plot may make an ʿar sacrifice at the door of a community's mosque or
the home of a big man in the settlement; an unsuccessful suitor may try to
constrain acceptance by an unwilling father through a similar act; shurfa or
marabouts may carry the coverlet of their saint's tomb to symbolize that they
bring God's possible curse when acting to mediate a dispute; and women will
tear strips of cloth off their garments and tie them to a fence or tree near the
shrine of a saint, thereby seeking to constrain his acceptance of their plea for
fertility or the good health of a loved one. Whether by animal sacrifice or
cloth oblation the symbolic constraint is clear. By offering up a life, the recipient can hardly refuse or give back that which is so irrevocably thrust upon
him. However, by acceding to the request for a form or quality of life—good
health, a child, peace—one at least responds, as it were, in kind. By offering
a bit of one's garment—that which covers one's nakedness, one's shame, and
hence one's honor—a person is rendered symbolically open and vulnerable to

---

12. See also Eickelman 1976, 149–53 and Hart 1976, 305–7. It is, I believe, somewhat
misleading to think of ʿar as relating mainly to an idea of "honor" (K. Brown 1982). For while
this usage may be found in parts of Algeria, and klam l-ʿar ("ʿar-bearing words") place a certain
shame on their recipient—perhaps because only a threat will accomplish what generosity will
not—the sense of supernatural curse remains predominant among users of this concept in the
Sefrou region. On this issue, see also the discussion and examples in W. Marçais 1911, 396 (ʿar
equates with protection, not honor); Bourgeois 1959–60, 2:55–56; Pellat 1970.

another, and the latter must now risk God's wrath if he fails to move symbolically to cover this shame by responding to the other's need.[13] The one who casts the ʿar on another does not, however, come as a powerless supplicant or petitioner but as a claimant: he or she is neither a beggar who entreats nor even an audacious mendicant who does the donor a favor by allowing that person to earn divine approbation through an act of charity. Rather he or she comes to constrain, indeed threaten, to benefit from a compact whose terms one seeks to govern though one is, in certain respects, clearly in the position of relative weakness.

As an institution the ʿar, as we shall illustrate later, affords many opportunities for calculation and manipulation, and its effectiveness, indeed its credibility, remains contingent on the broader context of personality and situation. For many people, especially educated urban Arabs, the term ʿar has lost its invocational power—in much the same way, and for somewhat similar reasons, that cursing has lost its force in the West. In contemporary usage it often conveys the sense of opprobrium or shamefulness, attributes which may, however, be invoked in highly manipulable fashion. As an institutionalized act, and to a lesser extent as an idiom of everyday parlance, the ʿar may, in addition to its other roles, perform two very interesting social and psychological functions. First, the ʿar may, as its root implies, set a test or standard for individual reliability. For the extent to which an individual responds in normative or exemplary fashion when the ʿar has been cast on him indicates to others the degree to which they can expect the ʿar recipient to be a reliable member of the community and their own network of obligation. At the same time, the ʿar is geared to a strategy of seeming depersonalization. By lifting the issue embraced in the ʿar out of the hands of both the one who cast the ʿar and the one who received it—by placing it under supernatural constraint and the standards of community morality—the parties can seem to render the actions involved immune to ordinary forms of manipulation while in fact reinforcing those highly personalistic elements of ordinary reciprocity. The ʿar can, for this particular transaction, equalize two otherwise unequal parties while giving support to the standards of reciprocity and tactical response it would be both shameful and impious to ignore. As an institution incorporating overtones of supernatural sanction and as an idiom for compelling desired action, as a unilateral contract or a shared solution the ʿar is wonderfully characteristic of Moroccan social life in its admixture of elements of obligation and negotiation, demand and ingratiation, sacred invocation and situational ethics.

13. Another highly potent form of the ʿar practiced among Berber tribesmen of the region, called *tʿaṭau rezez* (or *iḥemlaun* in Berber), consisted of the exchange of headdresses (*rezez*) between representatives of two groups in order, for example, to guarantee the peace of a marketplace or unimpeded use of a road. On the use of the ʿar in politics, see below pp. 105, 116.

The contractual qualities bound up in the concept of haqq as right, duty, claim, and title—and given ritual expression in such forms as the latif and the ʿar—point to what must be regarded as a still more fundamental aspect of haqq contained in the idea of obligation and reciprocity. For Moroccans, it may be argued, every relationship implies an obligation. To be related in a particular degree of kinship, to be another's neighbor, to be the client of a merchant in the bazaar carries with it certain expectations of potential recompense. Indeed, every act requires some form of reciprocation as an aspect of its very nature: every act creates an obligation or expresses a right asserted. To engage in any act that benefits another, or even causes him to alter his own acts as a result of such contact, carries with it the notion that a haqq, an obligation, has been formed and hence there is a need to reciprocate. The idea is so deeply rooted that Moroccans had to borrow the European word *fabor* (''favor'') to express the idea of an act for which no reciprocation is required or expected.[14] No relationship can escape this central ingredient.

The reciprocity involved is, however, subject to considerable manipulation. In most situations it is not necessary to reciprocate in exact kind or within a set period of time. Thus a person who, for example, gives aid in the accumulation of a kinsman's bridewealth payment may later seek support in a political election, or a client given favorable treatment in the marketplace may be pressed to offer his daughter in marriage to one's son. This interchangeability in the forms of reciprocation pervades all relationships and allows for considerable variety and tactical manipulation of those with whom one shares such bonds. Indeed, we may characterize the process by which individuals construct a network of obligations as one of negotiation. For not only does each person seek to place his acts, his obligations, where they may later prove most advantageous, but, as we have already suggested in other contexts, the very definition of a situation—as one involving one kind of obligation or another, as implying a haqq or merely a fabor—is itself open to bargaining. An example of just such an encounter will help illustrate this point.

> One day I went for a drive with Mohammed, a rural-born Berber now working as a caretaker in the city, to see the area in the countryside from which he came. Along one of the dusty tracks that led through his people's grain fields we encountered a distant relative who invited us in for tea. Mohammed demurred, over his kinsman's repeated imprecations, because, as he subsequently explained to me, he did not later want the

---

14. *Fabor* may be used, on occasion, as a euphemism for a bribe, along with the equally euphemistic *baraka* (''blessing'') or the forthright *ršwa.* The term *mziya,* given by Harrell (1966,94) as ''favor,'' is properly translated by Wehr, even for the Moroccan context, as ''advantage,'' ''privilege,'' ''prerogative,'' or ''superiority.'' Thus to perform a mziya for another is precisely to put oneself in an advantageous position vis-à-vis the other, a position made advantageous because it forms a basis for reciprocation.

man coming to Sefou and expecting to be put up by Mohammed and his already crowded family.

Several days later I was walking through the public marketplace in Sefrou with yet another friend from the countryside when the man who had issued the invitation for tea came up to us and, pointing at me, said to my companion (who was familiar to him only by sight and reputation): ʿandi ḥaqq f-had sid, "I have a haqq in this man" (i.e., he is obligated to me; I have a "right" in him). My companion asked how so? The man replied by recounting how he had invited Mohammed and myself in for tea during our tour of the countryside a few days earlier. My companion then asked if we had indeed had tea with him, or if he had provided us with a meal. "No," answered the other, "but I kept asking them to come in and they said no, they had to get back to town." "Ah," said my companion, "this is not a haqq; it is just a fabor." "Oh no," said the other, "this is a haqq: I invited them, and it was they who chose to go off."

The discussion continued in this vein for some minutes, my own presence being treated as quite secondary while the two bargained over the situation. It was far from accidental, too, that a group of people began to gather around us listening intently as the friendly dispute continued. Indeed, a certain amount of posturing toward the assembled accompanied the raised voice of my intended host. As the discussion continued, moreover, it became clear what the rural man sought by way of reciprocation for his show of hospitality—a ride in my car all the way to Khenifra and back, a distance of several hundred kilometers! My companion rejoined that this was excessive, certainly in the light of my not having availed myself of the proffered hospitality. After some more minutes of debate over the meaning and applicability of the notion of haqq, I proceeded to invite my intended host to be my guest at a nearby café for a cold drink, which, with the slight smile of an old rogue who knows you win some and lose some, he accepted with manifest grace.

Encounters of this sort are the lifeblood of Sefrou society. They happen in virtually every context and involve, by definition, virtually every relationship.[15] In the process of trying to build a network through ingratiation and one-upmanship, one must bargain over the definition of situations in order to be able to bring pressure to bear on how others will respond to you. Information about similar bonds of indebtedness tell a man how others are attached to people around him and how they are, therefore, likely to act toward oneself. There are, of course, conventions that govern the process—regularized ways that ties are formed with others, settled institutions within which activities are organized, broadly shared concepts that make it possible to comprehend the basic thrust of another's meaning. But there is also the element of free play,

---

15. It may be easier for negotiations of this sort to proceed about a third party, but they also take place frequently, as we shall continue to see, between the principals themselves.

the force of personality, the tactical manipulation of an entire vocabulary of relational possibilities, and the clear comprehension that some social or speech act must take place before a haqq, in the sense of potential obligation, may be converted into a tie that somehow may be characterized as "true" or "real." It is this transformation through act and speech that has brought God and man within the covenant conveyed by the Prophet. And it is in the manifold contexts of family, marriage, politics, and the marketplace that we must now consider in detail the way in which the Sefrou people negotiate their way to a reality of their own.

Negotiating Kinship

Since the middle of the twentieth century there has developed in anthropology an approach to kinship that, whatever its universal merits, suggests itself as particularly appropriate to the analysis of kinship in Sefrou. Rather than focusing predominantly on kinship as a vehicle through which the social, economic, political, and religious life of individuals and groups are organized into a functioning whole or seeking in kinship an expression of that deeper logic through which all cultural artifacts may be organized, the orientation applied here seeks to discern the dynamic connections that exist between the organization of social action and the conceptualization of meaningful distinctions. This viewpoint was neatly characterized by Lloyd Fallers when he wrote:

> Both "society" and "culture" are abstractions from the same phenomenon—social action. As [Gilbert] Ryle puts it, ". . . the styles and procedures of people's activities *are* the way their minds work and are not merely imperfect reflections of . . . the workings of minds. . . ." But the requirements of cultural consistency and of functional integration are somewhat different. Putting one's thoughts in order and putting one's affairs in order are rather different activities for either a person or a community. They proceed along different lines, but tend to react upon one another so as to produce not a one-to-one matching of ideas and social relations, but rather a continuing process of mutual adjustment and challenge. (Fallers 1969,316)[16]

What is central to this perspective, therefore, is the view of kinship as a set of concepts, beliefs, idioms, and ideologies that serve to guide and respond to actual relationships without constituting either a direct template or an unreflective mirror. Just as one may view language as an instrument which, by its very use, gives shape and purpose to the instrument itself, so, too, from this

16. The internal reference is to Ryle 1949,58. See also the discussion on cultural indeterminacies in Moore 1978:32–53.

perspective kinship may be viewed as an artifact that completes its very definition by its application.

This orientation is particularly conducive to an appraisal of kinship in the life of the Sefrou people. For, as we shall argue, in the Sefrou area relations of blood and affinity are most fruitfully seen not as fixed categories of affiliation allowing relatively little room for variation and manipulation but as a system of ideas and relationships that is noteworthy for its malleable, instrumental, and situationally applicable qualities. Kinship in this regard is characteristic of other aspects of Moroccan social and cultural life and closely linked to them. Just as the concepts of niya, haqq, asel, nafs, and ʿaqel possess distinctive features yet remain ultimately dependent for their implementation on the development of their situated meaning, so, too, Moroccan concepts of kinship are incompletely defined without the negotiations through which a range of possible implications can be fixed for a given relationship or purpose. It is not simply that individuals manipulate their ties of kinship—a feature common enough to virtually all societies. Rather, it is that at the very heart of the concept of kinship in Morocco lies the recognition that relational possibilities are inherently matters to be bargained over and that this is no less true of kin ties than of bonds of patronage, friendship, or political alliance. By focusing on the process by which concepts and actions are linked, by seeing how the people of Sefrou construct their particular kin ties from the limited yet open-ended conceptual possibilities afforded them, we can see that particular resulting forms—patrilineal descent groups, segmentary tribes, interlocking marital networks—must be understood as social forms whose apparent solidity usually belies a deeper contingency. Our purpose in this section is, therefore, less to enumerate the full range of factors that might be covered under the broad rubric of Moroccan kinship than to show how the domain of kinship is consonant with and integral to the general process by which the people of Sefrou bargain for reality.[17]

The malleable, indeed negotiable, aspects of Moroccan kinship are clearly inscribed in certain of the terms and usages associated with the concepts of descent and affinity. From birth each individual belongs to and traces his or her descent from a line of kinsmen who share a common patronymic designation. Although a child's naming ceremony may involve the use of the mother's name, and an entire line of a Berber tribe may take its name from the mother common to one set of siblings as opposed to those who trace descent through another of the father's wives, it is to the paternal line that one ordinarily looks for primary designation.[18] Yet, as we have seen in our discus-

17. The following analysis draws on the discussion of H. Geertz 1979a. Although specific reference will be made to a number of her analytic concepts, I wish to acknowledge the general influence of this work. See also Bourdieu 1977 and Rosen 1968b.

18. On personal names and the ceremonies connected with them, see Mas 1959–62,87.

sion of nisbas—those nomenclatorial designations that convey information of such diverse components of one's social being as patriline, place of birth, occupation, and religious brotherhood ties—the focus of Moroccan names is on affiliations as points of attachment rather than on incorporation in solidary groups through which many of one's interests are concentrated and met. This malleability of patrifilial attachment is central to a number of the key terms used for various kin groupings.

Let us take first the example of rural-born individuals, both Berber- and Arabic-speaking, who live near Sefrou or who have migrated to the city. The Berber term *iḡes* (pl. *iḡsan,* which like the comparable Arabic word *adam* means "bone") refers to a group of people who trace descent, usually through a series of named individuals, to a common ancestor some three to five generations past. The ighes is, moreover, almost always a localized group: its members may form the entire population of a rural settlement or encampment (*duwwar*)—except, of course, for those who have married in— or, more commonly, a single duwwar will be composed of several patrilin- eally related ighesan, all of whose members claim, but cannot necessarily enumerate, their common descent. This latter grouping, usually called a *fekeḍa* (from an Arabic root meaning "thigh"), may, in the past, have been the primary unit called upon to pay or receive bloodmoney (*diya*) and often partook of common defense or the exploitation of those pastures and waters lying within the territory under their control.

The crucial point to appreciate here is that since at least the late nineteenth century—and a close reading of the literature suggests for several centuries before that—none of the entities to which these terms apply can be regarded, in the Sefrou region, as solidary, corporate bodies.[19] That is to say, neither ighes nor fekheda refer to clear-cut associations, based on a simple principle of descent or recruitment, which engage in collective acts on a regular basis. Rather, the groupings, like the terms themselves, expand and contract, are covered by one of the above rubrics or bear no fixed term of reference: They do not depend for their distinguishable existence on a set of kin categories to which they are matched on an unambiguous basis. Rather, each of these terms, like several others to be noted in a moment, imply certain idealized forms of behavior and generalized bases of recruitment but are, at their very core, sufficiently open-ended and differentially applicable that the existence at any given moment of joint identity or activity has to be accounted for by principles other than those based on a simple notion of descent and affinity.

A similar absence of strict correlation between terms and groups applies at both a more-inclusive and a less-inclusive level. At the lowest level the term *ʿaʾila* may refer to the nuclear or extended family that shares certain resources in common and may reside within a single structure. Above the ighes and

---

19. For evidence in support of this argument for the Sefrou and Middle Atlas regions, see Lesne 1959 and Rosen 1968b.

ighsan, reference will often be made to the *ferqa* (literally, "fraction" or "division"), usually a set of dispersed ighsan that bears the name of an eponymous ancestor or place of origin. And at the most inclusive level is the *qebila* (Berber *taqbilt*), usually translated as "tribe," a loosely structured congeries of groupings whose claims of common descent and territorial integrity are asserted with a force and conviction that varies with the situation and utility of appellation. In the Sefrou area most Berbers identify themselves as belonging to the Ait Yusi "tribe."

It is, however, no accident that each of the terms we have cited—ʿaʾila, ighes/adam, fekheda, ferqa, qebila—should not admit of clear-cut referents since the units they might be said to represent are neither unitary, stable, corporate entities nor are they abstract propositions unrelated to actions "on the ground." In fact, the domain in which these terms operate is one of a sliding scale of references that is consonant with the malleable nature of group identification and collective action itself. Each term implies a degree of idealized behavior—the less inclusive the more intense—yet the groupings that may in fact perform such tasks may be precipitated into momentary existence, not by the invocation of a set system of kinship groups and their attendant obligations, but on the ability of given individuals to negotiate their way within the possibilities set forth in the sliding scale of kinship affiliations to create a group that can be made to perform in accordance with the conceptual ideals. The precipitation of such groupings, then, is itself a result of those same processes of creating obligations, balancing and manipulating debts and exchanges, fashioning bonds of common background and purpose that cut across such domains as kinship and alliance, domains that from a strictly social-structural viewpoint might be mistakenly assumed to partake of fundamentally different organizing principles.

In order to see how these particular concepts serve as both the instruments and objects of kinship negotiations, it may prove useful to cite several specific examples:

Hamed ou Azu is a Berber who lives in the settlement known by the name of its main patronymic group to which Hamed himself belongs, the Ait Alla ou Lahsen. The settlement includes sixteen extended families besides Hamed's, many of which stem from individuals who moved into the area since the turn of the century, bought land, and intermarried with the resident families. Together with two other patronymic groups—one that lives about ten miles away at Mezdgha Jorf and another that lives nearly forty miles into the mountains at Enjil—Hamed and his people also refer to themselves as the Ait Brahim "fraction" of the Ait Yusi tribe.

Hamed works primarily as a farmer, but he owns some sheep which he keeps not at his own settlement or in the care of one of the shepherds from the Ait Alla ou Lahsen but with one of the Ait Brahim living at Mezdgha Jorf. He explained that he prefers to do this because his own area and Mezdgha Jorf do not always get rain at the same time, because they lie in different administrative districts, because he has some maternal kinsmen at the more distant site with whom he likes to retain ties, and because placing his sheep at a distance makes it more difficult for local kinsmen to know his exact wealth and make further demands on him.

Hamed will often call the Ait Brahim as a whole his ferqa, his own localized patronymic group his fekheda, and the Ait Yusi as a whole his qebila. But he will also use the name Ait Brahim to refer to groupings all the way up to the level of the three dispersed fractions and will shift the referential terms as the situation suggests. Thus, when Hamed wanted help in finding a new shepherd he went to kinsmen at Mezdgha Jorf, spoke to them in terms of the ties they had as members of the same fekheda, and thereby signaled to them—and tried to conduce from them—the close aid and mutual security implied by a term that conveys the idea of co-residents who must protect one another's interests. He had to spend a considerable amount of time not only bargaining with his kinsmen over the terms of the caretaker arrangement but over the terms of relationship within which the general sense of reciprocal expectations could be cast. Yet to a fellow resident of his own settlement—albeit from a partriline other than his own—Hamed, who on other occasions would refer to their bond as that of members of the same fekheda, refused a request for aid in a political matter by saying that they were only members of the same ferqa, implying less inherent obligation. The colloquy went on for some time as each man sought to lay a basis for establishing a tie conceptualized in terms implying more or less distance and expectation. Indeed, when Hamed went so far as to say that he and his interlocutor were really only from the same *qebila men l-fuq*—from the same tribe at substantial remove—and the other tried to say that even though originally outsiders they were now from the same 'a'ila, "family", the bargaining extremes were clearly stated. In both cases, the terms employed were both an important resource in the negotiations and themselves contingent on a calculus of personal advantage and alternative resources to which both could orient their strategic moves.

A second example indicates one way in which such negotiations may proceed when a series of related fractions is involved.

Just south of Sefrou, in a valley of the lower hills of the Middle Atlas Mountains, lies the Berber settlement of Ait ben Assu. The two hundred individuals who comprise the Ait ben Assu are descended from a family the two Arabic-speaking fractions living in the valley invited to settle there, as neighbors and protectors, during the chaotic period following the death in 1904 of the great Caid Omar al-Yusi. The Ait ben Assu regard themselves as close relatives (ḥbāb) of the Ait Bouteyeb fraction that remained at Mezdou, the site some ten miles up in the mountains from which they moved down to the valley, and of the Ait Chou, another fraction that came part way down the mountains some years later. They also acknowledge kinship with two fractions located twenty to thirty miles farther into the mountains, one at Guigou and the other at Enjil.

They use the collective name I'awen to identify all of these groupings. The nature and extent of their ties are revealed by a number of particular incidents.

Before the establishment of the French Protectorate in 1912, the Mezdou fraction sought the aid of the Ait ben Assu in whose territory they sought winter pasturage for their flocks. Although close kinsmen who could easily stipulate their common descent, the Mezdou fraction made an 'ar sacrifice and asked for sanctuary for their flocks; the tie of kinship was not, of itself, regarded as sufficient to insure the desired result. When, several years later, the Mezdou people decided to hold out a bit longer before surrendering to the French, they did not demand or expect the Ait ben Assu to help them simply because of their relatedness. On other occasions, however, the Ait ben Assu joined the Mezdou fraction in the payment of bloodmoney and to this day refuse to raise a hand against the Mezdou people when they become embroiled in disputes with other allies of the Ait ben Assu. Individual members of the two settlements frequently engage in economic and marital alliances, and when they go outside their own territory almost everyone identifies himself with the collective name I'awen.

On several occasions, however, members of each of the various fractions of I'awen have established ties that would seem to contradict their affiliation with their kinsmen. Several years ago the I'awen at Guigou, many of whom pastured their animals near fractions of a completely unrelated tribe, sided with that tribe in a dispute that pitted them against a number of fractions of their own Ait Yusi tribe. Throughout the dispute these same people continued commercial relations with their "cousins" from Ait ben Assu, speaking often of their ties as fellow I'awen and Ait Yusi. Informants saw no contradiction whatsoever in their actions: they consistently maintained that ties of kinship are important and that they do indeed imply a generalized expectation of aid or nonbelligerence. But they were equally insistent that kinship alone does not dictate action. Identity and affiliation as an Ait ben Assu, I'awen, or Ait Yusi man are situational, negotiable, and, almost by definition, as variously employed as the persons they serve, in part, to characterize.[20]

What is true of kinship in the rural, "tribal" setting is no less true in the urban context. Not only does one find that kin-based corporate groups are essentially absent, but the range of terminological references have the same shifting quality found in the countryside.[21] Urban-born Sefrou people who

20. For a case study of the situated nature of descent ties in the context of a dispute between two kin groups over access to the waters of a lake in the Sefrou region, see Rosen 1979, 53–57. As in other arid regions of the earth, this example demonstrates that it is not unusual in Morocco to find instances in which water is thicker than blood.

21. For example, K. Brown (1976,60) notes for Salé, "I found no evidence of collective action by any patrilineal group or the existence of any effective social and political aggregations along patrilineal lines in the study of the city's social history between 1830 and 1930." The range of such terms as hbab and 'a'ila are discussed in H. Geertz 1979a:347–48, 380–85.

have no kin ties to the Ait Yusi do not, of course, identify themselves with any tribe. Like the Ait Yusi, however, they will often belong to extensive families and will bear that family's name and inheritance rights based on genealogical affiliation. As in the other instances cited, however, kinship constitutes a source of identity, a framework for individual action, and a malleable resource to be drawn upon rather than a widely ramified rule of recruitment for group action. Summarizing the role of kinship as ideology and rule in the Sefrou region, Hildred Geertz has said:

> What is foreign to Moroccan culture is not the notion of biological parenthood, but the idea of a position in a structure of categories of people sorted out solely according to biogenetic links. Both the idea of such a structure as an inclusive whole that is progressively partitioned and the alternative idea of a structure of strings of kinsmen knit together into a tree of branching and connecting lines are hard for a Moroccan to visualize. Social identity for Moroccans could never be built on such a unidimensional scheme. Kinship obligations and privileges cannot, in Moroccan cultural formulations, be separated from all other types of ties, such as patronage, as somehow qualitatively and jurally different. (H. Geertz 1979a,351)[22]

It is important, therefore, in discussing such issues as group action in Sefrou neither to exaggerate perceived distinctions nor to disguise polarity under the cloak of diversity. From what we have thus far described, two points stand out sharply. First, it is noteworthy that very little stress is placed on the tracing of genealogical ties except where, as we shall see, there is a question of sherifian status, inheritance, or access to a family trust. Although individual Ait Yusi and Sefrawis may be able to trace their descent with some accuracy, it is not a matter of great concern simply because groups are not formed or maintained on the basis of genealogical determinations. Thus, in the case of those with tribal attachments, we find no need for those devices familiar to us from many other tribal societies—genealogical manipulation, structural amnesia, fictive kin forms. Among the Ait Yusi one can often elicit an elaborate genealogical tree in which named groups are depicted as having a series of divisions which are in turn subdivided through a succession of branchings down to the present array of fractions known to the informant. Indeed, one may even be told that kinsmen should help one another in accordance with their kinship proximity. For all its appearance at one level, this is

---

22. This is not to say that individual informants among the Ait Yusi cannot visualize kinship relations in biological terms or that they cannot point to some groups who, they say, claim to mark descent largely in these terms. Rather, consonant with Geertz's argument, they themselves give no evidence of employing an exclusively biological view nor do they even think that other groups follow such lines strictly since they readily point to common instances where factors of patronage and friendship structure the actual claims of affiliation.

clearly not a segmentary system in any sense, for groups are not formed by or set in opposition or mutuality on the basis of a rule placing them within a nested series of genealogically specified units. Rather the Ait Yusi may be regarded as a "tribe" that is segmented—in the sense that it is *conceptually* divisible into units that have a genealogical or quasi-genealogical element to their definition—and, more precisely, as a people for whom the *idea of segmented affiliation* constitutes a cultural resource, among many others, that may be utilized by individuals in the formation of their personal networks. This latter point requires some elaboration.

It is possible to point to a number of instances, both historical and contemporary, in which a single individual has negotiated his relations using, in part, the idiom of segmented affiliation as one of several rubrics through which his relationships have been expressed. When successful, people may say that the groupings involved are related in a given genealogical fashion. But clearly this does not mean that it is because of a rule of recruitment based on descent that they coalesce, only that one of the underlying ordering principles by which such common involvement may be justified expresses itself in the language of descent. The momentary end result of networks built up through the balancing of elaborate ties of indebtedness within and beyond one's kinsmen may be a set of relationships that are expressed as segmentary. But such an expression has about it that air of make-believe by which a sense of legitimate order is temporarily acknowledged so that the relationships it implies may be rendered at once more predictable and more amenable to alteration in its terms.

Similarly, among urban Sefrawis, attachments within a given family may reproduce the pattern of mutual support, contiguity within a residential quarter, or transmission of prestige from father to son, ideally associated with blood relationship. Looked at more closely, however, the actual mechanisms by which such ties are reproduced or varied are essentially the same as those that are utilized in the formation of ties with non-kinsmen.

The second point warranting emphasis is that in the Sefrou area there are very few sanctions invoked for failure to conform one's behavior to ideals of proper kinship relations. To fail to support a kinsman in a given situation may call into question a person's willingness to recognize such ties as a basis for reciprocation, but virtually no institutionalized sanctions follow as a matter of course. An individual who does not give adequate support to kinsmen will find his or her behavior castigated as shameful (*ḥšuma*) and may encounter legal sanctions for failure to provide essentials to his immediate dependents. Although family members possess certain rights and duties under Islamic law, ties based on kinship are not unlike other relationships in that the idea of a right, a haqq, as a self-defining and self-executing moral or material entitlement is essentially absent. People may claim that they have a particular haqq—whether a share in an estate or support following separation or divorce—but they also know that there is little in the structure of kinship ties alone that will secure that right to them. Rather, as we shall see in more detail later, it is the way one builds a network and bargains out one's ''rights'' from situation to situation—even where the bargain struck looks like a ''standard kinship contract''—that is crucial. That rights should be few and sanctions severely restricted is, therefore, consonant with the view of kinship as a resource, rather than an ordering mechanism that operates according to its own highly distinctive principles.

It should be noted, however, that if kinship generally serves as a relational repertoire to be built on individually, there are certain relationships that are worked with great consistency and for which relatedness itself summarizes the material and symbolic resources to whose acquisition or maintenance it serves as one path. Thus we can constitute a continuum. At one end are ties of blood which partake of few sanctions or constraints and which may be thought of as ordinary kinship. More toward the middle are those relationships that, to borrow Bourdieu's characterization, partake of ''officializing strategies''—fairly regular use of given kin ties as a vehicle for working out one's personal ties, a strategy that is no less person-centered than others but that may require less effort to invoke and may appear less ''egocentric'' in design simply because it is a strategy that has been employed regularly over many years (Bourdieu 1977,38–43). At the far end of the continuum come those instances in which access to a particular resource is largely governed by consanguinity. Access to a family trust, entitlements based on inheritance, and descent from the Prophet or a saint thus constitute material resources that have been partially or completely removed from the free play of the individual and made the subject of an impersonal rule of attainment. Yet here, too, the strains of collective interest and individual effort that are so characteristic of Moroccan social life reveal themselves quite clearly.

Shurfa (the plural; the masculine singular is sharif, the feminine, sharifa) are those who claim descent from the Prophet Muhammad in any of a number of distinct lines. In Morocco, the most notable line is that of the Alawi, the line of the ruling monarchy, which is itself comprised of numerous branches. Most sharifian lines—particularly those with control over key resources—assign one of their number to serve as a recorder of the line's members. The legitimacy of the line will often be validated by royal seal, and each sharifian line will seek renewed validation of their authenticity from each succeeding monarch.[23] Many individuals lay claim to sharifian descent and seek to employ the honorific *sidi* (''sir,'' ''lord'') or *mulay* (''my lord''; the first person possessive of *mul*). Practically every man who comes to Sefrou from the Sahara claims to be a Drissi sharif. Except where the claim is given some

---

23. The request for documentation by the major saint of the Ait Yusi tribe, Sidi Lahsen Lyusi, constitutes a central part of the hagiographic accounts of his life (see Berque 1958 and C. Geertz 1968). The broader issue of validation will be discussed below at pp. 117–33.

authority by the recorder of the line, it will carry little weight. Indeed, designation as a sharif, like other nisbas, places a person contextually but by no means fully characterizes him or conduces particular forms of behavior in others. It is, in short, another descriptive feature which, depending on its possessor's conduct and connections, may add authority to the characteristics of moderation, spirituality, and learnedness—of a controlled nafs and developed ʿaqel—ideally associated with one who is close to the Prophet. As in other instances, however, each individual will have to demonstrate that such idealized features, though capable of transference by blood ties, have actually "taken" in his particular case. Whatever the amalgam of his personal and ideal traits and their effect on his claim to spiritual resources, a sharif properly inscribed in his line will be in a position to claim his share of any material resources to which this membership entitles him. In both of these respects— in the role of descent as cultural resource and material entitlement—the position of a sharif is not markedly different from that of a saint's descendant.

Moroccan Islam is often noted for the presence of individuals—usually, if somewhat inexactly, glossed in English as "saints"—who are deemed to have possessed that special quality of *baraka* (literally, "blessedness") which renders them capable of transmitting supernaturally sanctioned powers. These "saints" possess their powers individually yet, like the shurfa, may symbolically transmit their baraka to others by blood descent or through an act of transmittal.[24] But as in the case of the shurfa, the qualities ideally associated with actual or symbolic descent from a marabout must be determined on a case-by-case, and even observer-by-observer, basis. It is by one's act—of mediation, miracle working, curing—that one demonstrates that one has baraka; it is not a status acquired by formal acknowledgment but by common, though not by any means always uniform, opinion. It is, in short, an attribute dependent on the recognition by others who chose to acknowledge it out of personal opinion or relationship.

Those who claim descent from a saint—the *ulad sid,* "children of the saint" —will, by this descent also claim entitlement to gifts presented at the shrine of their ancestor. Because these gifts may be quite substantial, there is among ulad sid considerable interest in the designation of those who are to be granted a share of the proceeds. There may also be considerable dispute over the proper form for designating entitlements, disputes that are revelatory of the alliances formed by interested parties, and the interplay of conceptual forces and the negotiating strategies of the participants. A single example, drawn from the preeminent group of ulad sid in the city of Sefrou, will stand for many comparable instances.

On one of the hills overlooking Sefrou stands a small whitewashed

---

24. The discussion of baraka in North African Islam is extensive. To cite only a few of the works that discuss the issue in anthropological terms: Crapanzano 1973; Eickelman 1976; C. Geertz 1968; Gellner 1969, 1981; Gilsenan 1982; Jamous 1981; Rabinow 1975.

building with a green-tiled roof surmounted by a crescent-shaped orna-
ment. In shape and color, the shrine of Sidi Ali Bouseghine is barely
distinguishable from the host of similar shrines found throughout Morocco—from the squat and dilapidated rural sanctuary where a barely remembered saint once slept to the national monument where the body of
Muhammed V, the sultan who presided over the acquisition of Moroccan
independence, was laid to rest. Sidi Ali Bouseghine is said to have come
from Saquia El-Hamra, near Mauretania, and to have resided in Sefrou
for a number of years. Following his death various miracles were interpreted as an indication that he favored a particular family, the Ulad
Hamed Cherif of the Qlaʿa quarter, who in turn became the ulad sid.
Visitors to the shrine often make contributions of food and money which
used to be divided into three equal parts, one for each of the three sub-
segments of the ulad sid. In time, however, one of these segments grew
very numerous, one remained moderate in size, and one remained quite
small. The result was that some individuals were reaping more than others, each fraction's share being divided equally among its members both
male and female. Several decades ago a woman of the more numerous
segment, who married into a family close to the sultan, wrote to Muhammed V asking him whether the existing division was fair or if all of the
ulad sid should share equally. The sultan forwarded the matter to the
pasha, Si M'barek Bekkai, who (in the presence of my principle informant) examined the documents of the recorder of the ulad sid and concluded that the income should indeed be divided equally among all the
descendants, a decision that was subsequently ratified by royal decree.
At the time of my research, therefore, each of the ulad sid took turns
receiving the profits that came to the shrine that day. In the late 1960s
such daily income could range from a low of $10 to $12 to a high of
$300. With only several hundred descendants eligible, each person could
count on two days a year of income. However, since an individual becomes eligible from the moment of birth, a family with many children
will get more turns and more income. For example, one man has two
wives, both cousins from other branches of the ulad sid, and sixteen
children. His income, from ordinary sacrifices, donations, and special
gifts in fulfillment of vows, is enough for him to live on comfortably.

The example of the Ulad Sidi Ali Bouseghine is characteristic both in the
existence of disputes—often of interminable length, intricacy, and impu-
dence—and in the existence of greater group action where resource and personal strategy coincide.[25] Nor is it unusual for the ulad sid to be unrelated to

---

25. To cite only two additional examples involving Sidi Ali Bouseghine: Soon after the
commencement of the French protectorate, a number of Sefrawis pressured the French to end the
yearly festival (*musīm*) held in honor of the saint. They did not like having to feed and accommodate friends and relatives from all over the region while the ulad sid made all the money from the
event. The French, who did not otherwise ban such events, were nevertheless persuaded to forbid
the musim for a number of years. Around 1920 a challenge to the legitimacy of the ulad sid was

the saint himself yet for descent to be the key marker by which in turn membership is maintained.[26] Similar factors are in evidence when one considers the nature of family trusts administered by the religious foundation.

The institution for administering religious properties, called the *ḥabus* in Morocco, superintends real property left for the support of such religious institutions as mosques, schools, and the poor. It is also possible to establish a "family habus" (*ḥabus 'a'ila*) such that the income from the property continues to be paid to the heirs with ultimate title reverting to the habus foundation if and when the entire line ceases to exist. Such trusts were created in the past as security against mismanagement by particular heirs, in order to insure or deprive particular heirs—especially women—of a share in the estate, or to prevent the appropriation of property by the politically powerful.[27] For those Sefrou families who possess such trusts, genealogical reckoning is the critical means for determining eligibility. Although such a trust may aid in the continued identity of the family, it does little to retain family solidarity through an inalienable patrimony since demographic factors and economies of scale often diminish the per capita share in such trusts. Nevertheless, as an instance of corporate interest that may affect strategies of marriage and economic alliance, the family trust stands as an institutional framework that molds and is molded by the negotiation of personal networks.

Similarly, the control of resources within a given household or family constitutes a crucial framework within which an individual bargains out his or her particular network of associations. The woman who is financially dependent on her husband or male kinsmen, or the son who must rely on his father for aid in raising a bridewealth payment, operates in a context that shapes their choice of strategies. The range of resources that may be brought to bear—emotional, linguistic, financial, moral, etc.—are themselves extensive and varied, such that what may appear as a source of clear power in one situation may be appropriately checked in another. Nowhere does the full force of the

---

lodged by a group of Beni Azgha tribesmen from Sraghna. They claimed that their ancestor, Sidi M'hamed as-Sraghna, was the father of Sidi Ali Bouseghine and that they should, therefore, be granted a share of the shrine's income. They were unable to document their claim, whereas the ulad sid presented a number of royal decrees attesting to the legitimacy of their descent. The pasha of Sefrou and an appellate court in Rabat ruled against the claim of the Beni Azgha tribesmen.

26. Sidi Lahsen Lyusi, the major saint of the Ait Yusi, had no sons, and the present Ulad Sidi Lahsen Lyusi traces descent through a servant of the saint to whom his baraka is said to have been transferred. It is also worth noting that the Prophet himself had no sons and that his immediate successors sought to establish a legitimate line of descent through the Prophet's daughter.

27. Almost all of the habus endowments in Sefrou, both those that were for the exclusive use of the religious foundation and those whose income was distributed among the members of a particular family, were formed in the seventeenth and eighteenth centuries. On contemporary habus holdings in Sefrou and their impact on the marketplace, see C. Geertz 1979, 151–54.

negotiating process come more sharply to the fore than in the arrangement of a marital bond.

Marriage in Islam is an explicitly contractual affair. Indeed the defining feature of a marriage is not the performance of a particular ritual or the organization of festivities—although central moments in the process are accompanied by recitations from the Quran and celebrations surrounding the nuptials are often quite elaborate. Rather, a marriage is concluded by the signing of a marriage contract and the transmission from the groom to the bride—usually through their representatives—of a sum of money or goods constituting the bridewealth (ṣḍāq). The provisions contained in the contract, the stipulation of the bridewealth payment, and indeed the very choice of the bride or groom are all stages in a negotiating process that incorporates and summarizes a wide range of interests and concepts found in Sefrou society.

As in all realms of Moroccan life—economic, legal, religious, political, and social—the marital process begins with a search for information. At issue is not only—and sometimes hardly at all—knowledge about the personal qualities of a prospective bride or groom; for despite the natural concern and curiosity of the principles themselves, it remains true in Sefrou, as it was in the past, that the overwhelming majority of marriages are arranged by the parents or next-of-kin of the bride and groom. What they seek in a mate for their dependents is not always the same as the young couple may have sought for themselves. For fathers, information about the background (asel), economic status, personal ties, and general reputation of the potential in-laws is of considerable importance. He may be wary of entanglements that flow from the general rule of reciprocity now given a significant base in the creation of the marital tie—or he may actively seek it as a vehicle for enmeshing those with whom an affinal bond will be forged. Like his manipulation of the term for close kinsmen (ḥbāb) he—to say nothing of his dependent—may be able to use the term nsāb (roughly, "in-laws," "affines") to imply and perhaps conduce forms of reciprocation. He will also, in the vast plurality of cases, be genuinely concerned that his son's or daughter's marriage yield a peaceful and productive relationship within their own home and between the families so united. His quest for information will be carried out through friends and acquaintances, the intensity of the search being a function of his prior knowledge, his present concerns, and his emotional, financial, and personal stake in the outcome. Much of his information—and indeed much of the information gained by the principals themselves—comes through the women of each family.

For the women of a household, few events present greater opportunity and danger than the marriage of one of their offspring. If it is a son's marriage and if the couple are to live in a portion of the paternal house—a pattern, as we shall see, of declining but still substantial significance in both urban and rural areas—it means, for the mother, a new daughter-in-law and her entire group of visiting, inquiring, perhaps even dominating and prying claque of kinswo-men—a new presence that under the best of circumstances will alter and under the worst undermine the order of the house to which she comes. A mother must ask herself and others many questions: How helpful will the bride be with the tasks of the household? How tractable will she be to her mother-in-law's directives? How much will she seek to secure herself against the repercussions of a divorce by trying to increase her own assets at the expense of domestic order and material balance? As the queries are multiple and varied, the quest for answers are often intense and wide-ranging. Visits by the women to the public bath—which are often made at the request of the potential groom—afford an opportunity to view possible mates. Similar visits to a young girl's home by a close relative or someone serving as an intermedi-ary for one of the interested parties will yield still further data. And children, often so used in other situations, will be sent back and forth among the houses, serving as messengers and spies in the search for a mate.

But just as much of the data one seeks in the marketplace or in the quest for personal alliances is made more accessible by the conventions associated with these domains, so, too, much of the information relevant to the choice of a mate is rendered more available through particular institutions and rela-tionships. Kinship, residential proximity, and common economic interests, therefore, may provide contexts within which the answers to marital concerns can be found. The lives of one's neighbors or kinsmen are generally well known and relationships already exist with them that may give an element of predictability to a newly forged marital link. Often, therefore, we see the same families repeatedly exchanging mates, not, however, because there is a marital "rule" or even "preference" that works as a settled and institu-tionalized principle but because the coincidence of perceived interests and available information often favor such unions. In each case, however, many people will actively be weighing the relative advantages and disadvantages of the marriage.

Take, for example, the marriage of two cousins, in particular the marriage of patrilineal parallel cousins (i.e., those whose fathers are brothers). This union, which is regarded as highly desirable among many Middle Eastern Arabs, has been the subject of extensive anthropological discussion (see Bourdieu 1977,30–71; Cuisenier 1962; Khuri 1970; Murphy and Kasdan 1959). From the parents' perspectives it may have clear advantages: property, which at death or divorce might otherwise pass out of family control, can remain within the kin group; brothers, who might otherwise fall out with each other, can be united in their common grandchildren; a mother-in-law can hope for greater control over the new bride in the house or the new groom in the family, because she can adduce a substantial amount of deference by virtue of her role as the newlywed's aunt. The disadvantages are no less readily marked: faced by an argument with his wife, a husband may very well find that she complains to her mother, who complains to her husband, who tells the young man how to act—something he would not allow his father-in-law to tell him; but when his father-in-law is also his uncle, and he must feel "shame" (ḥšuma) in front of his uncle, he may be forced to accede and thus may not feel that he is really the boss in his own home.[28] Often delayed into their mid-thirties by the exigencies of raising the needed bridewealth and frustrated by the entanglements of conflicting familial interests, young Moroccan men often express as their ideal marriage with a foreign woman who, though not a Muslim, requires no bridewealth payment yet would still be subject to unilateral divorce.

Clearly, then, in the calculus of marital possibilities certain general conclusions are self-evident. Pursuing similar lines over the course of many marriages—following, as Bourdieu says, "well-trodden paths"—the accountability of changes wrought by such a union may be given an air of the regular, the predictable, and the controllable (Bourdieu 1977,52–58). Chaos (fitna), ever present in matters of sex, social entanglement, and (at least from the perspective of men) the raging impulses of women, may be channeled by a well-placed marriage. Indeed, the alliance forged may suit current needs or strategies and thus become the forum through which broader sociopolitical interests are brought into contention. Even the intended bride, whose formal agreement is required by law but whose obstinacy can galvinize opposition and create a noteworthy inconvenience, may be able to extort terms favorable to herself or her supporters in the process of holding up the union.[29] Power—ever diffuse, ever embraced in a wide variety of material, symbolic, and tactical resources—is played out in every element of the marriage formation. And everything is open to negotiation, however much the actual range of bargaining may vary from one marriage to another.

A number of aspects of the relative power and negotiating strategies of the parties may ultimately be inscribed in the marriage contract. Often, as we shall see, the terms involved reflect an attempt on the part of the bride or her kinsmen to check the husband's almost unlimited power of unilateral divorce. Among the most common stipulations not directly concerned with property are, for example, the understanding that the woman need never move more than a specified distance away from her family of origin, or that, at her option, she must first be granted a divorce if her husband ever seeks to take an additional wife. The woman's family may even stipulate that the marriage will actually be subject to termination at the pleasure of the wife herself. Court officials rationalize this apparent breach of Quranic law (which grants the power of repudiation to the husband alone) by saying that the woman has

28. Bourgeois (1959–60) thus found intense opposition by male students to parallel cousin marriage, an opposition that, for reasons he did not explain, was greater in Sefrou than in any other town or city in Morocco.

29. A similar process is described in an East African society by Mayer 1950.

actually contracted a situation similar to that in which she gains release from her husband through some form of remuneration. But here the "payment" is with the words the husband himself agreed to have placed in the contract rather than with a sum of money, custody of a child, or some other form of consideration.

The most common stipulation found in marital contracts, however, refers to the payment of the bridewealth (sdaq). The value of the payment may vary from that of a simple token to any sum of money or goods agreed upon by the representatives of the bride and groom. In 1978, for example, the sdaq of a previously unmarried girl from a well-to-do urban Arab family of Sefrou was in the range of $1200 to $1400. Daughters of wealthy Fez families often received payments of $2000 to $2500. A rural Berber woman, by contrast, might be married for as little as $40.[30] These sums are scrupulously registered in the marital contract, the original of which is given to the bride, since the sum involved may figure prominently in events following the death or divorce by her spouse.

It is important to note, however, that although payment of the sdaq is indispensable to the lawful formation of a marriage, it is not necessary that all of the bridewealth actually be paid at the time the marriage contract itself is signed. Rather, a portion of the bridewealth (called the *baqia ṣdāq,* the "remainder of the sdaq") may be left unpaid until a divorce actually occurs or, if so phrased in the contract, until the woman herself chooses to demand it. Clearly this latter condition gives a woman considerable leverage in curbing her husband's right to summarily dismiss her. Any man who has contracted a marriage with this provision in it will think twice before arbitrarily exercising his right of divorce or indeed of provoking his wife in any way that might move her to demand the outstanding portion of her bridewealth.

The extent to which a man may find himself obliged to acquiesce in the inclusion of such contractual provisions as these is, for the most part, a function of the relative power, particularly economic, of each of the parties concerned. If a man is attempting to marry above his social or economic rank, and if at the same time the bride's family suspects that the prospective husband may mistreat his wife or try to make life for her so miserable that she will pay any sum to secure her freedom, the family of the bride may leave part of the brideprice unpaid or require certain other contractual stipulations favor-

30. These figures are drawn from interviews with informants and court officials, and from the analysis of court records. A quantity of jewelry and personal items worth an equivalent amount is often given to the bride by her fiancé and his family during the engagement period (see Al-Amin 1968:43, 44). In the administrative district encompassing the nearby village of Bhalil, community representatives in the mid-1960s fixed bridewealth payments at $100 for a virgin and $50 for a widow or divorcee, regardless of economic status. Fathers were not expected to provide much in the way of furnishings for the marital home. Reportedly, there was not uniform adherence to this agreement although bridewealth prices in Bhalil have a tradition of being very low for the area.

ing the bride. In some parts of the countryside whole communities customarily use the deferred-brideprice clause as a means of insuring some degree of marital stability.

Marriage contracts are, as we have implied, often written in contemplation of divorce, a realistic view given the frequency of divorce and the legal powers possessed by husbands. As embodied in the Code of Personal Status adopted two years after national independence in 1956, the Moroccan laws of divorce reflect fewer significant changes from the traditional rules of the Malikite school of Islamic law than do the codes of, say, Algeria, Tunisia, or even Egypt, which were heavily influenced by French and Swiss legal codes. The Moroccan husband's rights of divorce remain very considerable. In fact, a husband may divorce the same wife three different times. The first time a man repudiates his wife, the courts will not only uphold his right to do so, they will also sanction his power to call her back to his bed and board at any time during a three-month period. If the three months go by without a reconciliation—a period of time during which any pregnancy on the woman's part will be attributed to the husband—the divorce will be declared final. If, however, the husband exercises the right to call his wife back, and then for some reason thinks better of the idea, he can repudiate her a second time. But if he divorces the same wife a second time—no matter how much time has passed since the first divorce—he must have the wife's consent in order to bring her back. Moreover, the husband will have to give her some gift as a sign of their reconciliation. If the husband repudiates his wife for a third time, the law will not permit them to take up residence together once again, even if both parties desire it. Only after the expiration of the three-month waiting period and the formation and dissolution of a marriage with another man would the woman be eligible to remarry her first husband.

One Moroccan characterized the differences between these three forms of divorce as being similar to the situation of a man who holds a small bird in his hand. To repudiate a woman for the first time, he said, would be like releasing the bird with a string attached to one leg: provided the bird does not get three-months distant, the captor can reel it back whenever he chooses. In a second repudiation, however, the bird has been released completely unfettered and will return to its master only if properly enticed. And after a third repudiation the bird will fly away altogether to seek a new and more congenial source of sustenance.

In each of these cases the legal powers of the husband are indeed absolute, but there are several other forms of divorce in which the initiative actually lies with the wife and the officials of the local court. If, for example, a woman can prove to the court that her husband has failed to fulfill one of the defining duties of the marital contract—if, say, he fails to support her or mistreats her excessively—she can petition the court for a judicial decree of separation. In another instance the woman may secure a divorce by getting her husband to agree to accept some form of remuneration for releasing her. Acceptance of such an arrangement by the husband carries with it an inherent and irrevocable repudiation. Clearly such an arrangement places a great deal of power—verging at times on extortion—in the hands of the husband, but the bride and her family, as we noted earlier, may have hedged against such an eventuality by placing additional terms in the contract.

The relative power of husband and wife is, moreover, affected by another aspect of the bridewealth payment. For upon receipt of the bridewealth for his daughter or marital ward, a man, in the vast majority of cases, will add a substantial sum of his own and use the combined amount to purchase a dowry for the bride. This dowry itself is called, quite significantly, "the furnishings of the household" (*'attat l-bit*). It is these goods, whether actual furnishings, items of personal jewelry, or raw wool, which will be considered the personal property of the woman and will leave the marriage with her in the event of divorce of widowhood. In addition to their security value these goods, rather than the bridewealth itself, are made clearly visible to the entire community as well as to those who later visit the couple's home. Indeed, on the day a bride moves to her husband's home the goods comprising her dowry are paraded around the streets of the city to the accompaniment of oboists and drummers, chanting relatives, and screaming children. Poorer families carry the goods in their hands and on their heads while wealthier people may display the entire dowry—down to the last fragile teacup—on the beds of several pickup trucks. As bridewealth payments have increased sharply in recent years— well above the rate of inflation in Morocco—it has been said that bride- wealth payments have become a matter of competition, a vehicle for demon- strating prestige. To the contrary, it may be argued that the Moroccan system has gradually been shifting from a bridewealth system to one that predomi- nantly stresses the dowry. In point of fact it is the goods that comprise the dowry, which represent both the status of the bride and a real source of her personal security, for which the competition directly expressed in bridewealth is being carried on. The mother of the bride is usually the most insistent that her daughter's dowry should be as substantial as possible. She will nag her husband to increase the bridewealth demanded, while he, seeking both respite from the nagging and a vehicle for emphasizing his own social standing, will increase the payment accordingly.

In addition to setting up an index of relative social status, it is also impor- tant to note that the law automatically assumes that all of the "household furnishings" except for the most personal possessions of the husband (such as his clothing and tools) are the sole property of the woman and may be taken away by her when she leaves. Since the woman's family generally does not allow the precise content of the dowry itself to be entered into the marriage contract, this legal fiction gives the wife a potentially powerful lever to use against her husband. Indeed, insofar as they can do so without creating an unbearable strain on the marriage itself, Moroccan women frequently try to pressure their husbands into buying them as many things as possible in order to insure themselves against a sudden divorce. Everyone is well aware that the more a man has to lose financially by divorce, the less likely he will be to exercise his legal powers arbitrarily. And if such a divorce means not only the loss of those goods bought during the marriage and any outstanding portion of the bridewealth, but also means incurring a whole new set of social and financial debts associated with the collection of a new bridewealth, a man will certainly hesitate before making use of his power of instant repudiation. The extent, then, to which a husband may be put at an economic disadvantage by a wife who is herself at a clear legal disadvantage will be a function of the relative power of the persons involved, particularly their respective financial positions.

In addition to the legal prerogatives and economic pressures affecting marital relations, there is a host of ways in which different social ties may be utilized by the parties involved. We have already seen how the bride's mother may cajole and conspire to elicit from her husband the largest dowry possible for her daughter, and how a husband may be reluctant to divorce his wife because of the degree of personal independence he may have to give up in seeking help with a new bridewealth from his relatives and acquaintances. Similarly a wife who wants her husband to abandon his plan to divorce her may turn to commonly shared friends and relatives—neighbors or some individual "in whose presence her husband feels shame." For example, if a husband and wife are first paternal cousins, the wife may utilize the position of her father as the husband's uncle rather than simply as his father-in-law to constrain the husband to act as a nephew properly should. Or by galvanizing the opinion of neighbors or threatening a public court action a woman may hope to induce her husband to give her more substantial support, abstain from occasional beatings, or spend less of his time at a nearby café. Again the success of her endeavors will vary tremendously with the social, economic, and legal positions of all those involved. What remains constant in this system, however, is neither the forms of behavior associated with certain relationships nor the groupings that are crystallized at any given moment to accomplish an ad hoc task but simply the ways in which persons can indeed relate to one another without overstepping "the bounds of permissible leeway" as they pursue their individually and pointedly defined goals.

As an example of the subtle interplay of social, legal, and economic factors associated with divorce in Morocco, it may be valuable to consider the case of a young friend of mine who was experiencing some difficulty with his wife. Mohamed, a clerk in the local administrator's office, had married a girl from his hometown of Fez and settled down to live with her in his father's house. Almost from the start, however, his wife and mother began fighting with one another as each tried to maintain greater influence over Mohamed's actions.

The situation created great strains among the members of Mohamed's own family and between all of them and his wife's kinsmen. Mohamed finally decided to move away altogether in the hope that setting up a household in a nearby town would solve the basic problem. But his wife continued to nag him and demand his complete attentiveness to her every wish. Mohamed tried go-betweens from his wife's family and from neighbors, but in each case his wife's agreement to behave herself was, he claimed, quickly followed by a renewal of her bossy and nagging attitude. Mohamed was hesitant to divorce her since he would then have to pay a very substantial sum of remaining bridewealth and begin all over again to collect money for a new wife of the standing he deemed appropriate for a man of his background and position. He thought that having children might make his wife more tractable but was equally afraid that if this did not settle the problem and he still had to divorce her, he would then have the additional burden of long-term child support. Quite literally, he said, he could neither live with his wife nor without her. He finally decided that since it was an independent identity of her own and an ability to have a say in her own future that was at the root of his wife's problem, the only workable solution was to allow her to finish enough of her education so that she could find some work outside of their home. Although he had the power and even the desire to repudiate his wife forthwith, Mohamed recognized that he was effectively constrained from doing so by the social and financial implications of such an act.

The features that are discernible in Mohamed's marital difficulties point up several important aspects of social practice and law in Morocco. Mohamed and his wife live in an apartment of their own, separate from both sets of parents. This pattern of neo-local residence is increasingly common although precise statistics are not available.[31] Given the sharp rise in the Moroccan population in recent decades and the increase in such separate residences, pressures for urban housing have increased significantly. In the new-medina areas of Sefrou, for example, many of the new houses have been built to accommodate families comprised only of a husband, wife, and their children. This does not necessarily obviate familial pressures but it may reduce some elements of friction. Regardless of residence, when divorce does occur it is less because of a division of loyalties between one's family and one's spouse than because of the numerous tensions that develop from the economic, social, or legal struggle among all those who have a stake in the union.

The Moroccan government is itself aware of the fact that these tensions are often at the root of the country's high divorce rate and has tried to take certain

---

31. Using data from the 1960 census, roughly 40 percent of all households were composed of a single conjugal family, the proportion ranging from 51.6 percent for Bhalil-born Arabic-speakers to 35.4 percent for Fez-born Arabic-speakers. For an analysis of these and other figures on household composition, see H. Geertz 1979b,494–500.

legal steps to ease the situation. The law does, therefore, recognize the woman's right to demand that her husband find living quarters for the couple outside his parents' home and in an area sufficiently well populated with respectable people to enable the woman to call upon the necessary witnesses to substantiate any case she might bring alleging misconduct on the part of her husband. With full recognition that husbands may act without due consideration in moments of great stress, the law also denies the husband the right to divorce his wife three times all at once. And, recognizing that fear of financial loss is the greatest dissuader of hasty action, the law also requires the husband to make a "conciliatory payment" of unspecified amount to his wife upon divorcing her. But insofar as local courts generally fix this sum at roughly one-third of the registered bridewealth with a ceiling of several hundred dollars, it is clear that this relatively insignificant sum has not greatly affected divorce rates, though it may have increased the frequency with which a husband and wife use this payment in maneuvering for positions of greater strength in a marital dispute.

It should also perhaps be noted that the whole negotiating process involved in forming a union is set against a background that includes the conception of men and women as substantially different creatures and a certain distrust of the marriage bond itself. We have already seen in our discussion of the nafs-ʿaqel paradigm the vision of men and women as essentially different, and we shall later consider how alternative concepts of reality may be sustained within the context of a broader cultural unity. Even where the relationship of a husband and wife is one of emotional warmth and affection—something my own impressions tell me is very common, especially if a marriage lasts beyond the first few years—it is always a relation between people who are not equals, and whose inequality is inscribed in their very nature. "In everything there is partnership," says a Moroccan proverb, "except marriage and divine prayer."

The view of the family as a congeries of competing interests and of marriage as a source of conflict in which action must be reconciled with the image of male superiority is a frequent theme in Moroccan popular culture. In addition to the tales and skits of professional storytellers in the marketplace, Moroccans have found in modern comedy a dramatic form that is especially well suited to their themes. Almost daily on Moroccan radio and television—and on cassette tapes that are readily available in the marketplace—one can find plays and "sketches" (the word used by the Moroccans themselves) that would be categorized in America as family or situation comedies.[32] Characteristically they involve a scenario in which a weak father is manipulated by

---

32. A number of the individuals associated with these "sketches"—among them Bouchaib Al-Badawi, Abdeljebar Laouzir, Hammadi Amor, and Abderrauf—have become nationally famous as a result of their work.

his voluble and omnipresent womenfolk. Escaping their strategems occasionally to commiserate with his equally henpecked buddies at a nearby café, the men hatch an ingenious plot to circumvent the women and reassert control, only to find that, notwithstanding their folly and ineptitude, their desires prevail in spite of themselves. In Morocco this type of comedy reaffirms the social conventions: Love is always placed in the context of marriage, the rebelliousness of women and children always comes round to the socially correct position, and conflict is resolved in ways that reinforce male privilege and familial stability. It is no accident, moreover, that these comedies are situated in the home rather than in public. Within the house there is a rough equality of the sexes, not because of any innate parity but because in this private environment the resources men and women can bring to bear on one another—financial, emotional, and social—are in greater balance. Comedy, George Meredith suggested, requires and encourages equality of the sexes— only then can their conflicts and society's be seen clearly, only then can each of the antagonists stand as a full person to be pondered, cajoled, avoided, or seduced.[33] Moreover, in Moroccan comedies, as in the assessment of others in everyday life, the focus is not so much on a sequence of causally related events as on the delineation of a person's "character" by showing him or her in a series of seemingly disconnected contexts. For the Moroccan viewer or listener, the "sketch" is a rather full portrait—one in which the individual is revealed by changing situations and society is strengthened by portrayal of its supreme capacity to channel social and familial chaos.

The analysis of Moroccan kinship thus recapitulates themes that resound throughout Moroccan culture: the centrality of the individual as the fundamental social unit who engages in a series of dyadic contracts within and beyond his kinsmen to construct a web of indebtedness that links him to others in his world; the importance of language—in the sliding scale of reference, in the set of associations conveyed by the ramified nature of Arabic root forms, and in the need for negotiation to complete the meaning of terms employed;

33. The Victorian novelist and critic argued that women must be treated equally with men for there to be true comedy and that comedy may thus further as well as reflect increasing sexual equality (Meredith 1956:14–15, 31–32). Meredith, who incidentally says that his remarks were spurred by discussion with "an Arab gentleman," says: "Comedy is the fountain of sound sense; not the less perfectly sound on account of the sparkle; and comedy lifts women to a station offering them free play of their wit, as they usually show it, when they have it, on the side of sound sense. . . . The heroines of comedy are like women of the world, not necessarily heartless from being clear-sighted; they seem so to the sentimentally reared, only for the reason that they use their wits, and are not wandering vessels crying for a captain or a pilot. Comedy is an exhibition of their battle with men, and that of men with them. . . . Where the veil is over women's faces, you cannot have society, without which the senses are barbarous and the Comic Spirit is driven to . . . grossness, . . . There never will be civilization where comedy is not possible; and that comes of some degree of social equality of the sexes. . . . Cultivated women [should] recognize that the comic Muse is one of their best friends."

and the multiplicity of resources through which individuals can attempt, through complex strategies, to fashion a relatively predictable and secure haven. As we have seen in kinship as well as in other analytic domains, the regularizing force of concepts and institutions places a framework around the process of social construction. In order to show further some of the characteristic patterns the networks of personal affiliation take, and in order to suggest how they become manifest in still other social domains, it may prove useful to consider, in somewhat greater descriptive detail, how networks are built by some of the Sefrou people whose activities I was able to observe most closely.

Building Networks

As they set about the task of building or servicing a network of personal attachments, the people of Sefrou will draw in different ways on the repertoire of relationships open to them. Since they are dependent on a common store of conventions, the results of their efforts will bear innumerable similarities yet will possess features that often set them off as individual and distinctive without being eccentric or unprecedented. By exemplifying some of the features characteristically encountered in the lives and strategies of the people of Sefrou, our purpose is neither to suggest the entire range of possible relationships nor to develop a typology that would account for all instances encountered. It will suffice if, by means of a few concrete examples, the articulation of concept and network can be suggested and some of the distinguishable qualities of Moroccan attitudes and social relations can be highlighted for subsequent analysis.

Tahar Marawi: An Urban Arab Merchant

Tahar Marawi was born in 1933. His family had lived for many generations in the Qla'a, the separate quarter located a short distance from the main part of Sefrou. Tahar and his older brother Hamed are the offspring of their father's second marriage, their mother being a sharifa from one of the most respected families in the city. Their father was a successful mason but, because he was the principle source of support for the children of his two successive marriages and often was cajoled into supplementing the income of a number of other relatives, Tahar remembers their nuclear family as having been quite poor for the times. Tahar himself attended Quranic school from the age of six, but after his father died in 1950 Tahar lacked the money—and, he says, some of the desire—to go on to the Qarawiyin, the great mosque university in Fez. Instead, he began to work as a hod carrier, then as an apprentice mason, and was a master mason in his own right before he was twenty. While Tahar learned his craft, his brother Hamed went to school five days a week and worked on construction jobs the other two days. Between them they were able to provide their household, consisting of themselves and their mother, with a good income.

Around 1952 Tahar became the foreman for a contractor and was given a motorbike by his employer so he could get around to the various projects. Soon, he went into business for himself, hiring a couple of masons and—through contacts with several Frenchmen his brother knew—serving as contractor for the construction of several villas in the Ville Nouvelle and other buildings in the medinas of Sefrou and Fez. He often worked alongside his men ("to encourage them," he says) and profited handsomely. His customers in those days were Frenchmen and Jews—the only ones who were doing a lot of building and who, he says, did not take up all your time bargaining over the price of everything.

It was during these years (1951–57) that Tahar also spent a lot of his time in Fez and attended many lectures at the Qarawiyin. He enjoyed the study of Islam—as is clear from the lengthy passages he can still recite by memory from the Quran—but much preferred to be out in the working world earning money. It was perhaps at this time too that Tahar began to see connections between Islam and business, to which he would often refer in later discussions. "The people who lived before Islam," he said, "worked very hard. But when they learned about the Islamic religion they shoved this world aside, ceased to work, and instead began numerous wars in the name of religion." When asked if the world would have been better off without Islam he replied by saying no, that you have to have a religion that recognizes the existence of one God, but you must not cease concerning yourself with this world. Moreover, he noted, "People who are very pious are also very much at ease, they are not nervous or uncertain, they are not plagued by the pursuit of wealth. The trouble with the Arabs is that they are always asking Allah to do things for them and do not help themselves as they should." Like many of his associates, Tahar could often find benefits to health, if not always to business, in religion, and he remembers these youthful days as an entrepreneur—making and spending a lot of money, working with his brother to establish their home, finding an occasional young lady who would ride with him into the country on his motorcycle—as a time of great enjoyment.

When Morocco achieved independence in 1956, however, the French and the Jews pulled out or drastically cut down on their construction expenditures. For several years Tahar and his brother Hamed continued to build houses—including the villa in the Ville Nouvelle where they still live—but they saw little hope of regaining their former level of business. When the opportunity was presented to do something else, they readily took it.

In the late 1950s, one of the wealthiest contractors in the Sefrou region—in partnership with a French general—bought a building on the main street of the Ville Nouvelle and asked Tahar and his brother to manage a movie theatre and run a grocery store in the structure. This entrepreneur, whom we shall call

Si Mokhtar, was from the Qla'a and had known Tahar all his life. The sister of Tahar's father had married into Si Mokhtar's family. Tahar and Hamed took on the big man's enterprises and even accepted Si Mokhtar's offer to be the guarantor of their debts, but Hamed, who never liked working in the store, soon took up a position as Si Mokhtar's general accountant. Tahar, however, liked dealing with the French and Moroccan elite who patronized his store, and he worked hard to show that he was more settled and responsible than in his youth. He particularly admired Si Mokhtar whom he saw as the sort of entrepreneur who would be instrumental in the economic development of Morocco.

Tahar's store also became the meeting place for a small group of Tahar's friends. Included were the principal of the local high school, the second in command to the rural administrator, the caretaker and cook for an elderly European living in Sefrou, several masons, and a schoolteacher who also worked with the local branch of the government-sponsored union. Together, these men shared in common gossip and news and made occasional outings to the hot sulphur baths at Zerhoun or picnicked among the Roman ruins at Volubilis. Although roughly the same age they are by no means of uniform economic standing or political importance. Tahar is clearly the common node in their ties, and, though they would seem to be very close, some of the friends have drifted in and out of the circle over the years. An occasional visitor to the store, but hardly ever to their home, is the elder brother of Tahar and Hamed by their father's first marriage. Indeed, it was only after months of daily contact with Tahar that I learned from one of Tahar's intimates the identity of this visitor.

Although Tahar and his brother clearly formed ties to others in which they were the dominant figures—as employers of help in the store, as intermediaries for masons trying to get certain contracts, as men who could lend their financial, accounting, and construction knowledge to those whom they favored—they were, in many respects, dependent on the man they themselves referred to as their "patron," Si Mokhtar. In time, a number of people came to refer to the brothers as *ulad Mokhtar*, the "children" of Mokhtar, even though they knew full well no familial connection existed. Rather as informants said, they were so-called because they obtained much of their nurture, their support, their importance from their connection with this "big man." How much this was true—and with what consequences—was revealed in the circumstances surrounding Tahar's first marriage.

Tahar was thirty-three when he became engaged, by no means an unusual age for Moroccan men to marry.[34] His fiancée was none other than the

---

34. Abu-Lughod 1980,275–304 offers an analysis of marriage patterns in Rabat-Salé that is consistent with field data from Sefrou which suggests that many men are in their thirties before marrying and that Moroccan men tend to marry at a somewhat later age than men in many other Arab societies.

daughter of the senior member of the Ulad Sidi Ali Bouseghine, descendants
of the city's main saint, a man of considerable wealth and prestige. And it was
Si Mokhtar who arranged and helped finance the union. All the principals had
a common origin and identity in the Qla'a and various marriages had occurred
among them over the years. Through his client, Tahar, Si Mokhtar could
forge a stronger tie with the Ulad Sid and, indeed, with the bride's father, who
was preparing to commission the construction of a hotel to house pilgrims
near the site of the saint's shrine. Since Tahar's own father was dead and there
were no paternal uncles, Si Mokhtar also served as the go-between (*wasīṭa*)
negotiating the bridewealth and engagement gifts. Ultimately, a sum of approximately $1,000 was paid as bridewealth, an equivalent sum being ex-
pended in gifts of jewelry and wedding costs. The bride's father, in return,
purchased household goods worth roughly $2,000 as dowry. Si Mokhtar him-
self contributed substantially to the bridewealth payment.

On the afternoon of the wedding night a procession of a dozen cars and two
trucks brought the dowry from the bride's home to Tahar's. On the back of
one of the pickup trucks a band of musicians played while on the floor of the
other were spread out a number of fine and fragile utensils. The procession
took a long, circuitous route between the homes, thereby affording many
people the opportunity to see the wealth of those involved.

The marriage, however, proved short-lived. Within eight months Tahar
registered his unilateral divorce with the court. People close to Tahar's family
said that the bride fought a lot with Tahar's mother and with his brother's
wife, both of whom, it will be recalled, were from the same sharifian family.
Some said the young wife was lazy and refused to do any household chores.
Others attributed the problem to the perfidious nature of women. But one of
Tahar's own friends saw the matter differently. He said that Tahar kept his
young wife cloistered in the house and even after a number of months would
not let her visit her own family. When he first arrived in Sefrou, the friend
said, he was not sure how much to allow his own wife to go about in public. It
was Tahar who counseled his friend against letting a wife be seen at all in
public. His remarks reminded me of an occasion when Tahar told me about a
dispute between a mason and the man whose house he built. The house had
been constructed with windows placed in such a way that one could see into
the house of the man across the street. The owner of the latter complained to
the head of the masons association who saw to it that the windows were
changed. Although this result was perfectly predictable and "normative," I
was struck by the extent to which Tahar was incensed by the contractor's
placement of the windows. "We do not do things this way," he said heat-
edly. "A man should never be able to see another man's wife; he should
certainly never be able to see into his home." But, said Tahar's friend, Sefrou
was not as conservative as Tahar had led him to believe: women do go about
in public, and many of the younger women wear scarves but no veils. Tahar,

he said, thought himself better than others, cloistered his wife, and left her always under his mother's thumb. No wonder, he concluded, there were fights.

The dissolution of Tahar's marriage also led to the termination of his business relationship with Si Mokhtar. The latter was offended at Tahar's repudiation of his wife and the breach of an alliance he found desirable. When he saw that Tahar was adamant in his refusal to take his wife back, Si Mokhtar made it clear both to Tahar and his brother that he regarded them as ungrateful and unreliable. In turn, Tahar left the store, his brother ceased working as Si Mokhtar's accountant, and together they opened a new *épicerie* farther down the street.

It was more than six years before Tahar took a new wife. When he did, he chose a poor but respectable young woman from the nearby town of El Menzel. A relatively uneducated Arab tribeswoman, she was undoubtedly more accustomed to the veil than a Berber woman and probably grateful to move into the villa of a successful urban man. When she died soon after, Tahar quickly took another wife from the same family. He now has a baby daughter over whom he dotes. When asked where he would seek a husband for her when she grows up, he points to the example of his brother Hamed. When the latter's daughter, an intelligent student who was given every encouragement to go to college and prepare for a teaching career, reached marriageable age, Hamed found her an educated young man who would let her continue her studies at the university. Indeed, when her first child was to be born, it was planned to send the child for a year to its grandmother in Sefrou while the daughter finished her schooling in Rabat. This pattern—wives veiled and cloistered, daughters modern and public—is, of course, the pattern followed by King Hassan II and is one with which both Tahar and Hamed can identify. In their store prices are fixed; in the marketplace they always bargain. In choosing partners for their children's marriages they insist on paternal privilege but seek modern mates from outside their own entangling family circle. In forming their friendships they do not hesitate to ingratiate and indebt, but they seek ties with no single level or segment of society. In short they have consciously, yet with that sense of compromise characteristic of Moroccan life, sought in their household, their business, and their vision of the future to resolve to their own satisfaction some of the central issues facing their generation of Moroccan men.

Omar Lyazghi: A Countryman in Town

Omar ben M'hammed Lyazghi is only a couple of years older than Tahar but his life and his relationships reveal other themes and variations. Born and raised in the Beni Azgha territory to the east of Sefrou, he presently runs a tiny shop in one of the quarters just beyond the gate of the old city in which he sells sugar, tea, cooking oil, and cigarettes. At the age of seventeen, Omar, like many of his companions, joined the French army and served in Indochina for four years. Many of the Moroccan soldiers were Berbers, and they were often formed into separate units in which Berber was actually the language of command in battle, but Omar served in platoons that spoke French and Arabic. Omar had originally intended to stay in uniform for the fifteen years necessary to qualify for an army pension, but after duty in Vietnam he quit the army and set up shop in Sefrou. He thus joined a large number of people who emigrated to the city in the years after World War II. In the case of the Beni Azgha, their reasons for coming to Sefrou were not untypical: the decline in employment possibilities in the countryside, the machinations of a local administrator who used his position to steal the land of many of those in his area of control, the desire to educate one's children at the Sefrou schools, and the sociability of the city—its baths, cafés, movies, and other amenities—made a return to rural life seem unattractive. Like many such immigrants, however, Omar still has one foot solidly planted in the countryside.

When Omar's father died, he left his offspring a house and several hectares of land in the Beni Azgha territory. After a certain amount of haggling, the assets were divided among the heirs and Omar took sole title to a small parcel of dry land. With some of his army pay he added to this a second parcel, for which he hopes someday to buy a share of water from a nearby irrigation system. In the meantime, he has a sharecropper raise grain crops on the land. The sharecropper—called a _kammās_ in Arabic, from the word meaning "one-fifth"—receives 20 percent of the crop in return for his labor. Omar supplies the other four elements of a sharecropping arrangement—the seed, the plowing, the ownership of the land, and the rental of the land—although during some years the sharecropper has supplied the plowing animals in return for an additional fifth of the harvest. If he were more wealthy, says Omar, he would have an arrangement in which the man who worked his land would receive the security of a fixed salary and free accommodation on the land, while Omar would receive the whole of the income from the harvest. For now, however, he and his sharecropper both carry the risk of crop failure. Although Omar was careful to register his title to the land through the government land registry, he has no written agreement with his sharecropper. Everyone knows about their arrangement, he says, and registration through the local court would just add an unnecessary expense.

Omar is, however, somewhat uneasy about his prolonged absence from his country holdings. He cites the popular saying "if a man is away, his right (haqq) is away" and points to instances of territorial encroachment and wrongful conversion that occur if one is unable, directly or indirectly, to maintain a presence in the area. He prefers, both in his property arrangements and in his social ties, to keep his close relatives at arm's length, bringing them occasional gifts from the city but indicating that he would prefer his children to marry outside the confines of their own extended family. His caution about

the pretense of familial aid recalls the remark of the sixteenth-century Moroccan poet Medjoub "the Sarcastic": "Give me what is mine as if I were your
enemy and afterwards you can chew me up as if I were your brother." Omar
further underscored his feelings about familial entanglements by employing a
common saying, itself a play on two similar-sounding Arabic words—
l'aqārib kel l'akārib—"close kinsmen are just like scorpions."

Omar's shopfront, like Tahar's more substantial establishment, is a gather-
ing place for a number of Omar's fellow veterans. Those who stayed in the
army to retirement or were wounded receive substantial pensions and, like
Omar, have often used the money to open shops or build homes for themselves in the new-medina quarters.[35] The veterans talk a good deal about their
days in Vietnam and teased me, in the mid-1960s, about how it was now
America's turn to be there. Together we would listen to newscasts about the
war, and they would ask me to translate for them the English-language reports
we heard, insisting that if a number of sources say the same thing it is probably the truth. Often, too, they told of Moroccan soldiers in Vietnam who, like
the great rural caids and saints of the past, were impervious to bullets, their
magical powers being so great that no weapon could kill them.

The men at Omar's store also talk a great deal about politics and the ways in
which men grow rich and powerful. There is talk of corruption and the need to
have friends in important places. "In the past," says Omar, "everything was
a matter of haqq; nowadays, it is all a matter of 'friends' (*shāb*)." One of the
others agrees, citing as proof a dispute he had with several neighbors over
irrigation. Ultimately, he noted, he was able to go to a fellow veteran who
was related to an assistant in the local office of the agricultural ministry in
Rabat, who in turn had a colleague in the local office of the ministry make
threatening noises to the people with whom my informant was fighting such
that they backed down. A substantial amount of the daily gossip that took
place in front of Omar's store was taken up with the exchange of information
about who knew whom and hence how something might be done.

The attitude of Omar and his companions toward authority was quite clearly expressed. For example, during the 1967 Middle East War, when there was
some question as to what, if any, action the Moroccan government would take
in the situation and how it might respond to any threats against the local

---

35. In the mid-1960s a retired officer received approximately $80 to $120 per quarter, a
noncommissioned officer $50 to $100, a wounded officer $300 to $1,000, a wounded noncommissioned officer $80 to $300. Amputees received about $1,100 per quarter and paraplegics over
$2,000. All of the pensions from the French army continue for life. According to Benhalima
(1977b:148, 400–500), pensioners, most of whom are military, received 720,000 dirhams (approximately $145,000) per year through the Sefrou disbursement office. When added to the 1.5
million dirham remitted home by some five hundred individuals working abroad and 120,000
dirham per year sent relatives in Sefrou by the three hundred *fonctionnaires* working elsewhere in
Morocco, these sums constitute a significant factor in the economy of the Sefrou region.

Jewish population, it was Omar who said to me: "You have to understand the custom in this country. People do whatever the big men tell them to do. *What they are told doesn't matter; what counts is that someone takes hold of things and tells people how they should act.* It doesn't matter that there aren't many people who have much sense ('aqel) because even those who do have sense want someone to tell them what to do. There is a saying: 'A leader without a leader, though replete is empty of direction.'[36] A student has a professor over him; a master craftsman, a representative of all craftsmen. The trouble nowadays is that the big men don't have the say-so [*klam*, literally "the word"] they used to; they don't give much of any direction so people accept the words of anyone who tells them what to do."

Omar was not optimistic about his future nor that of his country. When, in the early 1970s, economic conditions worsened, he had to close his tiny store and move back to the countryside. He had begun to be a man who knew others and could help himself by helping connect others, but as his own fortunes turned he became more dependent and was forced to seek help from relatives he had earlier kept at a distance. He was wistful about these changes when last we talked, remarking on how men rise and fall depending on whom they attach themselves to, on their own abilities and effort, and, of course, on the will of God.

The Election of an Agricultural Representative

The third example of network formation centers around a single event rather than a single individual and demonstrates, within a specific context, some of the mechanisms by which alliances are formed and employed. The situation in question was the election, held in the fall of 1966, for the post of representative from a rural constituency near Sefrou to the Chamber of Agriculture of the Province of Fez. Although the position itself has undergone considerable change in subsequent years, the features characterizing the election itself have, as we shall see, continued to appear in other electoral events.[37]

The office of representative to the provincial Chamber of Agriculture is of importance on several different levels and for rather diverse reasons. On the local level, the elected official may be instrumental in pleading his constituency's case for new roads, improved market and agricultural cooperative facilities, the fixing of various boundary lines, and the distribution of certain irrigation rights. Should the question arise as to what should be done with any

---

36. Šaik bla šaik wakka iʿammar jabhu kawi. The reference here to a sheikh is generally used in the context of the leader of a religious brotherhood and represents a proposition that, in its implications of religious hierarchy in such Sufi organizations, many contemporary Sefrawis reject.

37. For this reason the present tense will be used in this description, notwithstanding subsequent alterations in the governmental structure.

former colonial properties seized by the government, his voice may also be one of those raised to express the feelings and interests of the farmers of that region. And perhaps most importantly, it is the agricultural representative who frequently plays a major role in obtaining government loans of seed and fertilizer for the individual farmers of his constituency.

In all of these respects, however, it is not so much the minimal powers associated with the office itself that account for the interest taken in this post, but the informal potential associated with it. For besides his role as representative of the agricultural interests of his district's farmers, the agricultural representative is also in a position to do a number of valuable "favors" for his constituents and, indeed, for himself. In an area such as the rural environs of Sefrou where rainfall is as irregular over a given span of years as it is within any one year, any elected official is, by virtue of his powers of patronage and his connections with other politicians, usually capable of pulling certain strings to help those in his favor to hedge against a host of natural and sociological uncertainties. Request for and aid in the distribution of American grain allotments, a major factor in sustaining people through bad crop years, is, though not officially in the hands of this representative, certainly amenable to his influence. He may also have a say in the selection of the sheikhs and their helpers (sing. *jari*) who serve under the local administrator (caid) and help to distribute grain supplements, grant authorization of poor status (thus enabling people to be eligible for certain labor projects and fee waivers), and so on. Through his official role in the production and marketing of agricultural goods and through the informal powers he may develop for indebting others to him, the representative to the Chamber of Agriculture may indeed be a figure of some significance in a particular region. What determines his true importance, however, is not the fact that he holds a certain office or even that that office affords certain opportunities for personal aggrandizement, but the extent and success with which he as an individual is able to cumulate a wide range of personal ties, to display to others a number of highly valued personal characteristics, and, in this particular instance, to merge them into a larger framework of political importance reaching up to the very highest of government levels.

As is the case on the local level, so too on the national level the importance of agricultural representatives has both formal and informal coordinates. The Moroccan Constitution adopted in 1962 by popular referendum specifies that in addition to a lower house of Parliament elected by popular suffrage, there shall also be an upper house, or Chamber of Counselors, one-third of whose members shall be elected from among the representatives to the chambers of Agriculture, Commerce, and Artisans as well as from the college of representatives of salaried workers. The local agricultural representative may, then, actually become a member of the upper house of Parliament and will, in any event, have access to some of those who are elected. Given the frankly minimal importance of even this formal position and the highly tenuous formal tie any representative might have to it, the implications of this fact may not seem particularly impressive. But when one considers the informal factors associated with this link to the national political structure, some of the potential inherent in this position becomes more apparent. The representative to the Chamber of Agriculture may, in certain circumstances, have ties to one of the nation's major political parties or to persons seeking the support of his constituency in other elections, particularly the election for the lower house of the national Parliament. Or, given the structure of direct bureaucratic administration of the local level, the election of agricultural representatives may constitute a mechanism for discerning public sentiment, bringing into the open local power figures, and eliciting an informal political structure based on local support that can complement the political structure of the national bureaucracy in the administration of any particular rural locale. And it is precisely the dynamics of this interplay of national politics and national political structure, on the one hand, and local power politics and local political structure, on the other hand, that were revealed so sharply in the election of this particular representative to the provincial Chamber of Agriculture.

The election for agricultural representative from the district in question was only the second such election to be held since the promulgation of the new constitution in 1962. In accordance with the law, one-half of the twenty-eight representatives in the province were to face reelection every three years, and among those chosen by lot to face reelection first was the representative from the constituency under consideration here.[38] In addition to specifying the procedures for the election itself, the law also establishes that only those persons who are at least twenty-one years of age, own and work their own land, or hold contracts as sharecroppers are eligible to cast votes; nonworking partners and agricultural laborers are not considered eligible to vote. The roll of authorized electors is fixed by the local caid, who consults his sheikhs and local experts on the eligibility of any marginal case. Since only those persons were eligible to vote who possessed land in the rural district—which does not include the irrigated gardens surrounding the city of Sefrou itself—only about 20 of the 1,928 ballots cast were those of city-dwelling owners of rural farmlands.

Interest in the election ran high throughout the campaign period. The field quickly narrowed to four candidates whom we shall call Moulay Arabi ben Mohamed el Alawi, Qacem bel Lhussein, Moha Hamou ou Said, and Ali ou Lahsen. The contest was, in effect, a challenge by each of the latter three—all of them Berbers, all of them rural residents, and all of them possessing only

38. The establishment of the Chambers of Agriculture under Title III of the 1962 Moroccan Constitution and the specific laws governing their structure and powers are detailed in Breton 1963,107–8.

quite modest financial resources—to the candidacy of the incumbent Moulay Arabi, a wealthy urban Arab whose large local landholdings and intimate connections with important figures at all levels of Moroccan government and society had long given him a position of significant, but by no means dominant or all-pervasive, political importance throughout the Sefrou region. Given his wealth and power, his position as incumbent, and his desire to maintain that position, it was with reference to the candidacy of Moulay Arabi that each of the other contenders had to orient himself in the process of building up a local following.

Already into his early seventies, with the countenance and bearing of a man of great authority, Moulay Arabi looked and acted every inch the winner. As the scion of one of the oldest and most notable families of the city of Sefrou, as a man who had some years earlier undertaken the pilgrimage to Mecca, and as a descendant of the Prophet Muhammad in the line of the ruling Alawite dynasty of Morocco, Moulay Arabi embodied many of the inherent characteristics most fully associated with the Moroccan ideal of leadership. Yet as one who shared fully in the Moroccan sense of values and who recognized that in Morocco no single, inherent feature of one's being, whether the nobility of one's blood or the spiritual potential of one's descent, was sufficient to guarantee support in any given venture, Moulay Arabi knew that he would have to actively seek the votes necessary to assure his reelection. Being neither a Berber nor a rural resident, he was, however, unable to focus even a portion of his appeal on ties of kinship or sentiments of ethnic and geographical affinity with his rural constituents. Thus, whether by necessity or by positive inclination, Moulay Arabi sought to consolidate his support almost solely through the utilization of his financial resources.

As the owner of several large, modern farms in the richest sector of the electoral district as well as numerous properties within the city of Sefrou itself, Moulay Arabi was indeed able to call on a rather formidable reserve of financial resources. Although relatively few of the people in his constituency (and virtually none of the electors) were in his direct employ, the economic repercussions of Moulay Arabi's presence in the region were, nonetheless, quite significant. In addition to renting some of his smaller properties to resident farmers in the region, Moulay Arabi was in a position to lend or give allotments of seed, fertilizer, grain, and even the use of his tractors to any of the local farmers he chose to favor. Thus, in addition to his formal powers as agricultural representative to arrange loans for the farmers of his constituency, Moulay Arabi's own holdings placed him in a position of considerable strength vis-à-vis his political opponents.

This economic strength was given even greater significance in the fall of 1966 because the region in which Moulay Arabi was running for reelection was at that time experiencing its second poor harvest in as many years. Therefore, Moulay Arabi was apparently convinced that under the circumstances all that would be required to assure victory was the flexing of a bit of his financial muscle. Accordingly, close associates were sent around the countryside to remind people of the advantages that would accrue to them if they supported the incumbent's candidacy—and the difficulties they might experience were they to fail in their support—and to invite a number of the more influential members of the various rural settlements to dinners held at the candidate's house in Sefrou. After each of these dinners the big man simply handed out "gifts" of money around the table. Since money is generally regarded in this part of the world as one of the many convertible forms that physical, social, or cultural resources may take, and since the use of all such resources are recognized as more or less legitimate in the quest of a political goal, none of the guests showed any particular reluctance or embarrassment in accepting this token of Moulay Arabi's beneficence.

By contrast, each of the three Berber candidates pursued a course of action significantly different from that of Moulay Arabi. Lacking the incumbent's wealth and properties, but nonetheless able to capitalize on the multiplicity of social ties that bound them to their fellow electors, each of the three was able to call for support on his kinsmen, his neighbors, and the many friends and relatives to whom each had ingratiated himself over the years. Each of them was well aware of the fact that in Moroccan society all acts require reciprocation, but that the forms of reciprocation are sufficiently interchangeable that aid rendered, say, in the form of financial help in time of need or as an intermediary in the acquisition of a third party's favor might later be called up in the form of requesting the hand of a particular kinswoman in marriage or aid in a forthcoming election. Each of them also knew that although one should in theory be able to rely on the help of close kinsmen for any particular venture, in point of fact there is a wide range of permissible behavior associated with any inherent relationship and that it is, therefore, both possible and necessary to contract and not merely implement a wide network of personal ties that have been formed with individual members of one's own kin group as well as with outsiders. Thus, although each of the Berber candidates started with a network of personal kin bonds that could conceivably form the core of his personal following, each of them had to service these individual links with great care and to forge ties with nonkinsmen through a variety of distinctive institutions and strategies.

Ali ou Lahsen, for example, seems to have concentrated his efforts almost entirely on solidifying the support of his localized kin group and on calling up certain outstanding debts among his close neighbors. These social debts stemmed primarily from the fact that some years earlier, Ali ou Lahsen had been employed by a nearby French farmer; over the course of the years he had managed to utilize his position to do a number of favors for his various relatives and friends—finding jobs for some, arranging loans for others, and, eventually, seeing to it that when the farm was broken up and sold, it was the people of Ali ou Lahsen's choice who received the first option of purchase. After the departure of his former employer, Ali ou Lahsen, who owned very little good land in his own right, earned his livelihood primarily as a Quranic schoolteacher and practitioner of the art of magic. Therefore, Ali ou Lahsen could count on a number of different ties binding the members of his own localized kin group to the support of his candidacy. However, this support was largely restricted to one small section of the electoral district, a restriction further aggravated by the fact that the candidate did not have access to an automobile or the resources with which to hire one.

If the ties linking Ali ou Lahsen to his supporters were multiple in kind but restricted in scope, those of Moha Hamou ou Said were somewhat more specialized and extensive. Moha Hamou was, in effect, a small-scale political broker. His primary political resource lay in his friendships with a number of petty bureaucrats and influential members of the Mouvement Populaire, a Berber-oriented national political party. A camp follower and flatterer, a tireless gadabout and a practitioner of obvious ingratiation, Moha Hamou was, nonetheless, a man who understood quite well what sorts of knowledge and connections each of his acquaintances possessed and, therefore, just who was in a position to do what for whom at any given moment. By distributing his own favors over a wide area and by demonstrating that he was already in control of some of the channels of communication that would only be further enhanced by his election as agricultural representative, Moha Hamou, for all the dearth of his own financial resources, was able to generate a rather extensive network of supporters and potential supporters.

Qacem bel Lhussein, on the other hand, was neither an accomplished middleman nor a wealthy landowner. Although his ties to his own kinsmen were probably as strong as were those of Ali ou Lahsen to his, it was clear to Qacem that however loyal the core of followers drawn from his own settlement might be, they were simply not sufficiently numerous to assure his own election. Qacem's electoral tactics were, therefore, more varied and, as it turned out, more imaginative than those of any of the other candidates. The course of his campaign is in many ways the most interesting and the most revealing of them all.

Perhaps the bulk of Qacem's influence and power stemmed from his relationship with a Frenchman who owned and operated a large farm near Qacem's home settlement throughout the latter years of the Protectorate and the early years of Moroccan independence. Like Ali ou Lahsen, Qacem, who became a trusted employee and indeed a close friend of the French farmer, had for some time been in a position to dispense favors on behalf of his *colon* patron. Qacem's most important opportunity, however, came several years earlier when, having decided to sell his own holdings and retire to the Continent, the Frenchman was convinced by Qacem not to sell all of his property to a single person (like Moulay Arabi), but to break up his farm into a number of pieces that would be purchased by various native farmers from the surrounding countryside. Qacem arranged the entire matter in such a way as to facilitate the sale for his employer and allow a number of people Qacem wanted in his debt to benefit from the transaction. When election time came around, Qacem did indeed have a legitimate basis for expecting their support.

In arranging the sale of his employer's farm, Qacem was, moreover, very careful to see to it that some of the choicest sections were made available to the local leaders of the Aisawa religious brotherhood. Although many of the *sufi* brotherhoods fell into disrepute for their involvement with the French during the Protectorate period and remain for the most part either moribund or in a state of suspended animation, in this particular region the Aisawa lodges remain active social and religious institutions, and many of their leaders are thought to possess supernatural powers. When, therefore, Qacem called up the personal debts of these brotherhood leaders by asking them to have their followers cast their ballots for him, even those members who claimed to prefer another candidate said that they felt constrained to accede to their leaders' requests.

Qacem also made very effective use of the ʿ*ar,* the act that, to recall Westermarck's comment, "intrinsically implies the transference of a conditional curse for the purpose of compelling somebody to grant a request" (Westermarck 1926,1:518). In this particular instance Qacem sacrificed sheep as a form of ʿar at the doors of several mosques in settlements whose members were not otherwise committed to supporting him. It is, of course, very difficult to measure how much these acts actually contributed to the plurality of votes Qacem did eventually draw from these communities, but it can at least be noted that by his use of the ʿar Qacem was not only giving symbolic expression to his identity as a fellow rural Berber but was also forcing the question of the applicability of such an institution in a purely political context—an institution that, as Qacem must surely have appreciated, was not so fraught with factional opposition that people who make use of this practice in a wide variety of other situations would be willing to sacrifice its ongoing social utility for the sake of a single, rather short-term, political gain.[39]

Qacem also phrased his appeal to certain individuals and groups of individuals in ways that implied a sentiment of cooperation and interdependence underlying a traditional bond of affiliation. To his neighbors, for example, he referred to their aid in the forthcoming agricultural election as a form of

---

39. It might also be noted that if another man were to make a second ʿar sacrifice to the same person or group, it would have no binding force. As one informant put it: "The first man has filled our glass and there is no room left in it for what another man would try to pour in. His gift would be meaningless and wasted." That informants should explain this custom by reference to analogies involving a source of sustenance, ingratiation, and the implied need to reciprocate is particularly appropriate.

tuayza, or mutual aid offered in the planting or harvesting of a crop.[40] And to those members of a local descent group with whom the ancestors of his own group had once formed a sort of mutual defense pact (*uṭada*), Qacem appealed for aid in the election in terms of this compact of interdependence and co-protection.

But if some of the tactics used by Qacem were more varied and creative than those employed by his competitors, it is also true that he was not above the use of certain stratagems similar to their own. Thus, early in the campaign a fifth candidate—a man from Qacem's own settlement—was induced to drop his candidacy altogether in return for considerations involving both the payment of a sum of money and the promise of future benefits if Qacem were elected. Similarly, a wealthy native farmer who had benefited from Qacem's earlier aid in acquiring some of the properties of Qacem's French employer—and who was still regarded with some disfavor by his fellow Berbers for having failed to support the activities of the Army of Liberation during the struggle for national independence—was convinced that neither his financial status nor his overall reputation was likely to suffer for his making a hand-some contribution to the campaign treasury of the man who was certain to be the next agricultural representative.

Throughout the course of the campaign each of the candidates concentrated on forging and solidifying a wide range of personal ties rather than on making any direct ideological appeals. Not only was there virtually no reference to the agricultural policies of any of the major political parties, there was very little reference at all during the campaign to any partisan ideas or affiliations. All three of the Berber candidates considered themselves supporters of the Mouvement Populaire, the "Berber party," but attachment to a political party in this area was, at this time, far less an adherence to some body of ideas and programs than yet one more affiliation or attribute that may be adduced or ignored, utilized or avoided in establishing sets of personal ties and displaying valuable personal characteristics. It is true that previous efforts by Moha Hamou on behalf of the Mouvement Populaire were rewarded in this election by a small contribution from the head of the national party to his campaign effort, and it is also true that some of the voters were careful to appreciate that the victor would be in a good bargaining position with any of the political parties in the event of a national parliamentary election. But whatever their later political implications might be, attachments to national political parties were, throughout the course of this election, clearly subordinated to the much more general issue of competition for a highly personal and local base of political importance.

40. The practice of tuayza is discussed in the Algerian context in Bourdieu 1977,60. During the nationwide drought in Morocco in 1981, King Hassan II used the term to refer to efforts to replenish herds and rebuild the nation's agricultural base through cooperation among the different regions of the country.

The de-emphasis on party ties came out most clearly in one minor incident in which two young men, one a staunch supporter of the Mouvement Populaire and Qacem, the other of Moulay Arabi and the Istiqlal party (which Moulay Arabi himself did not support in the 1963 parliamentary election, but one of whose local officials did a bit of campaigning on his behalf in this election), exchanged blows at the polling station on election day. The entire incident was regarded with great amusement by everyone, not simply because of the histrionics associated with it, but because it showed so clearly how much these young men had mistaken the lines along which this election was being contested and how much they had failed to appreciate that party affiliations were incidental rather than central to this struggle for personal political importance on the local level.

By the time election day rolled around, each of the candidates had lined up his personal support in the way he hoped would prove most efficacious. The polling place itself was off limits to all of the candidates, but each of them sent some of his friends to keep an eye on things. Each voter was given a set of colored slips of paper and deposited the one symbolizing the candidate of his choice in the ballot box. Outside, some of the candidates' friends asked to see the remaining slips of people who had promised to vote for their candidate in order to reassure themselves that the person had indeed voted as promised. Many of the voters tried to slip quietly away, while others who had switched their allegiance engaged in a quick swap of remaining ballots with others who had made a similar but alternative turnabout.

The ballots were counted as soon as the polling station closed. In the early evening hours a small crowd gathered to hear the clerk read the final results of his tabulation: Qacem—549 votes; Moha Hamou—517; Moulay Arabi—510; Ali ou Lahsen—350. The effect of the announcement was electric, and the word quickly spread that Moulay Arabi not only had been defeated by the upstart Berber Qacem but that he had only managed to finish third in the field of four candidates. Rumor had it that upon hearing the news, Moulay Arabi immediately cloistered himself in his house and said that he wanted to die for shame. Many people rejoiced in the fall of the big man and many simply regarded the course of events as further evidence that "the game" in which, as one writer put it, "one can be a liar in the morning, a vizir in the evening, and perhaps hanged on the following day" was still very much in force (quoted in Monteil 1964,141).[41] But perhaps the most typical, and indeed perceptive, remark came from one man who told me: "Now it is somebody else's turn to get rich!"

41. Monteil himself, however, claims that Moroccans regard "the game" as no longer in force, whereas all my evidence indicates that while some of the lines along which it was formerly played are regarded as no longer effective, the opening up of new channels of endeavor, such as political-party maneuvers, has only served to reinforce the image of a highly fluid social and political structure.

The rejoicing that followed in the wake of Moulay Arabi's defeat was, however, to prove short-lived. Soon after the results of the election were announced, Moulay Arabi, with the aid of some of the most important figures on the national political scene, moved to have the entire election invalidated. In order to understand who the personalities involved were and why this very minor local election should have had such repercussions on the level of national politics, it is necessary to review a bit of Moroccan political history.

The importance on the national scene of the election for agricultural representative from the Sefrou area should actually be understood in terms of the parliamentary election held in 1963. At that time three candidates stood for office from the electoral district which included both the city of Sefrou and the countryside around it, a territory that encompassed most of the Ait Yusi Berber tribe and the Arabs of the Beni Azgha tribe to the north. The three candidates represented the three major political parties of Morocco at that time: Istiqlal, the parent independence party led by and having its greatest appeal to the traditionally oriented and largely urban Arab population, a firm supporter of the institution of the monarchy but often opposed to the specific policies of King Hassan II; FDIC (Front pour la Défense des Institutions Constitutionelles), a recently formed coalition committed to supporting the king's programs in Parliament and itself composed of the Parti Socialiste Démocrate, the Parti Démocratique de l'Indépendence, and the Mouvement Populaire, or "Berber party"; and finally the UNFP (Union National des Forces Populaires), the main leftist opposition party, whose primary strength lay in the highly industrialized cities and which was headed by Mehdi ben Barka until his kidnapping and presumed murder by unconvicted assailants in Paris in 1965.

Political-party affiliation is, as we indicated earlier, only one—and not necessarily the most important—of an individual candidate's attributes; the cumulation of personal traits and personal ties as differentially perceived and evaluated by the members of one's constituency must be taken into consideration as well.

Certainly the most important figure in the 1963 election in the Sefrou district was the candidate of FDIC, the then minister of commerce and industry in the national cabinet. The minister was, moreover, a distant relative and close personal friend of the king, a widely publicized national figure, a descendant of the Prophet Muhammad, a member of one of the most notable families of Fez, and the brother of the highly respected pasha of the city of Sefrou itself.[42] His opponent from the UNFP was a local entrepreneur whose father had years earlier placed him in the UNFP party and another son in Istiqlal—not for any ideological reasons, but simply as a hedge against being without connections in the winning faction. Accordingly, the UNFP candi-

---

42. The official in question has held various cabinet positions from the 1960s to the present.

date's minimal support came not from some radical fringe of the district's population, but from those people living on or near his large country landholdings and those receiving benefits from the olive-oil mill he shared with his brothers—although some of his support also seems to have come from the numerous war veterans of rural origins who operated small shops in the city and were disillusioned with all the other political parties.

The main opposition to the government minister came, however, from the Istiqlal candidate, a man who was then head of the local poorhouse through which food allotments to the indigent were made. His support came mainly from those who benefited from his control over the sacks of American surplus grain, from the Beni Azgha tribesmen who lined up solidly behind the Istiqlal candidate, and—most importantly—from all those who felt that government officials were simply out to line their own pockets and that, therefore, the minister of commerce and industry was a candidate whose lack of local ties and local interests would not constrain him to share the benefits of his office with the members of his local constituency.[43] So great was this feeling, in fact, that the voters of the Sefrou district—primarily the people from the countryside—voted against the minister of commerce and industry and elected as their representative to the lower house of the national Parliament the candidate from the Istiqlal political party.

Although fascinating as yet another exemplification of the political processes with which we have been dealing in the agricultural-representative election of 1966, the details of the 1963 parliamentary election need not concern us here. What is relevant for our present purposes are the implications that the king's man, the government minister, had been defeated by a rather minor local figure of the opposition party, thus depriving the king of having one of his closest associates hold a seat in Parliament. When, following the suspension of Parliament by the king on June 7, 1965 for failure to settle its internal differences to the king's personal satisfaction, it was rumored that new parliamentary elections might be called sometime in 1967, and the nationwide agricultural-representative elections took on added importance.[44] Not only were they the first major elections since Parliament was suspended but, as we noted earlier, if the local representatives would indeed be local power figures capable of turning over their constituencies to a particular candidate in the parliamentary election, the king would have not only a public indication of how such a parliamentary election might go, but what steps might remain to be taken so that those elected to such a Parliament would be more responsive to the king's proposals.

43. The usual way of phrasing this was to say, "Huwa maši mul l-bled" ("He is not a mul of this area," where mul means one who possesses some control over the resources that sustain a particular person, group, or region).

44. For the complete text of the proclamation suspending Parliament, see Hassan II 1965.

The defeat in this local election of Moulay Arabi was, then, of some significance on the national scene. Moulay Arabi had been a firm supporter of
FDIC and the candidacy of the government minister—who would probably
have stood from the Sefrou constituency in any new parliamentary election—
and was himself bound by distant ties of blood and close ties of political
affiliation to the palace. His loss to an upstart Berber candidate was taken as a
harbinger of possible defeat for FDIC in subsequent elections and a situation
amenable to exploitation by opposition parties. That such possibilities were
viewed with the gravest concern by the king and his political advisors was
dramatically underlined by the events immediately following the agricultural
election.

In the dead of night just a few days after the election—with all the conspir-
atorial airs that reminded one of my informants of the days of the struggle for
independence—Moulay Arabi was host to a group of dignitaries arriving from
Rabat, a group that included the minister of commerce and industry, the gov-
ernor of the province of Fez, and the director-general of the royal cabinet.
During the time they remained in Sefrou, as later events would seem to indicate, they apparently decided to contest the results of the election in court.
Accordingly, a suit was filed before the court in Fez charging that several of
the sheikhs in the electoral constituency had conspired to stuff the rolls of
eligible electors with the names of a number of ghost voters. Qacem was
barred from taking his seat and the sheikhs in question—all supporters of
Qacem's candidacy—were suspended from office pending the outcome of the
court's decision. In the meantime Moulay Arabi began applying additional
pressures in the region to remind people that he was still an important force to
contend with. For example, he drove up the bidding price for a particular farm
owned by the religious foundation (*ḥabus*) which had long been rented by a
man who had failed to support him in the election, and he meted out pecuniary
punishment to several other small farmers who had surreptitiously switched
their allegiance.

Now it may seem ungracious to say that one seldom has to look far to find
some irregularity in a Moroccan election, but one cannot help but feel that the
basis upon which the court finally did decide to suspend the electoral results
does appear a bit farfetched. Rather than declaring the election void by virtue
of any stuffing of the electoral roll itself, the court latched onto the fact that
the clerk of the polling station had stepped outside briefly during his lunch
break. On the assumption that under such circumstances the ballot box may
indeed have been stuffed (and not because any irregularities in the ballot box
itself had been proved), the court temporarily set aside the entire election,
ordered the representative from the adjoining district to act as interim representative for the constituency in question, and reserved judgment on the final
deposition of the case and the possibility of calling any new election.

As events would have it, however, the court was not to comment on the case again for more than two years. Initially, it was rumored, the supporters of Moulay Arabi thought it wiser simply to indicate to the electorate that if the latter were not prepared to reelect Moulay Arabi then at least no one else would be allowed to occupy his office. At first, too, it was made clear to the farmers of the area that only those who were prepared to back Moulay Arabi would find themselves receiving agricultural loans, but when this only prompted outraged appeals by the Berbers of the area to the leadership of the Mouvement Populaire and the whole issue was threatened with being turned into a partisan affair, the threats of discriminatory agricultural loans were quickly dropped. Following the June 1967 Middle East War, during which the opposition tried to rally potential electoral support on the basis of its disagreement with the king's stand on Middle Eastern affairs, the whole question of calling new parliamentary elections was set aside and a general moratorium on partisan politics was encouraged. Sometime later the authority to decide on loans to farmers in the constituency was taken out of the hands of the agricultural representative altogether and placed entirely under the control of the bureaucrats in the Ministry of Agriculture. Thus when the court finally did break its silence to comment that pending legal proof of any irregularities, Qacem was to be regarded as the duly elected representative of the district, it was to a position almost totally devoid of any formal power or importance that he acceded. True, there was still the question as to what would happen when the three-year term ran out. But for the most part everyone claimed to have lost interest in the affair; however, their general interest in politics had, no doubt, been rendered only momentarily dormant.[45]

The networks forged by Tahar, Omar, and the participants in the agricultural election are, like those of their compatriots throughout the region, characterized by a series of distinctive features.[46] We have already noted that

45. It should be noted that for a short while after the election Qacem did indeed take an active interest in the affairs of his constituency, influencing, for example, the paving of several roads leading to markets in his district. In this respect, however, he was no doubt exercising his general leadership rather than demonstrating his rights to a particular office. Similarly, when the government proposed to plow all the farms in the district with tractors and charge the farmers accordingly, it was Qacem—still barred from any official position—who arranged a settlement by which only those farmers who wanted to would participate in the government program. In general, then, Qacem continued to extend his local political influence irrespective of his role as agricultural representative and interest in the formal office itself virtually ceased to exist. (I am indebted to Clifford Geertz for some of the above data.)

46. A sense of how typical the Sefrou examples are for Morocco as a whole can be obtained from the numerous biographical sketches contained in the following works: K. Brown 1976; Charhadi 1964; Crapanzano 1980; K. Dwyer 1982; Rabinow 1977; Waterbury 1972. Indeed, these studies demonstrate the extent to which American scholars in particular have been struck by the importance that individual personality plays in the structure of Moroccan social life. For an excellent account of a famous Moroccan political figure of the early twentieth century, see Forbes 1924.

in the Sefrou area the fundamental social unit is not some aggregate of persons, but the single individual acting as the locus of a set of personal ties and personal attributes. Using a vast array of resources—his inherent ties of kinship, his control over physical and symbolic reserves, his capacity to cajole or manipulate others, his rhetorical skills and force of personality—he forges a range of personal, contractual, and often ad hoc ties to others that are as distinctive in their particular patterning as they are typical in their modes of construction. Whether it is a ''big man'' using his assets and manipulating his dependents toward some preconceived goal or a ''little man'' choosing among those upon whom to depend for his well-being, each person will draw on the flexibility inherent in all relationships to create his own network of affiliations. Provided he remains within what Llewelyn and Hoebel once called ''the bounds of permissible leeway'' (Llewelyn and Hoebel 1941,23), he can utilize the limited number of regularized ways in which ties can be formed and traits ascribed to build a structure as distinctive and ephemeral as the person who stands at its center.

Networks thus crystallize and dissolve as circumstance and purpose shift. Tahar and his brother can, for a time, build their world around their tie to the wealthy Si Mokhtar, Omar or his acquaintances can tap into their connections with other veterans to get support from a government official, and the candidates in the agricultural election can form political coalitions based on the interchangeable nature of mutual obligation. What may at one moment appear a structure of enduring quality—hedged round with gifts and exchanges, reference to longstanding kin ties, and physical gestures redolent of immutable attachment—often proves, in the kaleidoscope of everyday affairs, to be brittle, transient, and replaceable. This does not, as we shall see, imply either a lack of sincerity or truthfulness in Moroccan social ties. Rather, it underscores the commonsense belief in the need to respond to changing conditions, the potentially chaotic quality of human life, and the need to judge men and events not by a series of abstract and bloodless standards but by the contexts in which their words and acts impinge upon the world at large. It is not surprising, therefore, that in a social universe of shifting configurations, few tasks should take on more significance than the attempt to find, in one's ties to others, those points of attachment, human or supernatural, enduring or expedient, to which one can cleave for support.

It is against this backdrop that one must, in part, understand the role of big men. Big men (*l-kbar*) draw together and embody the skills and connections that less favored or imaginative men find it difficult to embrace with equal verve and success. Like others, but to a more inflated degree, they are dependent on acknowledgements of their reliability and forcefulness. Characteristically, it is in the metaphor of speech as act, word as deed that such reliability is encompassed. A big man is, therefore, one who ''has word'' (*klam*)—that is, one who has the ''say-so,'' whose word is both his bond and his instrument. Because the resources upon which one can develop a dominant position are so varied, a big man must not only marshall his knowledge and connections effectively, he must also demonstrate, in a society that gives limited emphasis to inherent rights and great attention to the capacity to make those rights that are asserted stick, that he does indeed possess the wherewithal to convert the ingredients of implicit exchange and explicit contract into a set of relations that are binding, predictable, and "real." Indeed, he must constantly demonstrate his willingness and effectiveness on behalf of his clients lest his ever-present competitors seize on the moment to divert his support.

The relation of big men and dependents may be thought of as patron-client ties, provided that this frame of reference is understood in its Moroccan manifestation. As we saw earlier, the term *mul* means "owner" or "patron" in the sense of a person who contributes substantially to one's nurture. One of the features that separates the believer from the unbeliever is the fact that, as the Quran says, "the unjust have no patron and no helper" (Quran 42:6). On Judgment Day, when the peoples of the world are arrayed in their respective groups before Allah, those to whom God's prophets have appeared will be spoken for by these patrons. Saints, whether alive or dead, are patrons, too, both in their nurturing capacity and in the personal relation of reciprocity and contract by which men are linked to them.[47] Certain features, must, however, be underscored. It must be remembered, for example, that because resources on which relationships may be based are varied, it is by no means true that the terms of the relationship can be permanently set by only one party. As Kenneth Brown (1977) has pointed out: "It is not the case that the values in circulation are always chosen by the patron. . . . It [is] crucial to emphasize the diversity of interests and resources adhering to these social relations. The transactions amongst clients and patron vary as much as the individuals and the situations in which they interact." Thus a resource that may be central in one situation may be rendered irrelevant in another. A rich man finds that where the question is one involving the cleaning of irrigation ditches in the village, it is not wealth allowing the hiring of substitute labor that matters but, as a rhetorically skillful poor man gets others to see the matter, whether one shows up to demonstrate solidarity in the collective venture. Moreover, it is

47. This is not the only feature that saints share with big men. Like big men, saints must demonstrate—through their effects in this world—that they do indeed possess the qualities to which they lay claim; they, too, are held to a kind of justification-by-acts standard. Similarly, the powerful political figure must move with serenity through a whirlwind of activity while the saint must trail serenity in the wake of his pulsating presence. Not only must each exhibit some of the qualities that are also associated with the other, but it is precisely in the cumulation of these features in a single person—the saint who is also warrior, the king who is also marabout—that these qualities achieve their highest embodiment. On the qualities of Moroccan saints in their cultural context, see C. Geertz 1968.

the dependent who, by responding in a very particular way to a show of generalized support by a big man, may be able to set the terms for future exchange. Since the relationships are so personalized and so little institutionalized—in the sense of perduring structural ties—and since the very terms of all relations remain open to negotiation, it is far less fruitful to concentrate attention on the momentary result of such relationships than on the regularized means by which, through language and consequence, they are constantly being formed and re-formed.

It is in this light, for example, that we can view the quest for political supporters in the agricultural election as a specific form of the more general process of seeking social dependents and supporters. In that election, as in many others, the goal to be achieved, the prize to be won, was more than just the acquisition of a particular political office. It was also a contest for recognition as a leader, a person who could be depended on to further the well-being of those who were bound to him in any of a variety of different ways and at any one of a number of different levels. Some of the candidates may, therefore, have been focusing their attention as much on solidifying their image as real and potential leaders of the settlements or areas from which they came as on actually acquiring the contested post. Others more or less had to make the attempt or risk losing some of their generalized leadership to one of those persons who are always ready to make the challenge. Thus the incumbent, Moulay Arabi, once he had decided to compete for the post of agricultural representative, could not have failed to realize that far more was at stake than the loss of the office itself. For if it is indeed true that in a system of this sort one is, in effect, only as good as one's last performance, the definitive loss of this election could only serve to call into question the big man's reliability as a patron in the very broadest of sociological terms. Qacem, on the other hand, though excluded from office for more than two years and allowed to take his seat only after the post had been deprived of its most important formal powers, was nonetheless generally regarded by the people of his district as their spokesman in agricultural matters and a man whose own reliability would now be under constant test.[48]

48. This is not to undervalue the fact that in this particular election it was apparently the intention of the central government to institute a position in the official hierarchy that was not part of the regular civil service but in which local personalities could exercise a degree of officially sanctioned authority over one aspect of the life of the members of their own home territory. By allowing various local men to utilize all available means to form personally centered coalitions, the government hoped to allow such political followings to develop "naturally" in the full public light and then to channel the followings into the support of particular government policies or government-favored parliamentary candidates. The election for agricultural representative was, then, less an attempt to fill an important functionary position than it was a tactic for discerning the present state of the rural political process, pinpointing local figures who might play a role in any future political situations, and focusing the dependence of these figures on the governmental hierarchy through which their distribution of political capital (in this case agricultural loans) would be directed.

The election also points up another feature of Moroccan network formation, namely the desire to avoid ties that are so entangling as to reduce the possibilities for creating associations along other, possibly conflicting, lines. Political-party affiliation stands as an example. Political parties in Morocco are generally perceived by people in the Sefrou region as amalgamations of individuals bound together by a multiplicity of different personal ties rather than by any all-pervasive organizational structure or ideological commitment. Such parties are, therefore, considered to be organizational frameworks whose flexibility and differential utility are not unlike those that revolve around and are expressed through the idioms of kinship and economic relations. Ties to particular members of the party hierarchy—ties based, for example, on ethnic, familial, and economic relations—are frequently of great importance insofar as these persons can serve as intermediaries for still wider networks of affiliation leading up to the very highest of decision-making levels. The ties centering on such party figures are, however, quite personal and varied, and while it may be possible to crystallize a field of supporters around a particular leader or the momentarily shared interests that he represents, political-party organization as a whole has had no greater persistent success in this constituency than have any other formally institutionalized social groupings.[49] Indeed, in this and other elections the people of the constituency have

---

Insofar as the election did indeed elicit a meaningful degree of participation on the part of candidates and electors alike, it certainly lived up to its expectations. But insofar as the result of this and other elections—as well as a series of extraneous political occurrences—indicated to the central government that they could not fully control the outcome or implications of such elections, the election results were regarded as somewhat less than satisfactory. Moreover, attempts to alter the results of the election in this particular district in favor of the defeated government supporter—as well as other attempts to enlist the commitment of the actual winner—were shelved when it seemed that such acts might only create more problems than they would solve. Similarly, the recognition that the highly personal support gained by a candidate in an election such as this might not easily be translated into support for candidates in other elections contributed to the government's decision to avoid the possibility of open partisan confrontations and to concentrate instead on the development of the existing bureaucracy.

Noting the post-independence lack of any important official post that combined local power and position in the official hierarchy, Gellner (1981,204) wrote: "The only locally recruited office-holders were headmen at village level, or at most clan level where the groups involved were not very large. This did have an enormously important consequence: there was no outlet, in the official hierarchy of the state, for the ambitious local who wished to operate locally, or whose local interests or lack of formal education prevented other than local activity. Admittedly, there were the village headmanships—but the power, prestige and perquisites attaching to these were not significant."

49. In the immediate post-independence period, political-party organization was, however, of somewhat more pervasive importance than it is now. According to Ernest Gellner (1981,204), this emphasis on political parties was due precisely to the fact that "the parties provided an organization, a hierarchy, and a channel of information leading right up to the provincial and national capitals. The rural regions were now incorporated in the national community, and local politics were not, as under the French, locally circumscribed. Hence it was now important to have a line to the capital, a friend at court." See also Waterbury 1972,130–48 for an example of the role of party affiliation in the electoral politics of one candidate.

specifically avoided firm partisan attachments.[50] The reason for this is quite apparent: it is generally recognized that if partisan attachments become so strong as to determine the axes along which people will have to line up in a wide variety of social situations, such a reification of social bonds would undercut the ability to contract various relationships across any social boundary.

The tendency to avoid issues or practices that might hinder one's ability to choose associates from any part of the total society for whatever situation might arise is, of course, not characteristic of partisan attachments alone. Throughout the election, candidates themselves avoided direct confrontations and refrained from phrasing their opposition to another's candidacy in terms that might appear too impassioned or inflexible. They knew that to do otherwise might well alienate those voters who recognized that today's opponent might be tomorrow's ally and that strict alignment in this situation might damage the flexibility of social relations everyone was desirous of maintaining. Similarly, many accepted the constraint implied in Qacem's use of the supernaturally sanctioned sacrifice, not because they were entirely convinced of its efficacy or were unaware of various ways they could have avoided its obligation, but because they were not willing to use this particular situation to deny or devalue a traditional bond of affiliation any one of them might wish to use in a different context later on.[51] In the context of political-party-ties prop-

50. This was true, for example, in the local council elections held throughout Morocco in November 1976. In the city of Sefrou, eighteen of the twenty-five seats went to candidates from the Socialist party (USFP). A highly placed member of the party accounted for this partisan victory not as a result of attachment to socialist ideology but because the disaffected urban middle class and rural immigrants who felt they were not getting their share of the national wealth saw in the party a well-organized group of local leaders willing to make efforts on their behalf. Local informants noted that shortly before the election, a bad flood occurred in Sefrou; the Socialists quickly sent aid while government assistance lagged far behind. Many of the socialist candidates were schoolteachers, and many people felt that a show of support for them would also demonstrate concern with local education. Lack of attachment to the Socialist party was demonstrated in the parliamentary election that took place the following spring. In an election generally described as very rough, the winner in a field of a dozen candidates was Caid Ali Lyusi, the nephew of Caid Lahsen Lyusi, the preeminent political figure in Sefrou for more than twenty years and the first minister of the interior in the post independence period. Caid Ali Lyusi professed attachment to the Mouvement Populaire, whose leader Mahjoubi Aherdane spoke to a large rally at which he said that Abderrahim Bouabid, the head of the Socialists, would promise anything but deliver nothing and that the Socialists were opposed to the king. Units of the Royal Air Force then flew overhead in formation. As one Berber leader told me: "Aherdane had airplanes and cars and money and everything and Bouabid didn't even have a donkey. So who would you vote for?" Therefore, except for a small number of party regulars, attachment to parties as such in Sefrou and its hinterland remains very tenuous indeed. On the municipal-council elections, see Zakya 1976. For a fascinating account by a candidate elected in the El Menzel (Beni Azgha) area east of Sefrou, see Lamghili 1976. See also Les elections communales 1977 and Santucci 1978.

51. The 'ar was also employed in various parts of rural Morocco during the 1976 local council elections. According to Zakya (1976,24): "In a village of the Atlantic coast where the population, though somewhat industrialized, is still close to its rural origins, a candidate walked

er we have already seen that when some of the young men tried to turn the election itself into a strictly partisan affair, they were laughed off because everyone preferred to maintain the ability to contract personal ties wherever they seemed most advantageous rather than allow partisan ties to drive a permanent wedge between momentarily competing social segments. Indeed, one of the factors contributing to the incomplete formation of political-party affiliations is the perceived need to close off no options unless the stakes are so high or the alternatives so few as to counsel to the contrary. Precisely because relationships are so negotiable and reciprocity so generalized, the people of Sefrou believe that relationships are inherently unstable and security lies in ramified networks.

The construction of personal networks of affiliation thus partake of a wide range of cultural assumptions and practices—the generalized expectations of mutuality and obligation, the running imbalance of asserted rights and proffered duties, the intertwined demands of generosity and ingratiation. Yet if these particular features form one part of that equation of Moroccan social organization summed up in the concept of haqq as duty and obligation, there remains another element in the meaning of this same term, an element that may be subsumed under the general rubric of "truth." And it is through this element of truth—and more particularly in the ways in which truth is attached to men's words—that we can comprehend an aspect of Moroccan speech and action that is central to an understanding of social life in the region of Sefrou.

Validation: Attaching Utterances to Actions

You tell me you are going to Fez. Now, if you say you are going to Fez,
That means you are not going. But I happen to know that you are going
to Fez. Why have you lied to me, you who are my friend?

Moroccan saying (cited in Bowles 1982, 55)

In the ongoing creation of their personal networks, the people of Sefrou demonstrate that the concepts through which they define situations and estab-

---

barefoot around several houses and cast the ʿar on the voters. He was elected." More suggestive of the convolutions that may accompany the use of the ʿar is Zakya's description of its use in a mountain community. "There, an entrepeneur cast the ʿar by sacrificing a sheep before each new candidate who sought to present himself. He obtained what he wanted, namely their withdrawal, and he thus found himself the only candidate on the ballot. He was duely elected. But the voters had made an alliance with a different party than the winner's. After the election, the voters then cast the ʿar on the winner demanding that he become the representative for their party. He did so." As indicated earlier, to many people in the Sefrou region the use of the ʿar carries implications of a supernatural curse as well as implications that, by failing to acknowledge the binding force of such an imposed obligation, one brings shame upon oneself. I do not, however, agree with the interpretation made by K. Brown (1982), that in the elections I discuss "there seems no doubt that in the circumstances, allusions to ʿār by the parties concerned is a matter of honor and not of curse, an inviolable trust and not a supernatural sanction." The fear of potential curse is still present for the Sefrou people; those few who express disbelief in it also express a lack of commitment to the practice in any form.

lish relationships are themselves the subject of constant negotiation. At their very heart the terms that imply some form of obligation or reciprocation—terms like haqq or "patronage," "friendship," or "tribe"—remain incompletely defined, open textured, until, by a process of mutual negotiation, an actual relationship comes to be conceptualized under them. Because such great dependence is placed on language for the arrangement of one's affiliations, the people of Sefrou are careful to distinguish between the role words play as one explores and assays the ties that are *possible* in any encounter and the role such words play in *fixing* a relationship—in linking an utterance so firmly to its consequences that one cannot, without serious risk to one's reputation and well-being, easily avoid its implications. What is at issue is nothing less than the process by which utterances that serve to define one's relation with another are transformed from mere verbalizations into statements that possess some attachment to the quality of truth.

To put the matter in this fashion is to sound a theme that would appear to be familiar in Western culture but which, in fact, contrasts sharply with it. Westerners may not believe all they hear or give voice to all they know to be so. But they do generally assume that when someone makes a statement about their relationship to another it is in some way connected to the truth—even if that connection is one of equivocation, dissimulation, or out-and-out lying. To say that someone is my friend or acquaintance, that someone owes me a favor or is connected to me by a particular bond of kinship or affection is to imply that what I say, even if a bald-faced lie, has some connection with the truth. By contrast, in Morocco it is tacitly understood that where relationships of obligation are being formed, mere utterances imply nothing about the truth of the thing asserted.[52] When, for example, the countryman who invited me in for tea later said that he had a haqq in me, he was not stating a truth in any sense of the word: he was making a declaration which, standing alone, was without any attachment to the issue of veracity. Similarly, for a man to say that he is attached to another in a way that implies some mutual right or duty (e.g., as his "friend," "client," fellow "tribesman," or other term indicative of reciprocal obligations) does not, by itself, convey any implication of its truth. Westerners may discount a statement as not having been serious or by saying that the speaker never meant what he said, and such characterizations may serve to avoid depicting the statement as a lie. By contrast, Moroccans see virtually all but the most absurd statements implying obligation as a serious and intentional but as being no more true or false than a price quoted in the marketplace. If the utterance is accepted—if a relationship can be suc-

---

52. I am indebted to Clifford Geertz for drawing my attention to this issue. For data supporting this assertion see Bourgeois 1959–60, 3:80 and the discussion of truth in Crapanzano 1980, 80–81. Gilsenan (1976) also draws a distinction between lies and utterances that bear no truth weight in the Lebanese context. It is interesting in this regard to compare the Moroccan situation with the philosophical approach to utterance and belief in Grice 1975, 1978.

cessfully shown to have flowed from it—the statement can be judged as true, in that it has been adhered to, or false, in that it has been contravened. Unless clearly a joke, the Moroccans take all such statements as serious but not subject to evaluation as true or false.

To capture the contrast between Moroccan and Western usage it may be helpful to formulate this issue on the basis of a distinction made famous by the British philosopher J. L. Austin.[53] Austin noted that in the process of making an utterance, we also perform an action. To say in English "close the window" or "I apologize" is not to describe what is being done but to perform an act—the act of issuing a command or engaging in an apology. Even a largely descriptive utterance like "the window is closed" or "John apologized" may, whatever its quality as a factual statement, serve to make others react in a particular way.[54] Yet between these descriptive (or assertive) statements and those in which the speaker tries to direct another or make a personal commitment or declaration, there is a significant difference: assertions are capable of being assessed as true or false while an order, a request, an avowal, or a plea cannot be weighed for its truth value.[55] It is thus possible to say of an

53. The fullest statement of Austin's views are contained in his book *How To Do Things with Words* (1965). See also Austin 1961. For a general overview of the issues associated with performative utterances, see Hartnack 1967.

54. Austin originally distinguished between utterences that can be either true or false (called "constatives") and those that perform an action ("performatives"). Austin (1971) later rejected this distinction, believing all utterances to be kinds of performatives even if, as in the case of an apparently factual assertion, the act performed is that of attempting to elicit a particular response from the hearer. Accordingly, he developed his famous typology of performative speech acts: locutionary, illocutionary, and perlocutionary. Although many critics agreed with Austin that the constative-performative distinction was not precise, others argued that there are contrasts this distinction serves to highlight. Thus, Sesonake suggests that constatives and performatives are not two kinds of utterances but two kinds of relationships: in the former the speaker specifies a situation in relation to himself, in the latter he indicates where he stands in relation to the situation. (Compare Sesonake 1965 with Fingarette 1967 on this point.) Similarly, Jacobsen argues that a constative like "I am a Dane" is not specifically tied to either speaker or hearer and can be transferred from one person to another, while a performative like "I promise you" is tied to the person making the promise to an identifiable other and is not transferable without a specific procedure (Jacobsen 1971; see generally Houston 1970). Although I have here adopted Austin's later formulation of all utterances as kinds of performatives, I believe the distinction between utterances as amenable or immune to truth evaluation, whatever its logical defects, accurately describes a critical distinction made in many cultures. Moreover, the implication that a truth-bearing utterance may also convey a sense of personal attachment and context, as Sesonake and Jacobsen suggest, is one I find particularly thought provoking for an analysis of the Moroccan concept of truth.

55. I am here borrowing the terms and distinctions made by Searle 1979, 1–29. It must be remembered that as in Austin's own taxonomy, truth is only one feature—and not the central one—for Searle's distinction, whereas truth is precisely the feature to which predominant attention is given in this discussion. My concern here is not with the drawing of logical distinctions but with the answers that Western and Moroccan culture provide to the question of the meaning of utterances about social relationships.

utterance like "it is warm" or "we are related" that however differently we view the matter, it is capable of being discussed in terms of whether the assertion is true or false; however, it makes no sense of a statement like "Close the window" or "Is it raining?" to say that it is true or false, only that it is fair, effective, adequately phrased, or appropriate to the situation.[56] What makes this distinction particularly interesting for our purpose is that utterances, which in one culture may clearly appear to be capable of assessment as true or false, may in another culture serve to perform the kind of act that is not subject to any evaluation whatsoever as true or false. Specifically, when Moroccans are engaged in forming their relationships, statements by which they seek to characterize their existing ties or future commitments are not, standing alone, subject to evaluation as true or false. For one man to say to another, "I have a haqq in you," "we are fellow tribesmen," "he and I are cousins," or "we are members of the same family," notwithstanding its appearance in English as a statement that could be characterized as true or false, is in the Moroccan context well understood to convey no more implication of truth than does the mention of a price between buyer and seller in the bazaar. Indeed, like the enunciation of an unfixed price, it is clear that such utterances about relationship, far from being capable of assessment as true or false, actually perform the act of establishing a negotiation between the parties involved—in this case a negotiation over the nature and terms of their relationship. To a Westerner the rather shocking conclusion results that whenever Moroccans are involved in forming a relationship, nothing they say—however definite it may appear, however forcefully it may be phrased—about their ties to one another or outsiders will be taken as having any bearing on whether what is said is in any way, shape, or form true or false.

In order for such utterances to have any bearing on the question of truth, something more is required: the assertion itself must be validated. This validation may take place in a variety of ways—by ritual confirmation or reliant acts, by evidence of reliability or conducing agreement. Until such validation takes place, the attributes of truth and falsehood are simply irrelevant; once validation occurs the concept of truth shows itself to be highly developed, seriously ascribed, and of a wholly different nature than mere utterance. It is this process by which utterances become attached to truth as a key ingredient in the formation of interpersonal ties that we must consider in some detail.

We have, of course, already touched on some aspects of the Moroccan concept of truth as embraced in the idea of haqq. Haqq, we suggested, can be understood as "truth" in the sense that what is true, or real, in the world is the distribution of obligations and reciprocal ties that bind individuals to one another and to the supernatural. Haqq, in this sense, is an objective quality—it

---

56. A series of social and linguistic conventions thus plays a critical role in the formulation and comprehension of any performative utterance. See, in this regard, Black 1968,141 and Skinner 1970.

is something that exists in the public world, an authenticity made tangible by the acts and covenants that engage those capable of understanding to one another. But truth is also a quality that inheres in those who traffic in it; a quality that is captured in the term *ṣidq,* and other ramifications of the Arabic root *ṣ-d-q.* "Haqq," as Izutsu argues, "represents the specifically objective side of the truth. Sidq is the opposite pole; it refers more particularly to a property in the speaker, which tends to made his words correspond with the reality, i.e., his truthfulness" (Izutsu 1966,89, and generally 86–101). It is not enough, however, for a man's words to conform to a reality that is "out there": "they should also conform to the idea of reality in the mind of the speaker" (Izutsu 1966,90). Whatever the reality with which he is concerned, a man's speech (or, for that matter, his actions) must link what is actually so with what the speaker conceives it to be in his own mind. Sidq is thus more than simply speaking the truth; it is the forging of total congruence between that which is overt and that which is affirmed within. As Wilfred Cantwell Smith, who has given thoughtful attention to this and related concepts, has written:

Ṣidq is that quality by which a man speaks or acts with a combination of inner integrity and objective, overt appropriateness. It involves saying or doing the right thing out of genuine personal recognition of its rightness, an inner alignment with it.

In other words, there is more to this virtue than mere outward propriety or correctness; and more also than mere sincerity or well-meaning intention. There is no room here for that kind of truth that leaves unaffected the moral character and private behaviour of those who know it. . . . Human behaviour, in word or deed, is the nexus between man's inner life and the surrounding world. Truth at the personalist level is that quality by which both halves of that relationship are chaste and appropriate; are true. (W.C. Smith 1969,12)[57]

This sense of the connectedness between the interior and exterior vectors of speech and acts pervades the terms that draw on this common root. To say of a man that he is *ṣādiq* is to mean that he is truthful in the sense of being "sincere," "accurate," "candid," and "reliable," and because he affirms within what he confirms without, he is "truthworthy" and "faithful." To use the intensive form *ṣiddīq* is to imply that he is so habitually accustomed to this quality that his deeds and utterances stand as testimony to the truth of a thing. In its more causitive form, *taṣdīq* imparts the idea of confirming or certifying something and someone as truthful. Again, Smith helps us sort out the implications; tasdiq, being so personalist in orientation, has as its primary object

a person, not a sentence; so that *ṣaddaqahu,* or he gave him *taṣdīq,* may mean "he held him to be a speaker of the truth"—he believed him, if you like, but because he trusted him. . . .

57. See also W. C. Smith 1971.

Another standard usage, moreover, is that it mean not "He held him to be a speaker of the truth," but rather "He found him to be so." One may hear a man's statement, and only subsequently find reason or experience to know that that man was no liar.

Thirdly, it may indicate this sort of notion but with a more active, resolute type of finding: that is, "he proved him to be a speaker of truth," or confirmed or verified it. . . . Thus *taṣdīq* is the term for scientific experimental verification although the notion of vindicating the experimenter as well as the experiment is never far distant. . . .

Throughout this *taṣdīq* form, the sincerity involved may be on the part of the subject of the secondary form, as well as or perhaps even rather than of the primary subject; so that if I *taṣdīq* some statement, I do not merely establish its truth in the world outside me, but incorporate it into my own moral integrity as a person.

Taṣdīq is to recognize a truth, to appropriate it, to affirm it, to confirm it, to actualize it. And the truth, in each case, is personalist. (W.C. Smith 1969,12–13)

Through the semantic range of sidq and its attendant forms one can see the crucial role of truth in Islamic conceptions—as the incorporation of divine revelation, as the characterization of loyalty and steadfastness in an uncertain world, as an instrument for confirming, by one's own words and actions, those of another. Given the extraordinary weight that truthfulness, in this sense, is called upon to shoulder, it seems less surprising that those who live by this concept should be cautious in its use. To hold open a situation, a relationship, without attaching the full import of truth to it—to retain one's options and mutual bargaining position by initially suspending all truth-value—can contribute both to one's maneuverability and to the greater force truth may have once firmly attached. To the people of Sefrou, for whom, as we are suggesting, utterances about relationships being formed possess none of the attributes of truth, the practical question is how to convert mere utterances into truth-bearing propositions and how to do this most advantageously. Although the forms of validation and the intensity of people's attachment to them vary somewhat even within the Sefrou region, it is possible to distinguish at least four basic modes of validation: ritual confirmation or constraint, affirmation through personal qualities or reliable witnesses, reliance on another's words or deeds and acting on that basis, and marshalling public opinion or conducing the actor's own agreement through the use of one's rhetorical skills.

Perhaps the most abrupt way to try validating an assertion is through a process of ritual constraint. As we have seen in our discussion of the supernaturally sanctioned 'ar, by sacrificing an animal at another's doorstep or thrusting a bit of one's clothing into his care, one can seek to constrain another's acceptance of one's request or force a particular obligational bond. Like all other forms of validation, the 'ar does not possess absolute certainty but is part of and subsidiary to the overall process of negotiation. Thus, as we noted earlier, the recipient of the ʿar may turn its full thrust aside by indicating, for example, that the request for votes by all of his dependents cannot be accomplished except by sacrifices to each and every one of them. Yet by its invocation of divine punishment, should the recipient fail at least to some significant degree to affirm one's claim, the ʿar certainly helps to verify or conduce verification of the assertion one has made.

Like the ʿar, the oath (ḥlaf; cl. Ar. qasam) calls forth a kind of ultimate verification in that it puts the matter of validation squarely in the hands of the Almighty. Although one may simply assert that what one says is true by swearing to its veracity in the name of the Prophet or a saint—such oaths being frowned upon when idly made and thus calling into question the swearer's truthfulness—really serious oaths are usually taken in the mosque or at a shrine with witnesses present. A number of people today claim to pay little heed to oaths since the world is so full of men who will swear falsely for their own gain. Yet the overwhelming majority of those with whom I have spoken express personal fear for the supernatural punishment that will follow a false oath, and the misfortunes of those believed to have sworn falsely are often recounted.[58] Since a man's general reputation for truthfulness deeply affects the value placed on his oath, it is often the case, to paraphrase Aeschylus, that it is the man who makes the oath believable rather than the oath the man. One informant, himself an officer of the court, analogized the man who will take an oath to a draft animal that has been shod; just as the iron horseshoes are an encumbrance yet allow the animal to traverse otherwise difficult or inpenetrable terrain, so too the man who will take an oath carries the weight of potential punishment if he has in any way misspoken himself, yet he will be able to move among all men as one known to be truthful, reliable, ṣadīq.

The use of oaths is perhaps most common in legal proceedings where conflicting claims cannot be independently verified. A complex system determines who may be called upon to swear the oath and in what order of priority (Rosen 1980–81,226–27, and references on 226, n.8; Pedersen 1961,226). If the oath serves as the ultimate determination of the case, it is taken at the mosque or saintly shrine rather than in court. Again, some people fear the oath even when they believe they are telling the truth because inadvertent error, misstatement of the oath, or impure acts may find offense with Allah. On several occasions in the field I have seen men who were clearly telling the truth refuse to enter the shrine or take an oath because they knew themselves to have violated the Quranic law in some wholly unrelated way. Significantly there is no punishment for perjury in Islamic law or courts of Islamic law in Morocco (see Westermarck 1926,1:509; Schacht 1964,159). But it is not as in some societies where litigants are expected to lie in their own behalf and the court's role is to sort out the various lies.[59] Rather, absence of perjury demon-

---

58. See, for example, those told by students in Bourgeois 1959–60, 4:32–35.

59. See, for example, the work of Ethel Albert cited in Hungerland 1960,237.

strates a recognition that utterances which will affect the distribution of obligations have no truth-value associated with them until validated. And this validation itself comes by the creation of a relationship, recognized by convention and sanctioned by the willingness of others to grant their reliance—a relationship that, in the case of the oath, takes on the character of a self-invoked covenant between man and God.

Although the ʿar and the oath draw on the threat of supernatural sanction, they clearly incorporate an independent element of personal credibility. This latter feature forms the basis for several other concepts and institutions through which validation takes place. We saw earlier how a man's background and connections, reflected in his gender, his names (nisba-s), his origins, and the myriad ties he possesses with others serve to define and characterize the individual. Such features also speak, though in different ways to different people, to the question of a man's truthfulness, loyalty, and soundness. This assessment becomes more formal when the question arises of a man's capacity to serve as a witness in a legal proceeding. In classical Islamic law, all evidence was conceptualized as oral in nature: even written documents were regarded as the reduction to writing of oral testimony. Just as the traditions of the Prophet recite the names of those through whom the original observation was passed—a chain (isnād) that gains and transmits credence by the reputation for reliability of those who form it—so, too, a legal witness had to be recognized as having qualities that made his word credible. A witness, therefore, had to be found by the judge to have the quality of ʿadāla, "reliability," from a root meaning "just" or "equitable." Relying on the word of those already deemed to possess this quality and the implications drawn from his background and actions, a man would be designated by the Islamic-law judge (qāḍī) as possessing or lacking the qualities of a reliable witness. Already by the end of the second century of the Islamic era, the characteristics of the reliable witness became institutionalized in the role of the court notary, the ʿadul.[60] When two notaries sign a document based on oral testimony, they are doing in the realm of the law what may be done by other mechanisms in social life: they are adding their stature, their word, as reliable witnesses to a bond that only acquires implications of truth by virtue of having received some form of validation. In a sense, therefore, the notaries render assertions relevant to the quality of truth in order that the court may assess them as true or false.

The institution of the reliable witness—the man who can validate assertions—is also found in domains other than that of the law. Until recent times an official, called the muḥtaseb, served in the marketplace as a regulator of market practices and as one who could be called upon to give acknowledged credence to what he had heard or seen. Similarly, each craft had a man (called

---

60. The translation of ʿadul as "reliable witness" is drawn from Tyan 1960,60. See also Heffening 1961.

the *amīn*) who was considered so knowledgeable and reliable that his word
could establish the facts in disputes involving members of his trade. The
muhtaseb has been replaced, in contemporary Morocco, by uniform weights
and measures, government regulations, and various bureaucrats, but the amin
and ʿadul remain important even though the domains of occupational associations and Islamic law have become reduced in scope.

Another validating institution that can still be found operating in some rural
areas is the group of co-swearers.[61] In a dispute between two parties the
plaintiff may designate as the lead oathtaker a man from among the defendant's kinsmen or allies who the plaintiff believes will speak truthfully. The
lead oathtaker, in turn, chooses an additional ten men who join him in the
oath. The co-swearers do not, however, swear to any of the "facts" in the
case but to their own assessment of the defendant as one whose statements are
known to be truthful. Thus, they serve to validate the defendant's assertions—to bring them into the domain of the true or false—and to add their
reputations to the proposition that in this case the defendant's statements are
indeed most likely to be true since he possesses the character of one who
should be accorded credibility.

It is also very common, particularly in economic arrangements, for one
man to serve as another's guarantor (*damen*). By adding his name to the
arrangement he is not only standing surety but underscoring, by his own reputation and affiliations, that when the principal enters into relationships in
which his statements might otherwise be regarded as irrelevant to the truth,
he, the guarantor, is assuring others that they may indeed interpret the statements as having truth-value and that he will back them up as being in fact
true.

In each of these situations, then, the form of validation centers on the reliability that should be attributed to the speaker or that may be created in his
statements by the reliable man who validates them. Once regarded by others
as truthful (sadiq) or as a reliable witness (ʿadel), a man's statements take on a
certain self-validating quality: if he declares that his statements are true many
people will take them as true. But this in no way means that the utterances of a
reliable man, absent his own insistence on their veracity, do not partake of the
neutral quality of all other unvalidated utterances. It simply means that both as
a matter of his own status and of the negotiating tactics of his interlocutors, he
may more readily attempt to have all of his statements taken as true or find
that others, eager to be allied with him, play on his reputation to make him
stand by utterances another might be able to argue were without any truthful
import.

In addition to confirmation by ritual and reliable witnesses, there exists a
third category of validation that may be designated as action in reliance. It is

---

61. On the practice of co-swearers, see Brunschvig 1960,180; Milliot 1953,737; Pedersen
1961:224, 226; Rosen 1980–81,224.

important to an understanding of this category to recall that it is only where ties of obligation are being formed that statements may be suspended from their truth implications until validated and that all forms of validation— whether an oath to Allah or the signature of a notary—themselves establish a bond, a shift in relations, a new form of obligation. Just as it is the element of sanction which takes preeminance in ritual confirmation and social character that is stressed for reliability, it is the relational component that receives particular emphasis when validation comes by reliant acts. What one is saying, in effect, is: "You said that we had an obligation or a particular kind of relationship to one another as a result of which I undertook certain relationships of my own. You cannot now disclaim your obligation to me since what I did confirmed what you said." Clearly there is great room for manipulation, negotiation, and dispute when such a claim is made. But, as in all other cases, convention offers a degree of certainty even as the open texture of the concepts and relations involved allow considerable room for maneuver. A specific example may help to illustrate this type of validation:

While seated in the café on the main street of the Ville Nouvelle, Hamed ou Lahsen, a Berber from the Ait Taleb fraction, mentioned to another man at the table, Aqa Boufar, that he was going to need an additional allotment of water for his rural plot and that he was going to have to find someone who could let him have it. Aqa, who lives in a neighboring fraction of the Ait Yusi tribe and who owns several gardens watered by the same irrigation system that runs down to the land of Hamed's group, said: "So, my brother (*iwa a-kay*), water is readily available (*l-ma mujud*); don't worry (*matkafšai*), we're all one tribe (*ḥna kullna men qebīla waḥada*), all friends (*kullna ṣaḥabīn*)." The discussion was dropped and all present went about their business. Hamed, relying (as he later claimed) on what Aqa had said, made some arrangements of his own for the purchase of various goods and for his daughter's marriage, fully expecting, as he said, that his irrigated crops would fetch a premium in so poor an agricultural year. When later he came to Aqa to borrow the quantum of water, Aqa said that although he remembered the conversation precisely as Hamed did, it was not an obligation formed but, as he asserted initially, a general expression of good will, or, as he said once the dispute was joined, "just words" (*ḡir klam*). The dispute became the subject of considerable debate by members of both groups. Some pointed out that if the whole conversation had taken place at one of the informal Friday gatherings when men of both groups often gather after the weekly prayer to share a meal, Aqa's response would, given Hamed's subsequent actions, have more of the quality of a binding obligation since it is precisely in this context and with this sort of informality that men arrange their affairs and let them be known. But a casual conversation in the café over so important a matter as this should have been much more specific to be binding. Others said that since Aqa was generally regarded as a man of his word, he should be held to his statement because Hamed had openly engaged in other ties, having told various people he was doing so as a result of Aqa's commitment to supply him with the additional allotment of water. Like most such disputes, things became vastly more complicated as old grudges, other relationships, and differing interpretations were brought into the conflict. And it ended, also characteristically, without really ending when someone else offered Hamed enough water to get through the harvest.

Here, then, one has an unvalidated utterance which Hamed regarded as validated by his subsequent actions—or which, perhaps knowing how shaky his base, he sought to make valid by his own undertakings. He could not have been ignorant of Aqa's regard for his reputation as a reliable man and may have felt his case strengthened when Aqa, who certainly regards himself as a man who speaks "with an undivided word" (*m'a klam waḥed*), was forced to disregard his own utterance as "just words" (*ġir klam*). Yet clearly Aqa did not want to be forced to have everything he said taken as an obligation that others could simply confirm by their reliant acts. Indeed, if I sensed any general opinion on the matter it was that a man "of word," like everyone else, must be free to make general expressions that may be regarded as not binding without in any way affecting the question of whether the relationship of which he spoke should be measured against a standard of truth. Thus, to draw again the contrast with Western practice, it was not simply a question of whether Aqa had committed himself but whether there is any basis for assuming that Aqa's statement had been sufficiently validated, by any of the means we have been discussing, that one could properly assess it as binding or true.

The example of Hamed and Aqa highlights the negotiable aspects of validation by acts. In some domains greater certainty of interpretation has been provided by a set of explicit rules. Thus in the law there are definite ways, centering, as we have suggested, around the use of reliable witnessing, to establish obligations. Similarly, regularity is provided in the law by a series of presumptions. To choose just one example, it is assumed in Islamic civil law that a positive act is more believable than a negative one, i.e., that it is preferable to give credence to someone's claim to have actually done something than to another's that he did nothing. The assumption here would seem to be not that occurrences are more easily proved than forbearance—which, if believed, would counsel the reverse procedure—but that acts have greater consequences than forbearance because the latter tends to maintain the status quo while the former lead to a changed set of interrelationships that may extend far beyond the immediate parties. Here one can see, as a matter of legal presumption, a version of that broader Moroccan assumption that every act is a haqq, a shift in the balance of obligations, and it is the consequences of an action by which society is affected and actors known.

In each of the three preceding types of validation, the opinion of others often plays a significant if subordinate role. In the final category it is precisely by getting public opinion on one's side or by conducing the antagonist's own agreement that one forces an utterance into the realm of the truth and claims for it a favorable interpretation. Here, argumentative and rhetorical styles play a crucial role. Faced by a dispute with another in which one is trying to get an assertion accepted as true, it is not uncommon to turn, often in a highly stylized way, to the people gathered around to affirm the statement. A personal example may prove illustrative:

Late one night I was awakened by the sound of a dish shattering against the wall that separated my apartment from that of my neighbor. As the noise of a domestic squabble reverberated through the common courtyard shared by four apartments, I heard the door of my neighbor on the other side open, a furtive knock at my door, and the quick closing of the door. Clearly, I thought, the Jewish woman next to me was signalling that I should be the one to do something about our neighbors' argument. Before I had a chance to consider the idea, the couple themselves burst into the courtyard knocking on everyone's door and, lest we miss their subtle invitation to the fray, increased the volume of shouting well beyond the limits of human inattention. In a moment everyone living around the small tiled courtyard had come out. It developed that the husband, a low-level civil servant originally from Bhalil, had just arrived home after an evening in the café. When his wife, a young Berber woman with no family in Sefrou, accused him of spending all his time in the cafés and not enough with her, the husband proceeded to accuse her of having male visitors in the apartment while he was away. Who threw the plate was never clear but the style of argument was instantly recognizable. With the neighbors assembled around, the disputants stood at right angles to one another and continued their shouting. They were speaking to and at each other but were also, more to the point, addressing the neighbors whom they sought to draw into the affirmation of their statements. It took no persuasion to accomplish this—the women of the assembled families unhesitatingly averring that they were there all day long and never saw a man come visiting the wife. The women also showed no hesitation in telling the husband that he should spend more time at home and less in the cafés. After much shouting and gesturing it became clear that the husband was losing. He muttered a few things more about the hardships of life and how he, hardworking soul that he was, was going to bed.

The style of this argument, like so many others in Morocco, had an almost choreographed quality to it. The raising of voices to draw neighbors or passersby, the angle of stance to one's opponent, and the mode of addressing the observers is replicated in almost all such disputes. The volubility and stance in particular are important signals of how serious the matter is: if the parties remain facing each other and not raising their voices, they are, at most, bargaining; if they shout while partially facing those who have assembled, they are looking for affirmation from the crowd but are more or less willing to abide by the collective judgment and get on with things; if either stomps away while the matter is, so to speak, before the crowd, it portends real trouble, even violence—the anger of one or both being too great to submit to anyone else's judgment.[62] For our present purposes the point to note is that in this argumentative style one finds an example of how people seek to have truth attached to an otherwise unverified statement by establishing a relationship with the bystanders that will result, first, in the statement being validated, in the sense of being regarded as touching on the question of truth, and, second, in getting their own version of that truth verified by the onlookers.

The forms of addressing viewers may also include a style of speech found in much more sedate circumstances of persuasion. It may be thought of as a form of Socratic dialogue because it consists of the questioner taking the listener through a series of propositions to which the listener is forced to respond before the questioner moves as cleverly as he can to his prearranged conclusion. Several examples may serve as illustration: I was driving up to the mountains one day on a main tourist road when I passed a stand at which a young boy was selling amethysts and other brightly colored crystals. My companion, an older man, began to mutter: "Lies, it is all lies" (*kdūb*). I asked what he meant. He turned to me and posed his questions: "Doesn't the government own all the mines? Do you think he has a permit to take those rocks out of the ground? Doesn't the government in America also own the rocks under its land? Isn't it a lie when you say something belongs to you and it does not?" At each point in this dialogue he paused and made me give some response, often persisting until the response was neither vague nor noncommittal, which he then took as license to go on to the next stage of his argument. Far from being rhetorical questions, his assertions forced me to engage him in negotiating the meaning of the situation and validating his statements. Similarly, one often sees a litigant in court try to put the judge through the same process. One man, accused of beating his wife, put on a particularly impressive (and to the court, mildly amusing) display as he kept forcing the judge to some gesture or response he took as favorable while asking: "Is it not shameful for a woman to have said the things she did about me to others? Isn't a man the 'chauffeur' of his wife? Doesn't the Quran say this? Would it be right to let her say such things and go unpunished?" Like the stylized argumentative stance, this form of questioning is not used where the questioner wants to leave the question of truth out of consideration. Like other forms of validation, it forces the hearer to respond and, by doing so, helps the speaker to achieve confirmation through the establishment of a relationship.

Each of the categories of validation we have discussed gives preeminent stress to one of the four components that run through all of them: ritual confirmation emphasizes the force of sanction; reliable witnessing, credibility based on social background and personal characteristics; reliant action, the rela-

---

62. To walk away also symbolizes that one is "quits," that the relationship is off altogether. And since the absence of any bond creates the potential for real chaos, this action may portend very serious consequences indeed.

tionships formed as the result of an utterance; and the opinion of others, the need to achieve negotiated agreement. Some mechanisms, like oaths, come closer than others to being self-executing; others, like notaries and guarantors, are more highly institutionalized; and still others, like argumentative styles and personal reputation, depend mainly on public perception and the arrangement of resources in such a way as to make a claim stick. What remains common is the idea that an utterance that has a bearing on the formation of relationships is not subjected to the rather stringent canons of truthfulness until others help to validate it. Standing alone, a statement about ties to others remains incomplete: the predicate of such an assertion can only be supplied by the relationship formed through it. Truth does not inhere in such a statement; it "happens to it" because those who confirm it have a hand in making it relevant to the truth (cf. Ezorsky 1967, 429). One may entice validation, as do litigants when engaging a judge in Socratic dialogue, or try to force it on another, as did the Berber seeking a water allotment. A subtle and extremely complex set of moves may take place simply because the relational concepts themselves are negotiable, their own completion coming only through the successful implementation of a settled convention or the marshalling of one's resources in such a fashion as to give backing to one's own view of the matter. By holding open the possibility of characterizing a statement as true or false until a relationship brings it into the realm of the real, each individual can avoid the entanglements implied by the general idea that relationships involve reciprocal obligations. If utterance and act are kept separate by holding off their connection through validation, one can retain the freedom to maneuver. And when an assertion has been validated, the extremely serious ideas of truth and lying, which add their own conceptual stability to an uncertain world of relationships, can now be drawn upon to greatest effect.

How, then, might we characterize Moroccan ideas about truth and lying once these issues have become relevant? In a sense, it might be argued that in their social and religious lives Moroccans do not *discern* the truth; they do not discover it from sources of knowledge which lie within themselves: they either *acknowledge* what is true (when it lies within the ambit of the religious life) or they *create* it (when it lies within the realm of the social). Whatever else they may be, Moroccans are not logical positivists; for them an expression refers to an object because it conveys something true about that object. In their view of social life, a thing is true as a result of the actions or consequences to which that assertion makes a difference. "The limits of God," the bounds set by divine ordinance, are true and real whether man acknowledges them or not; beyond that, what is true is the perceptible range of humanly created relationships and the inherent incompleteness with which men try to contain those ties, even as they seek to maintain the open-endedness of their concepts and their bonds with others.

What is true is also affected by the idea of what is possible. In colloquial Moroccan Arabic there are two words that we translate with the single term "if": *ila* applies to those situations in which the conditional occurrence is regarded as possible ("If it rains tomorrow I will go with you."), while *lu kan* applies to situations regarded as impossible ("If I were a bird I would fly.").[63] The choice of terms may reflect the circumstances of the person involved and their assessment or manipulation of a particular situation. In one story related by Pellat, three young girls muse over what it would be like "if (possible form) I married a king," while the king himself overhears their conversation. In another story, a Jew approaches a rich woman who is in debt to him and who is eager to marry, but she puts the creditor off by saying she will pay him only "if (impossible form) I marry a king" (Pellat 1955:44–45, 22–23). Depending on one's choice of "ifs," one can signal what is to be regarded as true or real. A child who says "If (possible) I had wings I would fly," may first be laughed at: if he persists, he will be the subject of open scorn and punishment. A man who speaks of situations as possible that are clearly contrary to fact will be held up to derision. People do not, however, seem to negotiate over their views of what is true by means of disputing over the applicability of one form of "if" versus another—perhaps because the difference, if resolvable, calls for one of the above forms of validation. Nevertheless the rhetorical use of one or another form of "if" can readily convey a sense of the concept or goal at issue for any particular speaker.

In addition to that which is unverified and that which is true, there is, of course, a well-developed notion of the lie. To lie is to contravene the truth in that a lie ruptures relationships and the precepts on which they are based. An unverified utterance cannot be a lie because no relationship has come to turn on it. A validated assertion that is untrue can lead to chaos.[64] Many of the statements Westerners might have to admit are lies and then dismiss as harmless or white lies, Moroccans need never characterize by the term *kdūb*, "lies", because they were never validated. Once an assertion has been validated, lying becomes a very serious matter indeed. Are there, however, any circumstances in which a person may justifiably tell a lie? According to an Arab commentator of the twelfth century, one whose words have a terribly modern ring, deception may be practiced only on three occasions: in time of war, for war is itself nothing but deceit; when one is trying to make peace between two conflicting parties; and, finally, "in the case of any man who has two or more wives!" (Donaldson 1943,276).[65] The focus then is on those

63. The form of these terms varies in different parts of Morocco. See Brunot 1952,736–37; Colin 1920,89–93; Ph. Marçais 1977,240–41; Harrell 1965:240, 243–44. The same distinction is made in various Berber dialects; see Pellat 1955,105–6. For comparable usages elsewhere in North Africa, see Ph. Marçais 1977 and Cohen 1975,260–61.

64. See the examples and arguments at Donaldson 1943,284. On the concept in Arab poetry that the poet must be part liar, see Broms 1972:25,70.

65. Donaldson (1943,277–78) also cites a tenth-century (A.D.) Shi'ite scholar's similar formulation of the circumstances under which lying is permissible, including, thirdly, "When a man promises his wife or family something which he will not be able to fulfill for them. The peacemaker is not to be considered a liar." See also Keddie 1963.

social consequences that are to be valued because they lead away from chaos, *fitna*. It is worth pointing out, moreover, that unlike some Middle Eastern groups, the people of the Sefrou region very rarely speak about honor and are not intent on maintaining a facade of silence or of lies through which their social selves may be preserved against attack.[66] For them, a man will not be held to the consequences of his utterances until his assertions have been made valid by interaction, and thus his honor and his flexibility are far less subject to attack than they might otherwise be. Francis Hutcheson once posed the problem in still more general terms when he said:

> Suppose men imagined there was no obligation to veracity, and acted accordingly; speaking as often against their own opinion as according to it; would not all pleasure of conversation be destroyed, and all confidence in narration? Men would only speak in bargaining, and in this too would soon lose all mutual confidence. (Quoted in Bok 1978, 18)

The people of Sefrou might agree with this formulation while adding that since men will always lie, it is best not to make everything a question of truth but to leave men a way by which they can, in good faith and without threat to all social harmony, bargain out the terms of their collective existence.

The issue of truth thus summarizes much of what is central to Moroccan social relations. By avoiding imputations of truth in the statements made about social ties while negotiating such matters with another, the force of sanction and strong claims of misdirection can be set aside in favor of maneuverability. By focusing attention on the completion of utterances through interpersonal agreement, the felt appropriateness of personal engagement can be solidified. From the perspective of modern-speech act theory it may even be suggested that the order of negotiating interpersonal ties follows a distinctive course: First comes a series of expressive utterances, formulaic utterances of etiquette, whose purpose, to quote Searle, is neither "to get the world to match the words nor the words to match the world," but to presuppose the existence of a world of truth (Searle 1979, 15). There follows a series of utterances by means of which the speaker tries to get the hearer to do something (Searle's "directives") or in which the speaker indicates a commitment to future action (Austin's "commissives") (Searle 1979, 12). In the Moroccan case, however, all such utterances are immune to assessment as true or false until some form of validation (operating like Searle's "declarations" to bring about "the correspondence between propositional content and reality") permits the utterance to become "real," i.e., attached to the world of human obligations (Searle 1979, 16–17). Thenceforth any utterance becomes a kind of "assertive," assessable as true or false yet uttered so as to bring about a fit

66. Contrast the Moroccan situation in this regard with the Lebanese data presented by Gilsenan 1976.

between words and world (Searle 1979, 12). Built into each step are not only the qualities of open texture of the central concepts that convey relationship, but a series of conventions associated with the construction of one's personal network of obligation. In turning, next, to a consideration of the relations between Arabs and Berbers, Muslims and Jews, we can see not only the distinctive qualities of these particular associations but, by regarding each as a kind of limiting case, further explore the range and force of the institutions and conventions that order life within the Sefrou community.

Special Relations: Arabs and Berbers, Muslims and Jews

In the enactment of their social bonds—and more particularly in their quest for them—the people of the Sefrou region rely greatly on their knowledge of the personal attributes and ties of those with whom they deal. Knowledge of gender or kinship, background or current attachments is, within even the most homogeneous of networks, richly varied and subtly arrayed. What is true about the search for and uses of information about others in any one domain is, in a sense, true of all: the question constantly before each individual is how another fits into his or her life and affects its shape and meaning. But where proximity of background or affiliation may contribute their distinctive qualities to the design of a person's network, so, too, certain features of so-cial-group identity may be seen to add to and extend the construction of each person's social world. To speak as we shall now of the social and cultural implications of identity as a Berber or an Arab, a Muslim or a Jew is, of necessity, to extend our study into a realm where difference is itself a key ingredient. But it is also, in the Sefrou case, to probe the limits of a concep-tual and relational world, to explore just what it is that these distinctions mean in the lives of the Sefrou people.

Throughout, we have argued that the lines of cohesion in Sefrou society are quite diverse and that while the actual range of one's contacts may vary enor-mously, it is a distinguishing feature of life in the region to engage and assess one another in terms of a range of characterizing features. If, therefore, we turn our attention to the place of "ethnic" and religious identity, several distinct yet related questions may be posed: Where does this feature of a person's identity fit into the broader range of features by which a person is known? Which of a person's actions can we say are significantly affected by the recognition of oneself or another as an Arab or a Berber, a Muslim or a Jew, and in what situations does this identification take precedence? Put somewhat differently, what kinds of information does an awareness of such identity supply and in what contexts is it relevant? Indeed, is it possible to look on the relations discussed here as, in some sense, limiting cases which are, by that very quality, particularly revelatory of the assumptions that per-vade relationships that do not span these lines? To ask these questions is to try to understand discrete events against a cultural background and to understand the reality of Sefrou society in its fullest complexity.

Arabs and Berbers

We have already noted some of the key elements of the Arab-Berber distinction: that it is primarily a linguistic distinction; that the range of social and cultural variation within the Arab or Berber linguistic communities is at least as great as the variation that may be discerned by comparing the one with the other; that until the recent flood of migration from the countryside, the vast majority of people living in the city of Sefrou has been Arabic-speaking while the predominant tribe of the region, the Ait Yusi, has long been comprised of a few Arabic-speaking settlements set amidst a population of Berbers.[67] Indeed, the reified division of the Moroccan population into Arabs and Berbers was itself, in no small part, a function of French-colonial perceptions and policies. In the years leading up to the establishment of the Protectorate in 1912, some French ethnographers—notably Edouard Doutté—were able to point out that the Arab-Berber distinction was of a linguistic, rather than racial or ethnic, nature.[68] In the first few years of domination the French considered the primary lines of division within Moroccan society to be those separating the regions under government control (*bled al-makzan*) from those (*bled es-siba*) that, for whatever reason, were actively engaged in opposing the policies of the sultan and his "protectors." As more was learned about the rural peoples and more functionaries of the Office of Native Affairs took up residence in their territories, the Berbers were seen less as anarchic and uncivilized tribesmen than as proud warriors whose manly qualities distinguished them from the truculent or obsequious Arabs of the cities. Familiarity with Berber tribesmen bred an appreciation of their political organization and an idealization of it as a form of indigenous democracy separate from the decadent autocracy of the urban areas. Similarly, the French found in the Berber's practice of Islam not only an independence from urban religious institutions but a less than rigid attachment to the faith of the Prophet. The issuance of the Berber Decree (*dahir*) in 1930, which allowed Berber communities to remain under their own customary laws instead of the formal Islamic law, was the most notorious (and disastrous) consequence of the French belief that Arab-Berber differences were so great as to permit a real divide-and-

---

67. Leaving aside the nearby villages of Bhalil and El Menzel, the countryside around Sefrou was approximately 80-percent Berber-speaking at the time of fieldwork.

68. "Le vocable de 'berbère' n'a de sens précis qu'en linquistique où il désigne un ensemble de dialectes étroitement unis par des caractères communs et c'est vraisemblement dans ce sens qu'il fût pris à l'origine. On peut donc si l'on veut répartir les Africains en berberophones et arabophones; en nomades et en sédentaires; en nombreux types anatomiques distincts: mais la classification ethnique, en arabe et en berbère ne correspond à aucun fait concret susceptible d'être précisé" (Doutté 1901,166). See generally E. Burke 1972.

conquer policy.[69] For as the nationalist activities of the following decades clearly indicated, this division was not nearly so sharp as the French had thought it to be.

Since the advent of independence in 1956, the Moroccan government has tended to avoid characterizing any of the axes of division in the country in Arab-Berber terms, while outside observers have seen the distinction as the underlying basis of various political difficulties, a remnant of the as yet to be completed process of Arabization, or a category distinction that inhibits an understanding of cultural integration.[70] Neither government aversion to Arab-Berber distinctions nor outsiders' inquiries framed in such terms should cloud the fact that the lines of social cohesion in Morocco are highly diversified and that no single feature of any Moroccan's social identity remains central to all situations. If, at least in the Sefrou region, people do not relate to one another in such a way that being an Arab or a Berber—or, for that matter, the member of a given family, region, occupation, etc.—is at all times equally important or relevant, it may prove valuable to look at some of the specific contexts in which these various factors are brought into play. In particular, one can look for the bearing of ethnicity on such relationships as those established through clientele relations, alignment in a specific election, and the formation of marriages across ethnic lines.

In the rather fluid social structure characteristic of both Arabs and Berbers in the Sefrou region, in which one builds on various inherent ties through a multiplicity of personally contracted alliances, almost all social relations are characterized by a rather high degree of competitiveness and even jealousy. Through ingratiation and role bargaining, manipulating intermediaries and performing "favors," each man plays on the expectation of some form of reciprocation to form a wide network of supporters and dependents whose potential aid will serve as a hedge against a host of natural and sociological uncertainties. The contracting of such social debts is, however, carried out with a certain element of caution. Men are particularly wary of becoming obliged to another if they feel that, in the absence of such cross-cutting ties as kinship or common residence, they will have no alternative channels through which to modify the demands of their social or financial creditors. It is not, therefore, a question of avoiding involvement in a web of indebtedness, for without such ties a social existence could hardly be maintained. Rather, the trick is to arrange ties in order to gain the highest possible degree of predictability, if not control, over the actions of others.

In the specific context of a bazaar economy such as that of Sefrou, this avoidance of undesirable obligations is coupled with the need to deal effectively in the marketplace. Lacking detailed knowledge of the quality of partic-

69. The text of the Berber Dahir of 16 May 1930 is reprinted in Halstead 1967,276–77.
70. Compare Lacouture and Lacouture 1958:83, 96 with Gallagher 1966.

ular goods, their purchase price by the dealer, and the consequent worth of various items presented for the bargainer's consideration, it is often the case that for certain major goods a man chooses the seller to deal with rather than the goods as such. In the purchase of such items as cloth, meat, furniture, and the services of a barber, people often form clientele relationships with particular merchants in order to have some personal basis for relying on the quality of the supplier's goods or services and in order to obtain more favorable prices. Some indication of the other's personal reliability must, therefore, be sought in establishing this kind of relationship. The expectation of exclusive patronage in return for high quality, low-priced merchandise or the extension of purchasing credit is, of course, of great importance to the establishment of an ongoing clientele relationship. But of at least equal importance—since what a person is buying is a relationship with a particular man rather than a simple commodity—is the quest for a basis of relationship with the other as a total personality. Ties of common background, similar residence, equivalent attitudes, or some such common bond may supply the necessary degree of assurance that the other's actions can indeed be induced to conform to their ideal. The absence of such a basis for a personal bond of reliability may inhibit or strain the establishment of a lasting clientele relationship. And it is the absence of such a basis of commonality that often puts a strain on relations between Arab merchants and their potential Berber clientele.

Initially at least there is often a tendency on the part of an Arab businessman and a Berber client for each to regard the other with a certain degree of circumspection. Berber countrymen often feel that the urban Arab merchant is trying to get the better of them, while the merchant himself often considers the Berber as a country bumpkin of questionable intelligence and morality. In fact, these gross stereotypes are almost always capable of being superseded once a face-to-face relationship is actually established, but in the absence of additional cross-cutting ties an element of distrust often tends to persist. Berbers express a certain reluctance to become financially or socially indebted to an urban Arab merchant, knowing that because he cannot be relied upon to treat them as fellow kinsmen or neighbors he will be less vulnerable to the constraints implicit, at least ideally, in these latter forms of relationship. Accordingly, in the past, when there were numerous Jewish merchants in Sefrou, Berbers clearly preferred dealing with them because the Jews were socially noncompetitive, linked in a clearly symbiotic relationship with the Muslims, and interested mainly in straightforward economic relations with the Berbers. As the Jews have moved out of the city, many of their shops have been taken over by Berbers now residing in town, and there is a tendency for them to acquire clienteles composed in great part of those with whom they share common social bonds.

Ethnicity, then, is a factor but by no means either the sole or even necessarily the primary factor associated with patron-client relations. The main consideration is the whole personality of a man as perceived by another, and in this perception and evaluation, ethnic identity is only one among a number of crucial variables. There are those who perfer to play on the ideals of mutual aid implicit in any common social bond in order to obtain a favored bargaining position. Others avoid compounding obligations within their own social groupings, preferring instead to deal with people who are not closely related to them by blood or social origins. Clientele relations often operate, therefore, as if social-group distinction were irrelevant, and insofar as it may be superseded by a personal tie and a personal evaluation of one another's whole social personality, the distinction may indeed recede into virtual irrelevance. But as a baseline for perceiving the lines of association with an unknown merchant, a difference in ethnicity also tends to project an image of uncertain and perhaps uncontrollable reliability whose precise impact is as difficult to measure as it is a somewhat ambiguous yet real factor in the perception by Arabs and Berbers of the initial bases of their economic relationships with one another.

After independence in 1956, political parties became a major vehicle through which members of the electorate sought to gain access to the national decision-making apparatus or through which they sought to acquire certain patronage benefits. At first, politically active Berbers worked largely within the context of the Istiqlal political party and, during the actual struggle for independence, within the Army of Liberation as well. Subsequently many of them supported the Mouvement Populaire (which was formed in 1957 but not granted immediate legal recognition) because they felt it more adequately represented their needs than the urban-Arab-dominated parties then in existence. The Mouvement Populaire, as a Berber-oriented party, received the support of a large number of Berber electors in subsequent political undertakings, but this does not mean that Berbers have uniformly supported the party as a simple function of their social identity. Indeed, since a host of other factors are usually involved, it often happens that when elections do occur there is some crossing of party lines. Such was the case, to choose only one of many examples, in the parliamentary election of the Sefrou district in 1963 to which we alluded in our discussion of the agricultural-representative election.

In the 1963 parliamentary election, it will be recalled, candidates were put forward from each of the three main parties, the two most important being Istiqlal and FDIC (Front pour la Défense des Institutions Constitutionelles). This latter was an ad hoc coalition, including the Mouvement Populaire, devoted to the support of the king and his programs. The FDIC candidate for this constituency was, as we saw, a government minister, a distant relative of the king (and thus an Alawite sharif), and brother of the pasha (appointed mayor) of the city of Sefrou itself. The Istiqlal candidate, on the other hand, was the director of the local poorhouse. More importantly, though, he was a local man with numerous local connections, as opposed to the FDIC candidate who was an outsider to this particular region. All of the candidates involved, however, were Arabs.

Now in theory the Berbers, who generally voiced strong support for the Mouvement Populaire and whose leaders had been urged by party officials to support the FDIC candidate, should have voted quite solidly for the coalition candidate. In fact, a large number did. However, a very substantial number of Berbers felt that the FDIC candidate, being an outsider, would be wholly concerned with his ministerial duties and would not be as amenable to sharing the benefits of his office with the electorate as his opponant might be. Consequently, for reasons that had little to do with either their Berber identity or their general support of the "Berber party" in other circumstances, many Berbers choose to cross over and vote for the candidate from the urban Arab-dominated Istiqlal party. And because he also drew heavy support from other rural groups as well, the Istiqlal candidate, in fact, did win the election.

In this particular situation no one felt that the lines being drawn were in any sense those of Arabs versus Berbers. Had one of the candidates been a Berber perhaps the situation would have been different, but when such instances have occurred at other times it has not been primarily in these terms that the elections were contested or the voters aligned. In more general terms, one can note that, as Joan Vincent has put it

> cultural pluralism becomes politically relevant only when differential access to positions of differing advantage is institutionalized in ethnic terms. The mere existence of social or cultural categories in the population is not enough to account for political cleavages: there must be politicization of ethnicity before we can talk of "the politics of ethnicity." Ethnicity *per se* is a cultural not a political variable. We must inquire, therefore, into the *process* of politicizing ethnicity and the ideology that validates it. (Vincent 1969,52)

In the Sefrou region—and for that matter throughout most of Morocco—the politicization of ethnicity, at least as it is expressed in electoral events, has never proceeded very far. In this particular locale the reason seems to lie in the fact that people prefer to be free to contract personal ties wherever they seem most advantageous, rather than to allow momentary social or political alliances to form barriers across which such personal ties cannot be contracted at will. The emphasis is on personal networks of affiliation in which ethnicity is but one among a number of factors, and there are few people in the Sefrou area who are willing to sacrifice long-term eventualities to the binding exigencies of a short-term alliance. Of course elections in Morocco are rather rare events; it might therefore prove more fruitful to consider the politics of ethnicity in terms of the lines of political influence (for jobs, patronage, etc.) rather than the lines of voting support alone. Identity as an Arab or Berber thus appears to be less a factor than ties of kinship, residence, and personally contracted bonds of association. In electoral politics proper, as in other domains of political life, ethnicity is not a major factor in Sefrou; but as situations vary, its relative centrality, at least as an idiom of expressing alignment, could conceivably shift as well.

If there is only a certain hesitancy associated with economic relations between Arabs and Berbers and even less associated with political events, there is, by contrast, a sharper sort of barrier of interaction associated with marriage between members of each group. The figures on this are quite clear. As table 3.1 indicates, in 1960 in the city of Sefrou proper less than one married couple in eight (11.3 percent) was composed of partners of different ethnic backgrounds. Within this group, marriages between Berber men and Arab women are found to occur three times more often (8.6 percent) than unions between Arab men and Berber women (2.7 percent). The figures thus reveal not only a high rate of endogamy but sustain the impression gained from many informants that some Berber men regard marriage to Arab wives as a form of "marrying up" socially.

These figures can, however, give a misleading impression of both the extent of ethnic-group endogamy and its relative importance when a series of more discriminating indices are taken into account. The figures in table 3.1 do not, for example, take into account such factors as economic background, residence, or length of time the various parties have lived in Sefrou. They do not show the frequency with which urban Arab men marry Arab women of rural origins nor whether the Berber men who marry Sefrou Arab women come from equal or higher economic backgrounds. When, however, we look at the gross figures concerned with the rates of endogamy for groups defined in terms of residential origins, it becomes clear that there is a general tendency for people to marry members not only of their own ethnic group but persons with whom they share certain other characteristics, particularly social origins

Table 3.1
Marriages between Arabs and Berbers in Sefrou (1960 Census)

	Arab Men	Berber Men	Total
Arab women	96.5 $N = 1,403$	38.7 $N = 160$	$N = 1,563$
	89.8	10.2	100
Berber women	3.5 $N = 51$	61.3 $N = 253$	$N = 304$
	16.8	83.2	100
Total	100 $N = 1,454$	100 $N = 413$	$N = 1,867$

Source: Compiled from data in Hildred Geertz 1979b, 501–6.
Note: Figures in the upper left-hand corner of each quadrant represent the percentage of men of each category married to women of each category, while figures in the lower right-hand corners represent the percentage of women of each category married to men of each category. Numbers of couples sampled are indicated in the upper right-hand corners.

Table 3.2
Social-Group Endogamy in Sefrou (1960 Census—Percentages)

	Sefrou-Born Arabs	Rural-Born Arabs	Rural-Born Berbers
Men marrying women of their own social group	83.4	63.0	62.9
Women marrying men of their own social group	71.7	71.9	79.1
Percentage of total population	34.9	23.4	12.1

Source: Hildred Geertz 1979b, 501–6.

(table 3.2). Thus, the rates of ethnic-group endogamy alone do not prove that ethnicity (as opposed, say, to economic background, residential origins, etc.) is the really crucial factor, but when one also considers certain qualitative data for each form of endogamy, a good case can indeed be made for ethnic identity alone being a significant if not all-pervasive factor in the selection of mates.

In the case of Arab-Berber endogamy, the attitudes expressed by informants make these figures quite understandable. Berbers often attribute their reluctance to marry their daughters to Arabs to the fact that Arab men seclude their women and do not allow them the freedom to which Berber women are accustomed among their own people. Arabs, in turn, regard Berbers as less cultivated and, given the freedom of their women, too used to dealing freely with members of the opposite sex to be trusted around their own women. The women in an Arab bride's family are reluctant to have as in-laws women who will speak another language and possess different backgrounds from their own, while Berber men often find it preferable to shore up existing relations with fellow kinsmen through the endogamous marriage of a son or daughter. A wide range of reasons is given by all the relatives of the principals for preferring one mate or another, but unless the person is a close neighbor or associate about whose homelife one has some detailed knowledge, there is a clear tendency to avoid interethnic marriages. The statistics themselves do not permit us to say that identity as an Arab or Berber is the only factor involved here, but there can be no doubt that it is indeed a significant contributing factor.

We are, therefore, faced with a far more subtle inquiry than would be necessary if the terms "Arab" and "Berber" simply corresponded to clearly bounded social groupings whose members dealt with one another exclusively in terms of a single feature of their identity. But, as we have seen, Sefrou society, both urban and rural, is a highly complex social terrain in which individuals forge their identity and relationships out of a diverse range of conceptual and relational possibilities. The question to be asked, then, is what one really learns from knowing whether another is an Arab or a Berber and how this particular piece of information fits in with and helps us to understand the larger process of interpersonal perception and network formation. Toward this end it may prove useful to consider two analytic constructs—Alfred Schutz's concept of consociational ties and Basil Bernstein's notion of elaborated and restricted codes.

Schutz began with the proposition that people do not perceive one another as generalized others but as particular kinds of persons and that the symbolic structures through which they conceive of their contacts with each other across time and space deeply influence their view of the bonds that link them. Specifically Schutz distinguished between four different types of people: predecessors, successors, contemporaries, and consociates (Schutz 1967a, 15–19; 1967b, 139–214). Predecessors are simply those who have lived before us and successors those who have yet to be born. Contemporaries and consociates, on the other hand, share a point in time together; but whereas consociates come into actual face-to-face contact with one another, contemporaries do not normally encounter one another directly. Now obviously each of these categories overlaps with the others and is, therefore, not precisely delimited, and it is equally obvious that for simply analytic purposes these four distinctions can be made in any particular society. What is perhaps less obvious—and what renders this set of categories useful—is that different cultures may view those who can analytically be distinguished into several different categories as if they were, in point of fact, particular variants of only one of these categories. Thus, if the essential feature of contemporaries is that they remain rather anonymous occupants of particular structural positions within a social and cultural world, it can, as Clifford Geertz has shown, be argued that the Balinese conception of other persons—regardless of the analytic category into which they can be placed—is one in which all persons are regarded

as stereotyped contemporaries, abstract and anonymous fellow men. Each of the symbolic orders of person-definition, from concealed names to flaunted titles, acts to stress and strengthen the standardization, idealization, and generalization implicit in the relation between individuals whose main connection consists in the accident of their being alive at the same time and to mute or gloss over those implicit in the relation between consociates, men intimately involved in one another's biography, or between predecessors and successors, men who stand to one another as blind testator and unwitting heir. Of course, people in Bali *are* directly, and sometimes deeply, involved in one another's lives; *do* feel their world to have been shaped by the actions of those who came before them and orient their actions towards shaping the world of those who will come after them. But it is not these aspects of their existence as persons—their immediacy and individuality, or their special, never to be repeated, impact upon the stream of historical events—which are culturally played up, symbolically emphasized: it is their social placement, their particular location within a persisting, indeed an external, metaphysical order. The illuminating paradox of Balinese formulations of personhood is that they are—in our terms anyway—depersonalizing. (C. Geertz 1973, 389–90)

In its concept of time as cyclical and repetitive, and in its display of highly formalized and climax-avoiding behavior, Balinese culture consistently sustains the view that people, events, and acts are to be regarded in terms of discrete and rather fully stereotyped cultural categories.

Now if one looks at the Moroccan situation in these same terms—and if, for present purposes, one limits the discussion just to the distinction between contemporaries and consociates—a sharp contrast can be drawn to Balinese culture. For whereas the Balinese perceive of all others as types of more or less anonymous and stereotypical contemporaries, the Moroccan Muslims would seem to conceive of all those with whom they share a period in time— whether or not they actually come into contact with one another—as kinds of consociates. Or, perhaps more accurately still, they see all people as bound together in what might be referred to as a chain of consociation. That is to say, in the Moroccan conceptual system even though two people have not yet come into direct face-to-face contact, such persons are regarded as linked together through a specifiable series of intermediate face-to-face contacts. Such intermediate contacts are posited as necessarily existing, and one need simply search around in the network of contacts a stranger possesses to determine where the actual intermediary links occur or can be construed as occurring. Sometimes these intermediate links are rather contrived, but no matter: what counts is that one simply has to uncover them in order to understand where, within the entire community of fellow humans, another's sphere of relations touches upon one's own. Such a conceptual system underlines both the nature of interlocking ego-centered networks and the importance of intermediaries as the bonding agents between persons who do not actually confront one another directly.

To know, then, as a fundamental presupposition of one's social existence that all men are united in a chain of consociation, whatever its psychological repercussion, is a knowledge of considerable importance. For in determining the intermediate links that bind one to a stranger, certain very important bits of information are obtained. One learns, for example, what kinds of ties the other already possesses, what kinds of personal characteristics he does or is most likely to display or acquire, what kinds of regularized ways (i.e., in terms of what particular customs) he is most used to relating to others, and most importantly, what kinds of bases now exist for the establishment of a personal bond between him and oneself.

Association with others who share certain features in common with oneself can, of course, be indicative of a broader range of social ties and traits, but whereas Westerners generally treat such information as indicative of the rather anonymous association built on a community of interests or block-group affiliations, Moroccans treat such information as indicative of the actual and potential ties that link otherwise unaffiliated persons into a direct relation of consociation. It is, therefore, rather easy to confuse individual Moroccans' social personalities with their membership in particular groupings insofar as a wide set of individual characteristics and roles may indeed typify a series of people who interact intensely. It was particularly true in the past, for example, that core groups of individuals shared the same family ties, religious-brotherhood affiliations, residential placement, and occupational type: for all the diversity of each person's social ties, there was a clumping up, an overlapping, of certain affiliations for certain groups of people. It was, then, somewhat easier to conceive of and refer to such groupings in terms of one or more of the institutions in which they were all involved or in terms of the symbols of such an institution. Since there was such a common overlap of ties, perception and expression of the symbols associated with any of the above institutions could serve as a sort of shorthand expression of a whole series of interrelated traits shared by many: to think of another as, say, a blacksmith was to imply his family background, the quarter where most blacksmiths lived, his financial status, and so on. This is not to say that people thought of individuals only as members, for example, of occupational groups and that it was to such groups as embodied in particular members that one related. It is to say that such group attachments, like other sources of social identity, supplied many of the characteristics that went into the make-up of each social personality, and reference to the symbols of a particular grouping formed a shorthand expression of a multiplicity of common but neither fully homogeneous nor completely corporate ties. There was, then, to use a linguistic analogy, a closer fit in the past between the surface structure of institutional relationships and the deeper structure of interpersonal relations on the basis of which expected normative behavior was perceived.

This emphasis on consociate relationships is relevant to the consideration of any feature of social identity, including the particular topic with which we are concerned here, namely Arab-Berber relations. It can be argued that since the regularized ways in which individuals form various personal and contractual ties with one another constitute the major focus of Moroccan social structure, knowledge of another's ethnicity serves to supply certain baseline data about another's most probable characteristics, ties with others, and customary ways of forming new face-to-face relations with others. The minimal, baseline information derived from the knowledge of another's ethnic background contributes, therefore, to the transition to that second level of conceptualization in which a particular consociate relationship is formed. In other words, the information supplied by a knowledge of ethnic affiliation, though it remains a relatively incomplete means of typifying another person, does indicate the bases upon which the implicit relation of intimate and personal consociation can be made manifest as an actual dyadic bond. The existence of this second stage of conceptualization, treated here under the rubric of consociation, thereby utilizes the baseline information of ethnicity, residence, kin bonds, and so on, but places primary emphasis on the superordinate level of perception and relationship in which all people have the potential for forming contractual ties with one another without being limited by ethnic origins or any other single feature of their overall social identities.

Therefore, the encounter of two individuals not otherwise acquainted consists of a quest for sufficient information to place the other in one's own commonsense scheme of things. What counts as relevant information and how it is elicited and amalgamated with other information is itself a culturally constructed and culturally characteristic process, a process, in the Moroccan case, in which identity as an Arab or Berber forms a baseline for still further inquiry. In order to see how, in part, this process works, consider the following hypothetical situation. Imagine you are an American man boarding a plane or bus for a trip to a distant city and taking a seat next to another man. If you strike up a conversation at all, it is very likely that early on in your attempt to place the other you will ask him "What do you do?" The word "do" could mean anything, but in fact it means what does he do for a living, what is his occupation. If he says he is a bricklayer, you are likely to call up a whole set of assumptions about him: that he has a given level of income and education, that he is more interested in baseball than ballet, that he holds a certain range of political views, and that he is or is not the sort of person you are going to be eager to see again. If, however, you look over and notice that on his lap he has a copy of the untranslated works of Livy, you might become more than usually quizzical and ask what that is. If he says that he found the book years ago and that it is just the right size for holding down the waxed paper while he is eating his sandwich when on the job, you might well find your initial stereotype of bricklayers confirmed and feel no need for deeper inquiry. If, however, he replies that he gets rather bored during his lunch breaks or between jobs and has developed an interest in the rhetorical style of Roman historians, your entire comprehension of the man is likely to be shaken and any assumptions based solely on reference to what he does for a living subjected to more searching inquiry.

Contrast this example to a similarly hypothetical situation in Morocco. Here it is far more likely that priority will be given not to a question about occupation but to one of social origins, asel. Just as occupation triggers for most Americans a range of features that are thought of as connected to what one does, a similar process applies in Morocco to the question of origins. But the exchange of information is not likely to stop there. Rather, a statement of origins will very often be followed by each party telling about who each knows from that or nearby places until they have discovered or concocted some actual set of persons, each of whom has face-to-face relations with the other—until, in short, they have discovered or created a chain of consociation by which they can see themselves as linked. To be able to place each other in this way—to find a set of coordinates of background and attachment—constitutes an indispensable first step for the formation of any more durable involvement: it gives each the baseline data he needs to gain some degree of predictability about the other in various situations. The inquiry is thus part of a process of network formation for which the analytic distinction formulated by Basil Bernstein seems particularly appropriate.

Bernstein argues that the particular forms of social relations that are operative in any one society give rise to rather different linguistic codes through which individuals transmit vital information about themselves. The codes, in turn, serve to orient the speakers toward certain kinds of relationships that bind them together. Specifically, Bernstein says, two main kinds of codes can be distinguished. Restricted codes arise from situations in which a tight-knit group of individuals—such as a prison community, a group of adolescents, or the members of an academic department—possess an "extensive set of closely shared identifications, self-consciously held by the members" (Bernstein 1964,61). In the case of restricted code usage,

> the speech is played out against a backdrop of assumptions common to the speakers, against a set of closely shared interests and identifications, against a system of shared expectations; in short, it presupposes a local cultural identity which reduces the need for the speakers to express their intent verbally and to make it explicit. (1964,60)

Because they share so many assumptions, those using a restricted code in any given situation are, in the context of this constraining form of communication, indicating their relative role and status positions far more than they are probing into one another's total personalities. Thus, "the unique meaning of the individual is likely to be implicit" in the communication, and the more restricted the communication the less one can predict another's individual attributes (1965,156). One has only to think of the almost ritualized forms of communication at cocktail parties, diplomatic occasions, religious events, or the shorthand idioms of a group of specialists to find examples of such usage.

An elaborated code, on the other hand

> will develop to the extent that the discrete intent of the other person may *not* be taken for granted. Inasmuch as the other person's intent may not be taken for granted, then the speaker is forced to expand and elaborate his meanings, with the consequence that he chooses more carefully among syntactic and vocabulary options. (1964,63)

An elaborated code thus "encourages the speaker to focus upon the other person as an experience different from his own. An elaborated code is *person* rather than status oriented'' (1964,63). Indeed, insofar as an elaborated code is not, like a restricted code, ''refracted through the implications of the status arrangements,'' it permits a far more highly ramified concept not only of others but also of one's own self as a distinctive personality (1965,161).

Now if one looks at the relations between Arabs and Berbers in the Sefrou region in terms of Bernstein's distinctions, several important features can be noted. In their initial contacts with and conceptualizations of one another, an Arab and a Berber are, fundamentally, dealing in terms of a rather restricted code. From the form of greeting and the recognition of one's dress and accent, through the routinized inquiry into the sources of one another's nurture (place of residence, occupation, etc.), to the inquiry into who one knows and what intermediate persons fill in the missing links between oneself and the other, an almost set scenario is played out. However, once this restricted code has indicated the bases of another's social identity and the grounds that are now perceived for establishing a face-to-face, personal relationship, the possibility exists for using a more elaborated code that probes into the other's overall personality and tests for the kinds of relationships that can be formed with him. And since it is the social relationship that precedes the entire communication, namely one in which all individuals are seen as linked in consociate forms that merely need to be uncovered, movement into an elaborated code is an almost inevitable result. Thus, even in what may seem the most casual of interactions—say, in the communication between a buyer and a seller—the initial use of a restricted code to determine the bases for further interaction is quickly superseded by the use of an elaborate code to discover a desirable form of interpersonal relationship. The choice and timing involved in the use of different codes elicits, stabilizes, strengthens, and models one person's orientations toward another. Ethnicity, then, defines, through the mediation of a restricted code, the bases on which an elaborated code can be implemented for establishing a particular kind of consociate relationship with persons of quite different ethnic backgrounds.

Bernstein himself has suggested that ''the ability to switch codes controls the ability to switch roles,'' and indeed there is a sense in which the emphasis of one's ethnic affiliation can be regarded as the playing of a role (1965,157). F. K. Lehman, for example, argues quite convincingly that in Burma ''ethnic categories are formally like roles'' and that given the political plurality of the country, it is to the advantage of ethnic minorities to possess several ambiguous identities that can be enacted, like roles, as the situation varies (Lehman 1967,106–7). Insofar as Berbers or Arabs may indeed identify with members of their own grouping, one can say that ethnic identity is at times given a rolelike quality in Morocco. But in most instances ethnicity is used simply to establish what another's most probable traits and ties are and how a personal bond of consociation, colored but in no sense wholly determined by ethnic background, can now be established. Only in such instances as intermarriage, where cultural differences apparently restrict rather free intermingling, does a significant barrier to full interaction exist. But even this eventuality may be as much a function of differences of education, economics, and urban-rural residence as of ethnicity as such.

In sum, then, ethnicity in this part of contemporary Morocco is a factor that varies with situational contexts and the additional affiliations by which each of the participants is characterized. Identity as a Berber or an Arab is not, however, in almost any context an all-pervasive typification in terms of which one views and relates to another person. Each of the social groupings is only quite imperfectly isolated in reality and hence only quite imperfectly insolable for analytic study. Nor are the categories themselves seen as mutually exclusive: those rural Arabs living in the territory of the Ait Yusi Berber "tribe," for example, see no more contradiction between their cultural identification as Berbers and the dominant Arab culture of the city than does a person of Irish or Italian descent necessarily regard the cultural features he displays as a member of a particular ethnic group as inherently opposed to his identity as an American citizen. To speak, therefore, of the Arabization of Berbers as if they had to dispense with their identity as the latter to achieve inclusion as a member of the former is to fail to appreciate that the two categories are simply not totally antithetical to begin with.

Indeed, as we have argued, the primary emphasis in this society seems to be placed on the regularized ways in which two individuals can contract a personal bond of affiliation in order to secure the bases of their own well-being. In order for each person to take fullest advantage of the contractual social ties available to him, he seeks information about others that is relevant to an understanding of who that person is and how he does or may relate to people like himself. Identity as a Berber or an Arab supplies some of this information, for each person starts not only with a generalized stereotype of other kinds of people but with an awareness that people of different backgrounds tend to possess different kinds of traits and ties and tend, therefore, to form relationships with others in terms of specific customary ways. Through the use of a restricted linguistic code this fundamental information is communicated to others. But almost immediately this fundamental data, this baseline conceptualization, gives way to a more elaborated, open-ended probe into the totality of the other's social personality. The possibility of such a probe is not only a necessary consequence of the fact that all men see themselves as linked in a chain of face-to-face relations that knows no totally impermeable barriers, but itself serves to establish the basis on which any particular dyadic relation is going to be formed. Thus the recognition of a common friend, an experience in the army, difficulty finding a job, or a broadly similar geographical origin may serve as a basis for a personal relationship as patron-client, political ally, or potential go-between. Once a slightly more than casual acquaintance has been established, this delving into another's being will progress through a highly ramified series of conceptual categorizations influenced, but not necessarily fully determined at any point, by the facts of any one particular trait or tie.

Treated as an ordered system of categories in terms of which the experience of another is perceived and articulated, ethnic identity serves to indicate some of the bases of possible relationship to those who choose to actualize such latent bonds while it defines in rather vague and minimal detail the essential features of those members of the opposite ethnic group with whom a direct tie of consociation has yet to be realized. Ethnicity, like other social indicators in Morocco, distinguishes individuals as kinds of persons without at the same time separating them from rather full social intercourse. Indeed, insofar as there is a clear tendency to resist the establishment of any sharp lines of affiliation and identification in this part of Morocco, all studies that confront the question of Arab-Berber relations are forced to view them as the Moroccans themselves do—as contingent and partial rather than complete and pervasive features of each person's social identity. To approach the question of social relations in Morocco mainly in terms of ethnic differences is to perpetuate the same error of misplaced concreteness of which the French themselves were so guilty: it is to give a reified and primary status to a distinction which, in actual operation, is of more ambiguous and subsidiary importance. By considering ethnicity as just one of the features that can be factored out for analysis without having its particular importance unnecessarily exaggerated and by concentrating primarily on the overall system into which such a feature fits, one can avoid dichotomizing the categories ''Berber'' and ''Arab'' and appreciate how each of these attributes relates to the whole conceptual and relational scheme so characteristic of contemporary Moroccan society.

Muslims and Jews

The relations between Muslims and Jews—perhaps more than any other relationship in Morocco—constitutes at once a very special instance whose unique elements must never be discounted and an examplary case, one which, by standing at the limits of Moroccan society, tests the very process of social construction within the Muslim community itself. Obviously, any attempt to grasp the nature of Muslim-Jewish relations in the Arab world poses a number of very special problems. In the present political climate of Arab-Israeli relations, arguments are frequently brought forth by disputants on each side concerning what each regards as the fundamental relations between Muslims and Jews, not as political but as social communities. Muslims insist that Jews who have lived in their midst have always fared better than those living in Europe and that their opposition is not to Jews as a religious, but as a distinct political, grouping. Zionists, on the other hand, consider as humiliating the treatment Jews have received in the Muslim countries from which most of them have emigrated and often regard the Muslims as fundamentally anti-Semitic, despite the latter's protestations to the contrary. Fact and myth, particularly in the hands of each side's propagandists, have become inextricably tangled, and attempts to tease them apart often fall victim to accusations that the author is less interested in a judicious presentation of the data than in serving some private and ulterior motive. Indeed, since most of the Jews have either left their homes in the Arab nations or found their positions drastically altered by the present conflict, it has become almost impossible to study firsthand the ways in which Muslims conceive of and relate to the Jewish minorities living in their midst as part of Arab society and not just as an extension of the Israeli nation or the community of world Jewry.

In Morocco, however, one finds a nation sufficiently distant from the Israeli frontiers yet bound by ties of language, religion, and primordial sentiment to the Arabs of that region where it has been possible to do on-site research into the question of Muslim-Jewish relations. Jewish communities have long occupied an important place in Moroccan social history and the numbers of Jews living in the country have always been significant. Thus, in 1948 nearly a quarter of a million Jews—about one out of every four living in the Middle East—resided in Morocco, and though the Jewish population has progressively declined—from about 45,000 at the beginning of my research in the mid-1960s to less than 17,000 at present—the effect of the Jews' presence continues to remain evident in Moroccan social life and thought.[71]

The nature of Muslim-Jewish relations is of particular importance to an understanding of life in the Sefrou region. As table 1.1 (p. 14) shows, the Jews of Sefrou accounted for roughly half of the entire population of the city until the formation of the French Protectorate in 1912; in the years after World War II the Jewish population grew to more than 5,700. As elsewhere in Morocco, subsequent events—the founding of the state of Israel in 1948, the advent of national independence in 1956, the death of the sultan Mohammed V in 1961, the Arab-Israeli wars, and a host of local events—contributed to the emigration of Jews abroad. As a result, when my own fieldwork began in 1966 there were about 750 Jews still living in the city; by 1972 the figure was 200; in 1978 it was fewer than a score. Yet even with the remnant community of the 1960s, many of the distinctive qualities of Muslim-Jewish relations in the region were readily discernible and it was possible to reconstruct much of the social history of community relations as they dated back into the pre-Protectorate period. Thus it becomes possible to see that an understanding of Muslim-

71. According to the national censuses, the number of Jews in Morocco in 1960 was 162,420 (1.4 percent of the population) and in 1971, 31,119 (0.2 percent of the total). See generally, Abu-Lughod 1980,239. A figure of 17,000 for 1979 is given by Tessler 1981,189. Since there was still a significant Jewish population in the city during the initial period of my fieldwork, I will continue to speak of that community in the present tense, notwithstanding its subsequent dispersion.

Jewish relations depends, in no small part, on our seeing how the concepts and modes of interaction that characterize life within the Muslim community deeply affect and in many respects remain broadly relevant to the relationships that Muslims have with their Jewish neighbors. The relations between Muslims and Jews in this city thus puts to the test of scope and relevancy a series of features about Muslim social life itself and allows us to understand how the conceptual framework we have been describing has informed Muslim-Jewish relations for a considerable period of time, notwithstanding situations and incidents that have led in other parts of the Middle East to the complete breakdown of relations between these two communities. Only by comprehending both its uniqueness and its culturally characteristic qualities can we see how the Muslim-Jewish relationship fits into the overall scheme of Moroccan cultural life.

If, in the eyes of the Muslims of Sefrou, a man's identity suggests the modes of relationship that may be negotiated with him, and if identity rests initially on the concept of social origins (asel)—that intercausal amalgam of nurture, settlement, attachments, and characteristic customs for relating to others—then surely the identity of the Jew as a member of a particular religious grouping remains the central, the unavoidable basis for determining that person's place in the Muslim social world. To be a Jew in Sefrou, certainly during the past three or four generations, has involved a far from unambiguous relationship with the Muslim majority. On the one hand Jews occupied the status accorded them under the Islamic law as a "people of the Book," a non-Muslim group of free people who, by the payment of an appropriate tax and the maintenance of the symbols of their subservience, were granted the protection of the Muslim community and its leaders. This status is generally referred to in the Islamic world by the term _dimma_, a word that actually means "compact" or "guarantee" but which in its root sense both of "censure" and "protection" conveys an impression of the differential power of the contracting parties and the self-limiting terms by which the superior party exercises custody over the weaker and more blameworthy.[72] Thus in Sefrou, as elsewhere in pre-Protectorate Morocco, the Jews had to manifest their dependency by dressing in distinctive clothing, removing their shoes when passing a mosque, and showing appropriate deference when greeted by a Muslim. If, as a sign of their subordination, Jews were forbidden to ride upon the back of so noble an animal as the horse, they could perhaps draw solace from the Muslim's assurance that they could travel in the desert serene in the knowledge that the most majestic of beasts, the lion, would never lower himself to eat a mere Jew. "Protection," of course, often meant reserving the skills or contacts of the Jews for the protector himself, and while this often led

72. On the concept of dhimma and its history in Morocco, see K. Brown 1980; Gerber 1980; Malka 1978,115–16; Stillman 1975a, 1979,83–85. See also Goldberg 1980,53–55.

to a close and interdependent bond, the extent to which the Jews were fairly treated or exploited varied in part with the power and personality of the sultans, their largely autonomous local representatives, and the "big men" of the city and its tribal hinterland.

Perhaps the most striking manifestation of the Jews' social distinctiveness was the existence of a separate Jewish quarter, the *mellāḥ*. These enclaves had been formed in other Moroccan cities, notably Fez, as early as the fifteenth century, but in Sefrou, as in a number of larger communities, the formation of a separate Jewish quarter dates only from the nineteenth century.[73] Unlike such quarters elsewhere in Morocco, which are located just within the city walls, the mellah of Sefrou is situated right in the center of town and could only be reached, until recent years, through a single gate at the end of a short bridge spanning the Aggai River.[74] Here the Jewish community maintained not only a separate physical existence but perpetuated an elaborate set of social and religious institutions.

Yet to isolate the symbols of social differentiation, residential placement, or incidents of communal strife from the full context of Sefrou society and culture can only yield the most itemized and truncated of analyses. For it is in the more subtle and complex realm of their actual relationships that the intricacy of Muslim-Jewish ties reveals itself. In particular it is important to appreciate that the interlocking, indeed symbiotic, relationship of Muslims and Jews in Sefrou is intimately related to the nature of reciprocity and social identity within the Muslim community itself.

Throughout this study we have noted that virtually every relationship between two Muslims incorporates an element of competition, an effort to acquire, through tangible or intangible resources, that degree of knowledge or control by which one can obtain a degree of predictability about another's behavior and hence an edge of security for oneself and one's dependents. While the process of acquiring such information and contracting such ties involves a variety of subtle modes of ingratiation, bargaining, and manipulation, each act is itself based on the assumption that every act implies that some form of reciprocation may later be expected or sought. While certain conventions help to shape the kinds and amount of reciprocation expected, and while some of these may even involve legal or religious sanctions, the process is itself comprised by the manipulation, negotiation, and choice through which reciprocity is asserted or effected. Yet one feature stands out sharply in this

73. For Salé, see K. Brown 1976,42; on Fez and other mellahs, see Stillman 1979,79ff. The word mellah probably derives from the word for salt (*milāḥ*), though whether this is associated with the fact that many Jews lived in salt-bearing locations or performed the task of salting the heads of decapitated prisoners is impossible to determine. On the history of the Jews of Morocco in the modern era, see generally Hirschberg 1981,188–326.

74. A photograph showing the scene will be found in Stillman 1979, photo no. 11 following p. 90.

highly flexible process, namely that the forms of reciprocity in which two Muslims may engage are highly interchangeable such that the possibility always exists that a debt created in a social, economic, or political context may later be called up in a similar or quite different form at a later date. Notwithstanding the extraordinary variability of intra-Muslim differences, in terms of their expectations for potential reciprocation all Muslims may be regarded as acting within a common pool of reciprocal obligations.

The Jew, by contrast, stands well outside of this sociological pool. Because he does not share in exactly the same goals and prestige resources as the Muslim—because he does not share with the Muslim exactly the same customs, values, and sociological capabilities—he does not enter into relationships that involve the same sort of social competition as that which characterizes the relations between two Muslims. Reciprocity between a Muslim and a Jew—though it may arise from similar forms of ingratiation and encounter and be either delayed or immediate—is not as generalized as among fellow Muslims; there is no real possibility, for example, that an economic exchange with a Jew might later involve a Muslim in a situation in which he would have to reciprocate, say, through a marital or political association. The competition for power and prestige that may inform dealings between two Muslims is inapplicable in the relation to a Jew: a Muslim can hardly compete socially with a person who simply is not a member of the grouping within which this competition is taking place. An economic dealing between a Muslim and Jew can, therefore, remain a relatively pure financial transaction involving none of the social competition implied in such a transaction between fellow Muslims. Indeed, an economic agreement between members of two such socially separate groups becomes less a contractual relationship than a symbiotic one: each party recognizes that his interests are more closely safeguarded by the controls inherent in their relation of interdependence than they would be by having recourse solely to external legal sanctions. A sense of mutual reliability was thus able to grow out of this social situation, and however much Jews may have been regarded as shrewd businessmen by the Muslims, they are almost never characterized as dishonest or duplicitous.

This relationship—of social symbiosis and religious contrariety—was further reinforced or made possible by the interstitial position Jews could occupy between two Muslims or, particularly, between urban Arabs and rural Berbers. Never quite sure how a tie formed for one purpose might result in obligations called up for quite another purpose, Muslims would often turn to the Jew for their economic attachments. Whatever hesitancy or distrust two urban Arabs may have felt in this regard was intensified in transactions between these urbanites and Berbers from the countryside. Many country people were, until recent years, at a linguistic disadvantage dealing in the urban marketplace and were mindful that many urban Arabs regarded them as immodest, irreligious, untrustworthy, and unsanitary. By turning to the Jew there was neither risk of unforeseen entanglement nor a potential loss of one's superior position of power. Whether as cause or result, Jews could thus form bonds with individual trading partners that were characterized by mutual economic advantage but devoid of social competition. This served the Muslim's wish to avoid undesirable bonds of obligation and the Jew's wish to maintain religious separation. A number of institutions and conceptualizations contributed to this symbiotic tie.

One of the more noteworthy institutions was the bond of protection formed between Jewish traders and Berber countrymen. Jewish peddlers generally obtained their merchandise from one of the few Jewish importer/wholesalers in the city and travelled around the tribal hinterland servicing their clients. For most Jewish peddlers, particularly those who made their home in a country settlement, a formal bond of protection would be contracted with a powerful Berber figure in the regions through which they travelled. Following Berber custom, the Jewish merchant would sacrifice a sheep at the home of a particular Berber—a form of the 'ar sacrifice—and the latter would make it known that this Jew was under his protection and that any attack on the Jew would be construed as an attack on himself as well. When the Jew led his pack train through tribal lands, his protector would send along an armed guard or place his own son on the lead animal as a sign to all of the Jew's status. Should anyone, even a member of the Berber's own family, dare to violate this sanctuary, he would pay heavily in blood or money for his foolishness.[75] Clearly more was at issue here than the economic tie between Jew and protector, important as that was, particularly during moments of "disorder" (*siba*) when the Berber's access to the urban marketplace was affected. The protector's word, his own authority, his reliability as one who will come to the aid of those who forge ties with him was called into question by an attack on "his Jew"; thus failure to meet such a challenge could have serious repercussions for his image as a reliable ally.

Whereas Jews living in the countryside were dependent on such ties of protection for their well-being, the Jews of the city could secure themselves not only through their intermediate and symbiotic economic ties to individual Muslims but by the multiplicity of institutions through which they organized their own communal life. It is one of the striking features of Sefrou that as few and as solitary as were the institutions in the Muslim sector, those of the Jewish community were elaborate, corporate, and all-pervasive. As Clifford Geertz has shown, within the mellah of Sefrou a central Comité drawn from the predominant merchants of the community supervized the division of the entire Jewish population into a pyramid of economically defined groupings, each of which was assessed charitable contributions that were distributed by

75. Examples of such unusual breaches are explored in C. Geertz 1973,6–30. See also C. Geertz 1979:138, 168–72.

the Comité to the poor (C. Geertz 1979,164–68).[76] Each Jew also belonged to a variety of cross-cutting voluntary associations, ranging from Bible-study groups and synagogue congregations to burial and marital-aid societies. The committee itself handled relations to the Muslim and French governments while the rabbinical scholars and courts, through the application of Jewish law and moral criticism, placed a check on both the committee and the voluntary associations. The result was an intensely institutionalized plutocracy in which the personal affairs of the Jews were kept under tight internal control, and relations between the Jewish community and the Muslim majority could remain unified, controlled, and responsive.

Yet as much as the Jew was considered by the Muslim to be a member of a largely separate community, he was also considered very much an individual. In the marketplace, for example, the Jews of Sefrou did not occupy a set of distinctive trades or crafts, as has been the case in many other instances of Jewish economic organization in the non-Jewish world. Rather, the Jews of Sefrou, with a few exceptions, were engaged in most of the same crafts and businesses as the Muslims, almost always side by side with them in the part of the bazaar where such practitioners were located (C. Geertz 1979,168–72).[77] Although a hierarchy of suppliers existed within the Jewish community— from the rich wholesaler who imported goods from the coast and abroad to the peddler working the most remote stretches of the Ait Yusi territory—individual craftsmen and retailers formed highly personalistic clientele relations with individual Muslim buyers. In pre-Protectorate times some of the Jewish merchants of Sefrou, like some of the Muslims, became protegés of European powers and were thus exempt from the taxation, jurisdiction, and predations of local Muslims.[78] In Sefrou, however, relatively few of the Jews—though some of the wealthiest—were directly covered by protegé status, and while many others benefited from the ties they possessed to those who were pro-

76. See also K. Brown (1980,191) who estimates that in Salé one-fourth of the Jewish population depended on charity from the rest of the community. However, this figure may be inflated due to the presence of non-Salé Jews seeking charity in the city on the occasion of Jewish holidays.

77. Some occupations however, were, almost exclusively staffed by Jews. Thus tinsmiths were Jews because tinsmiths did all the plumbing work, and Muslims were reluctant to allow another Muslim to enter their homes where they might see the women.

78. It has been argued that in some Moroccan Jewish communities, acquisition of protegé status created a disruptive elite within that community (see Bowie 1976). This does not appear to have been the case in Sefrou, if indeed it was true anywhere, in part because of the prior existence of a plutocratic elite in the Sefrou Jewish community, some of whose members were also those who acquired protegé status. Benhalima (1977b,30) cites a figure of eight Jews who were protegés in 1911. On the protegé system generally, see Bowie 1970; Meyers 1982. The influence of French culture on the Jewish communities of Morocco was greatly extended through the schools of the Alliance Israélite Universelle (see Laskier 1983).

tegés, far more emphasis was placed on the interconnections Jewish merchants and artisans maintained with individual Muslims.

To the Muslim the Jew in Sefrou society was, therefore, both an individual who could be dealt with in terms of many of the same concepts and negotiated ties employed in relationships with a fellow Muslim and a member of an inferior religious community with whom full ties of reciprocity were inapplicable. Nowhere is this pattern more visible than in the perceptions Muslims express about their Jewish neighbors. To this day, when one discusses the Jews with Arabs and Berbers of all economic, generational, and educational levels, one never hears remarks that suggest a collective economic cabal by the Jews: there is no notion that the Jews have tried to gain financial control of the marketplace to the detriment of the Muslims. To the contrary, one consistently encounters people from all sectors of Sefrou society who deeply regret the departure of the Jews from the region and blame the decline of the Sefrou economy in no small part on the absence of Jewish merchants.[79] The comments of one urban Arab are representative:

> Si Arabi, a middle-aged, unmoneyed hardware dealer and part-time musician, whose family has lived for generations in the medina, said that the Jews were extremely good for the business and prosperity of Sefrou. "The thing about the Jews," he said, "was that they didn't just sit on their money, they always kept it moving. They were always investing, always putting their money to work; they didn't hold back: they spent money as freely as if they were playing by chance (*kif swirti*)." The effect of this, he continued, was that the Muslims invested their money as well: "The Jews pulled people out and together they would get rich. Now with the Jews gone the Muslims are like stingy old men. They hold back their money and won't take any risks." He noted, for example, that apartments could easily be built over his shop in the medina. But the habus—the religious foundation—that owns the building wants the full sum for construction put down first and no Muslim wants to put out his capital that way. "Without the Jews," he concluded, "the Berbers have made the mellah a filthy place. Without the Jews the market doesn't work."

Si Arabi's remarks—whatever their wishful or factual merits—point up more than the attitude that without the Jews the economy of Sefrou has suffered enormously. They imply, quite accurately, that Jews often formed partnerships with Muslims for the purchase of real property and that their pur-

---

79. On Muslim regret over the departure of the Jews, see Malka 1978,104. In the late 1970s King Hassan II invited a number of Moroccan Jews who had emigrated to Israel to visit Morocco as part of an announced effort to encourage emigré Jews to return. A few Jews did return but the number, though perhaps not the gesture, was not significant.

chase of "green" crops—those as yet unharvested, and even unplanted—
were, notwithstanding the rates paid, a significant element in spreading one's
risk in a most uncertain environment.[80] No doubt such partnerships made
certain forms of investment possible for the Jews that would otherwise have
been less open to them, and no doubt the fact that a Muslim had a stake in the
enterprise—whether a parcel of rural land or the Jew's living quarters in the
mellah—helped to secure the Jew against certain pressures or depredations.
Whatever its source, the actuality of Muslim-Jewish economic interdependence found expression in the perception of Jews as clever, but eminently
human, beings. Jews were, in short, members of a community with its own
affiliations, customs, and beliefs. But they were also individuals, persons
with whom one could establish relationships that took account of their background and contexts in much the same way one did of a fellow Muslim.

Just as one hears comments about the Jews economic position that are not
stereotypically negative, so, too, one does not hear remarks implying that the
Jews are politically dangerous, that they are individually or collectively undermining the nation, plotting the overthrow of the kingdom, or that they are
responsible for the country's various political problems. It is, of course, true
that since the advent of the state of Israel and the beginning of Jewish emigration, the leaders of various political parties from far right to far left have tried
to associate Moroccan Jewry with the Jewish or pro-Jewish enemies of the
Arabs. Yet it is a matter of no small significance that there exists no well-
developed body of anti-Jewish literature in Morocco, or for that matter anywhere else in the Middle East, in which the Jew is portrayed as a politically
dangerous presence.[81] Those Moroccan politicians who have resorted to such
anti-Jewish diatribes have invariably, and only recently, imported their texts
from abroad simply because the Arabs lack a body of such literature of their
own.

The anti-Jewish comments one does hear in Sefrou are, therefore, neither
political nor economic in orientation; instead, they are, quite revealingly, social and cultural, the gist of such remarks being that the Jews' religion creates
a clear separation between them and the Muslims. Asked whether the basic
human nature of the Jews—their *nafs* ("passions") and *'aqel* ("reason")—is
like that of the Muslims, many informants, particularly more traditional urban
Arabs, say that the Jews are ruled more by their nafs than are the Muslims.
This, they say, is not because their nature is essentially different but because

80. This widespread regret at the Jews' departure takes many forms of expression. I have
heard the Jews' departure cited—almost always in sadness, seldom in anger—for everything
from the decline in business to the lowered level of the Aggai River.

81. See Goitein 1955; Malka 1978; Stillman 1979. On the absence of blood libels against Jews
in Arab countries, see Stillman 1975b,203. A few Jews who have remained in Morocco have
commented adversely on their coreligionists (see Lévy-Corcos 1968; Serfaty 1969). For an
answer to these commentors, see Malka 1978.

the Jews have nothing to guide them in overcoming their passions, in leading them to do good things. To Muslims, the power of the Quran lies, in part, in its ability to guide reason over passion; its legitimacy lies in the fact that it is the all-inclusive, precise, and unaltered word of God as transmitted through His last prophet. The Jews have their Torah, say these informants, but they keep rewriting it and have thus destroyed whatever truth that document once contained. Of course, one is also told, there are wise men among the Jews who can tell the good parts from those that have been changed and who, although not Muslims, know and respect the word of God contained in the Quran. But it is obvious, these informants conclude, that the Jews would be better people if they had not altered the truth given to them by earlier prophets. Other informants, particularly rural Berbers, when asked to comment on the nafs and ʿaqel of Jews, find this paradigm familiar but inapplicable. They too see no difference in the nafs of Jews and Muslims, but, perhaps given their own illiteracy, they see the written word as a less certain vehicle for containing human propensities. Indeed, they often say that the Jews are wiser in at least one respect than the Muslims—a Jewish man, they say, will always be faithful to one wife, and even if he does not get along with her he will not look at another woman. As one man, an important Berber trader, put it: "The Jewish officials work hard to patch up disputes and keep people from getting divorced while our judges and notaries just register divorces as fast as they can in order to get the fees." Muslim informants of diverse backgrounds also find in the Jews' revision of their sacred texts a confusion of identity and legitimacy. By manipulating their heritage, it is said, "the Jews no longer know who their grandfathers ["ancestors," *ždūd*] are"—a factor of no mean significance for those to whom genealogical attachment is a vital factor in the determination of filiation, inheritance, and the establishment of personal attachments. Muslims also cite as incest the fact that Jewish men marry their nieces, and one otherwise well-informed urbanite even insisted that Jews do not circumcise their sons, thus (quite mistakenly, but understandably) finding a symbolic basis for distinguishing Muslim from Jew.

One can see in the cultural perception of the Jews and in their interstitial role in the local society and economy that Jews were at once stereotyped as exemplars and incorporated as individuals within the scheme of this most personalistic society. Their position was inherently ambivalent and, like any such ambivalence, combined elements of the irrational and the arbitrary along with the guidance of commonsense understanding and the probing of acceptable standards of behavior. To the Muslim the Jew was at once an exception to certain categories of behavior—the pool of negotiable reciprocity, the precise demands made possible by membership in the community of Islam—and very much a part of the whole society and culture—individuals to whom one could and must relate on a highly personalized level, a category of people with whom one could share many cultural and spiritual activities. To grasp in somewhat more theoretical terms this interaction of stereotype and person, it may be valuable to recall our earlier discussions about personal and social identity among the Muslims of Sefrou.

In our analysis of Arab-Berber relations we saw that broadly speaking, at least two main conceptual constructs appear to be operating, one after the other, in the Muslim perception of other persons. In the first stage what we might refer to as the establishment of baseline conceptualizations is operative. Here information about a person's origins and general group associations is relevant. Knowing, for example, that a man is an Arab, a Berber, or a Jew tells one something about that person's probable traits and ties—the customary ways he forms ties to others, what if any broad impediments exist for interaction with this man, and what kinds of direct and personal ties are now possible with him. It is this last feature—what personal ties can be formed between him and oneself—that triggers into operation the second level of conceptualization, which we have been treating under the rubric of consociation. This shift to the level of consociation is made all the easier by the fact that, as we noted earlier, it is this feature of consociation that is culturally, symbolically stressed regardless of whether people have as yet actually come into face-to-face contact. What then takes place with the implementation of this conceptual level is the establishment of particular ties and the mutual evaluation of particular characteristics. The range of possibilities operative at this level will, of course, depend on how comprehensive the baseline data is in telling one what kinds of ties are possible or desirable with a given kind of individual. The critical factor in this society, however, is that such baseline information is invariably minimal and partial rather than complete and comprehensive. Thus when an Arab and a Berber deal with one another, there is a recognition that relatively few cross-cutting ties exist to weaken the outright competition that characterizes all relations between two Muslims. In the case of Muslim-Jewish relations, the Muslim recognizes that the baseline information gained by virtue of one's recognition of the other's ethnicity does not totally define all ideas about and relationships with that person. The sheer recognition on the part of the Muslim that a very significant proportion of his relations with a Jew is open to personal evaluations and relationships—just as they are with fellow Muslims—constitutes a recognition of the fact that a Jew is no more fully characterized by his religious origins alone than is a fellow Muslim by his ethnic or residential affiliation. Of course, the particular features that define baseline conceptualizations and particular kinds of consociate relations for persons of different backgrounds varies significantly. But the two stages of conceptualization themselves are applicable to all persons. Thus, in a way that is as typical in its underlying principles as it is distinctive in its resultant patterning, Jews are indeed treated as members of the community of men even though they are obviously not members of the community of believers.

As a category of person the Jew thus falls into a unique position. He is by no means altogether a stranger: The Jews' assumptions about reality are not thought by Muslims to differ radically from their own, and thus images of the Jew do not show him to base his actions on premises and practices utterly foreign to Muslim conceptions. Quite the contrary, Muslims tend to regard the customary practices of the Jews as perhaps more distinctive than those of other groupings in the society but not beyond the common bounds of the culture within which they all live. Jews, as we have noted, share many ritual foci in common with the Muslims. As elsewhere in Morocco, Muslims and Jews share a saint whose shrine, lodged in a cave just north of Sefrou, is visited particularly by women of both faiths who suffer from illness or infertility. When special prayers for rain are said, the Jews engage in a parallel ceremony of supplication. True, these spiritual events have been affected to some extent by that form of logic, the *trajetio ad absurdum,* that argues that God must acknowledge one's need if *even* a Jew has such a need.[82] But it is also true that the sheer coexistence of these rituals and beliefs renders the Jew more than a simple stranger. If it is true that the thinkers of the French enlightenment could never perceive the Jews as related to them in a bond of fraternité similar to that of other Frenchmen—and if this attitude in turn precluded the eradication of anti-Semitic beliefs—then Morocco may represent the converse situation, one in which unremitting anti-Semitism has not been able to put down solid roots in the presence of recognized cultural commonality.[83] For Jew and Muslim alike the confrontation with the other has not itself been a problematic confrontation with a stranger: it has been an encounter for which baseline identity and interpersonal attachment form an instrument, unique yet not alien, for disentangling the problematic.[84]

Nor is the Jew entirely like that other category of person whose status and power always carries an edge of the problematic for Moroccan men: Moroccan women. Like women the Jews are at once admired, feared, coddled, abused, treasured, expended, and only half seen. Jewish men are often explicitly likened to women: confronted by a strong man Jews are seen to be as "frightened as women," and the military victories of the Israelis are often attributed to Jews of European origins (who, like European women, are said to be "different from our own") or to foreign powers. To kill a Jew is to kill someone so inherently weak as to appear little more than a coward oneself. Yet like women, the Jews are often treated with caution since some of them—

---

82. See the discussion in Lewis 1970,19–20 and below on p. 178.

83. On Jews in the French Enlightenment, see Hertzberg 1970.

84. The formulation presented here draws on and is in contrast with Schutz's assertion that "the cultural pattern of the approached group is to the stranger not a shelter but a field of adventure, not a matter of course but a questionable topic of investigation, not an instrument for disentangling problematic situations but a problematic situation itself and one hard to master" (Schultz 1964,104). See also Simmel 1921.

particularly the learned men and the old women—are said by many to possess spiritual and magical powers both positive and dangerous. Undoubtedly, as Hart has argued, many Jews found "safety in humility," a safety of person and a refuge from the threat of cultural assimilation (Hart 1976,280). But weakness for the Jews, no less than for women, is not without its power. Not only is there the magical power of affecting rain and fertility, there is also the power to choose which among various patrons to depend on—whom to favor with one's apparent weakness. Just as a woman, though lacking formal powers, may be central to a man's good opinion of himself, so, too, the Jew, as a vehicle of supplementing a Muslim's view of his powers and attachments, could turn this symbolic resource to his own advantage. Sometimes, too, the very fact that the Jew is, in the full sense of social reciprocity, in a noncompetitive position with the Muslim allows a kind of intimacy that is less possible within one's own network of obligation, kinship, and gossip. For the Muslim the ease born of social superiority and interdependence can thus encourage a sense, or at least an illusion, of fellow-feeling.

If, then, it is useful to look at the relations of Muslims to Jews as a particular variation of the general Muslim paradigm of relational and conceptual constructs, the question arises as to how capable, particularly in moments of great stress, this paradigm has been for guiding the actions of those concerned. The answer is to be found in large part in the historical record. In numerous incidents—ranging from the political confusion following the deaths of nineteenth-century sultans to the struggles surrounding French penetration and the subsequent rise of Moroccan nationalists—Jews were subject to attacks by some of their Muslim neighbors. However, such attacks were, with rare exceptions, directed almost entirely against the property of the Jews rather than against their persons. Indeed, in many cases the Jews received the full protection of the community's Muslims and, like Jews in other parts of Morocco, were no more frequently robbed or intimidated than any other segment of the overall population.[85] In the only event that I witnessed personally—namely the period of the June 1967 Middle East War—the impact of outside events was rather quickly absorbed and enervated as the Muslims of this and other cities refused to allow the Jews in their midst to become wholly stereotyped in terms of their religious identity alone.[86] The vitality of the Muslims' view of the Jews as persons rather than as simple types and the relations of the Muslims to them as socially noncompetitive middlemen, mili-

85. Support for this argument can be found, for example, in K. Brown 1980 ("cases of violence perpetrated against the Jews were few and isolated"); Chouraqui 1968; Corcos 1976; Goitein 1955,74–76; Goldberg 1980,57. For a contrasting view, see Stillman 1975a; 1979,78–87; 1980. For discussions of these contrasting interpretations, see Centre National de la Recherche Scientifique 1980; Shokeid 1980; Shokeid and Deshen 1982; Zenner 1980; Zenner and Shokeid 1982.

86. For a detailed description of the events of this period, see Rosen 1968a. For a discussion of similar events see Malka 1978,66ff.

tated against a significant shift in the Muslims' attitudes and ties to their Jewish neighbors.

It should, however, be noted that there is some variation within the Muslim community itself on this issue. For example, there is clear evidence that anti-Jewish sentiment runs higher and is more persistently sustained among the urbanized middle-class segment of the Muslim population than among other parts of the whole society. These are, of course, the people most apt to seek their identity from just those cultural traits that are seen as so different—as necessarily so different—from those of Jews and Christians, differences that add a certain justification to their image of their own cultural superiority in a world that challenges both their values and their self-image at every point. Moreover, given the present economic and political circumstances in Morocco it is these people who are most likely to be moving into occupations in which there is more direct competition with the remaining Jews and who, accordingly, feel them as somewhat more of a threat. Whether it is for a job as postal clerk or small shopkeeper, radio repairman or large-scale distributer of European goods, there now exists a certain economic strain between the educated, under-employed Muslim and the Jew, which has contributed to some of the present tension between the two. The fact, however, that even this pressure has been largely enervated by the continuing stress on individual ties and the Jews' position as noncompetitor in the social sense has meant that Muslim-Jewish relations at all levels of Moroccan society have thus far remained at least relatively workable.

In addition to acknowledging that anti-Jewish sentiment runs higher among some segments of the urban Arab population than elsewhere in Morocco, one must also face up to the incontrovertible fact that about three-quarters of the nation's Jews have indeed left Morocco in the past two decades. The causes for this emigration appear, however, to be primarily economic (and to a lesser extent political) rather than because of any sharp alteration in the ways the Muslims perceive of and relate to their Jewish neighbors. The Moroccan economy as a whole has become rather depressed since the end of the Protectorate in 1956. Many of the occupations Jews practice have become less profitable. Many of the opportunities for jobs and schooling have had to be parcelled out among competing segments of the Muslim population. And many of the political decisions made with reference to the avenues of access to various resources have necessarily granted highest priority to different segments of the Muslim community. The attachment that had developed to French cultural life, the birth of the state of Israel and the recognition that they did have a real alternative to continued residence in Morocco, the sudden death of the sultan Mohamed V in 1961—these and other economic, political, and (for the Jews) attitudinal changes have all contributed to the departure of the Jews from this North African country.[87] What does not appear to have

87. See Malka 1978,72ff. For an argument that increased levels of education reduced Muslim

been the case, however, is that there has been any real alteration in the fundamental relational and conceptual schemes in terms of which most Muslims act
towards most Jews. Moroccan Muslims generally do not seem to attribute any
of their own misfortunes to the Jews, nor do they seek to remedy such ills by
the restriction, expulsion, or extermination of that segment of the population.
In a world in which whole groups of people are frequently stereotyped by
reference to a single feature of their existence and severely persecuted for it, it
is indeed important to understand how in a society such as this one a set of
ideas and relationships has had the sheer staying power to ward off shifts of
fundamental perception that could otherwise spell the violent end of so dependent a minority group as the contemporary Moroccan Jews.

Socially and culturally, then, one is confronted in this part of the Middle
East with a very different sort of relationship between the Jews and the dominant population than has been true for the West or, for that matter, many other
parts of the Arab world itself. For the Muslims of such Moroccan communities as that considered here, the Jew stands neither as an exception nor as a
contradiction to a social order founded on networks of dyadically contracted
personal bonds linking people whose inherent membership in any particular
group or category serves only to establish a baseline for interaction with others rather than as an all-pervasive typification. Where impermeable boundaries, reinforced by discriminatory practices, have impeded totally free social
intercourse between Muslims and Jews, such boundaries have also contributed to the relative security that the Jews have enjoyed as social and economic
middlemen between various individuals and segments of the Muslim population. In certain societies or sections of them, the individual may be seen as a
composite of parts, any one of which—ethnic origins, occupation, political
views—can take on such primacy in the eyes of all those (including the subject) who perceive others through the lenses of such a cultural system as to
identify the totality of an individual's being through a single feature of his or
her social character. In Moroccan society, however, neither ethnic identity
nor any other single trait or affiliation has come to stand for the whole individual in any given circumstance. The desire to form personal bonds wherever
they appear most advantageous has helped to support a conceptual system in
which baseline identities quickly give way to views of others as more or less
total social personalities. The question of typing is, of course, a question of
levels of analysis. But it is also a question of a cultural system, of a set of
symbols through which the categories of thought and perception are themselves formed and expressed, and through which action is rendered meaningful. And in his conception of and behavior towards the Jew, each Muslim
in this community clearly indicates that there is much that is similar to if

dependence on Jews and thus contributed to increases in the estrangement of the Jews, see
Tessler 1981:162, 176–78.

somewhat differently weighted and apportioned from his view of himself, his fellow Muslims, and his relations with them. The sheer vitality of such a conceptual and relational scheme in the face of numerous strains must, therefore, be accorded careful attention whenever broad assertions are made about the relations between Muslims and Jews in the Arab world.

Summary: Repertoire and Performance

Social scientists often rely on analogies and metaphors to capture and communicate the distinctive design of cultures notably different from their own. Finding in some societies' emphasis on genealogy a central principle of organization, they have at times spoken of descent as if it operated as a legal rule; seeing collective action as the result of recruitment based on group affiliation, they have likened the units of society to corporate entities. As many anthropologists have come to see that no single principle—of descent or residence, sect or class—forms a complete explanation for all of a society's life, and, as governing principles that lie beneath the observable—whether biological, mental, or material—seem unable to achieve their own proffered standard of scientific reliability, a more eclectic view of what gives order to particular societies has come to the fore. Thus, in the Sefrou case, as we have seen, the data lend themselves to a view not of corporate groups but of personally centered action groups, not of rules of descent but of an ordered struggle for dependents, not of ideology as a mask for reality but of concepts held in such a way as to facilitate meaningful action. The metaphors that come to mind incorporate images of process and procedure, theme and variation, repertoire and performance. In the next chapter we shall elaborate on two aspects of the order of Sefrou society—the ways in which individuals place one another in context as a central element in the process of defining and relating to others, and the particular assumptions and principles by which interpersonal negotiation goes forward. Before turning to those considerations, however, it may prove useful to summarize the view of social organization our analysis thus far suggests.

The central feature of social organization in Sefrou is the interpersonal contract. Since corporate groups are virtually nonexistent, individuals forge personal bonds according to conventions that are as well recognized as they are fraught with leeway for maneuvering.[88] In the formation of these dyadic bonds—whether between social equals or patrons and clients—individual activity is not reducible to a set of rules but is informed by regularized procedures through which the components of a culturally distinctive way of establishing ties may facilitate a socially recognizable form of individual and

---

88. There is, in this regard, some degree of similarity between my view of Sefrou society and that developed by Foster (1961, 1963) in his analysis of a Mexican village.

collective action. Different individuals may draw on the repertoire of relational possibilities differently and the resultant ties may or may not coincide with ideals expressed. What really counts, however, is that if a dyadic tie is formed in a recognizable way, it will introduce a set of expectations and results that will themselves be relevant to other interpersonal ties. Therefore, at each point in the social system it is not ongoing groups that are the locus of activity but those "action groups" that individuals have managed to precipitate to their own advantage. It is in this sense that one can understand T. E. Lawrence's assertion that "the Arabs believe in individuals, not in institutions."

The orderliness of Moroccan social life is, moreover, deeply dependent on each person's ability to gather information about others that may be useful for assessing the possibilities and consequences of their associations. Predictability of behavior as well as an indication of appropriate modes of constructing attachments may be supplied, in part, by elements of another's social identity. Knowing another to be a Jew or an Ait Yusi tribesman suggests possibilities and forms of interpersonal contract. Such knowledge may also serve not so much to keep people from perceiving some ultimate truth about themselves as much as to provide a basis for apprehending that, for all its uncertainties and latent chaos, the world is not inherently devoid of order. Locke's assertion that "the only fence against the world is a thorough knowledge of it" is not only readily translatable into the Moroccan experience, it underscores that in this particular society, it is the indispensable ingredient in each person's necessary effort to build a network of dependents and obligations.

We could, therefore, attempt to sort out the resultant networks either in terms of some statistical model or in order to posit normative and deviant social arrangements. To do so would, however, miss the dynamic quality of Sefrou social life: it would fix relational patterns without at the same time grasping the essential fact that there are regularized ways to form ties with others and that these regularizing principles are suffused with, indeed given substance and definition by, the cultural constructs that encapsulate them. To speak, therefore, of the range of meaning of haqq or asel is to consider the very concepts that, because people use them, manipulate them, and bargain through them, render it possible for people to act. It is to the elaboration of the context dependent and essential negotiability of these concepts and their consequent relationships that we must now direct our attention.

Four

Convention and Creation in the Construction of Social Reality

Homo Contextus: Situating Actors in the World

For the people of the Sefrou region the fundamental unit of society—the point of predominant attention, the locus of all activity—is the single individual, negotiating in and through the concepts that define that person's world. Seeing oneself and others within the parameters of one's origins and connections, residence and intentions, obligations and essential human nature, each person draws on the repertoire of relational possibilities to achieve personal and familial security in an uncertain world. There is a regularity to each person's actions as well as room for change and creativity. The features entailed in one's knowledge of another's background provide a baseline for association; the assumption of face-to-face contact reinforces personalistic inspection of those one encounters; the suspension of truth until a claim of validation can be fixed lends room for maneuver and constancy to one's assertions. At every turn, efforts are made to place the other, to understand who he or she is in terms of the people, the circumstances, and the traits that surround and shape each of the frames through which that person moves.

To know another—and to know how to operate in a world of others—is to know how to interpret these features and contexts and how to engage in their very definition. Seen from the Sefrawis' perspective, the individual is the embodiment of contextualized features. Although the world of human interaction is perilous and unpredictable, it takes a certain form and regularity through words and deeds—through the principles by which relations are forged and the concepts by which contexts are understood.[1] Just as in a language, where the context of a sentence becomes normalized by repetitive use yet is itself always open to additional meanings as other contexts arise, so, too, in Morocco the contexts by which individuals are known become stabilized in certain respects yet are themselves the result of a contingent and variable process of context formation.[2]

Moroccans express this interweaving of person and context with a term, *ḥāl*, whose broad range and implications (the entry in Wehr's dictionary runs to seven columns) have great currency and import. Hal is usually translated as "state," "condition," "circumstance," and "situation" and conveys the sense of what is actually and presently so. But hal, as present condition, carries overtones of the root verb which means "to undergo a change," "to shift," "to be transformed." To refer to a person's hal thus holds the connotation of a person presently set in circumstances that are subject to, and possibly the result of, shifts and alterations that transform and transmute what was into what is. Hal incorporates a general sense of how change and character and circumstance interact. To say "I know your hal" (*kanʿarf ḥalek*) is not only to say that I know your situation but what best suits you as well (Brunot 1952, 206). Circumstances being central to the conception of the individual and his or her social position, hal is also equated with "character," that set of contextualized features that inhere in and define a person. The situated person is, like the "weather" (another meaning of hal), subject to change.[3] But the change that is implied is that of a "shift" from one whole "state" to another, a "transmutation" or "conversion" (*taḥwīl*) that establishes a new context within which a person must be understood. It is as if a person's hal were like a snapshot, an instant that, regardless of its duration, shows a subject in the setting one defines and is defined by. The ordinary person lives subject to the vicissitudes of "the times" (*l-ḥāl*) while the Sufi mystic, for whom hal means a state of "trance" or "ecstasy," stands in a context in which time and circumstance take on transcendental meaning (see Gardet 1967; Macdonald 1961b; Massignon 1952, 1968). In each of its usages, the semantic realm of the concept of hal displays the intertwining of character and condition, of transmuted states and time as circumstance. That

1. In this respect at least the world of the North Arabian Bedouin, as assessed by Meeker (1979, 27), shares much in common with that of the Moroccan: "One cannot say that a world of uncertain relationships is a completely formless, chaotic world, one can only say that such a world takes a peculiar form. It takes the form of men who are dealing with other men in the form of 'personal deeds and words.' The person, as a political actor and speaker, emerges as a central conception."

2. See the discussion of language and context in Fish 1980, 268–92.

3. Brunot (1952, 206) reports that the idiom *ḥāl uḥwāl*, the singular and plural forms of the term, means to be of a changeable humor. It is perhaps in this vein, too, that some Berbers use hal as a designation for women.

individuals might be greeted or asked after in terms of each other's hal is, whatever its idiomatic force, a recognition of that joinder of person and situation that is so central to the facilitation of interpersonal ties.

The subtle interplay of context and person is, of course, subject to a set of organizing principles; mechanisms by which the general idea that a person's character, identity, state, or condition is shaped and revealed through circumstantial settings is given more concrete meaning and application. Nowhere is this interplay shown with more clarity than in the way the people of Morocco narrate accounts of action and event. Narrative, it has been said, confronts the problem of translating knowing into telling (H. White 1981, 1): it seeks to convey, in a comprehensible fashion, what is known about an act, an occurrence, a person, or a life. Moreover, the way the narrative progresses will supply clues to a people's ideas of time and causality and will often suggest, if not boldly assert, what is regarded as essentially true about its subject.[4] When we look at Moroccan narrative style, therefore, we can see how the individual constitutes and responds to his circumstances, his hal, and the ways in which the style of narration, the choice of significant qualities and events, and the designation of a privileged perspective contribute to the Moroccans' elucidation to themselves of the relation of humans and their world. As one listens to Moroccan narrative accounts, three characteristics stand out: (1) that people are known by their actions—thus an account of what people say or do, rather than what lies within them, is the fullest and most coherent form of describing them; (2) that the perspective sought is that of the reliable witness, to whom a privileged viewpoint is necessarily accorded; and (3) that since individuals can be known by the contexts in which they are placed rather than by any development they undergo, time is of secondary importance to the revelation of more or less invariant character through more often than not changing circumstances.

These characteristics reveal themselves in the style and content of a wide range of stories, descriptions, anecdotes, and literary texts. Perhaps no single, concise text embraces all features, but a sufficient number of instances are available in the literature to supply clear examples of the characteristics mentioned.[5] Consider, for instance, one of the descriptions contained in a recent sociolinguistic study by Ahmed Boukous (1977, 168–85). In an account en-

4. Ricoeur (1981, 165) states: "I take temporality to be that structure of existence that reaches language in narrativity and narrativity to be the language structure that has temporality as its ultimate referent." M. White (1963, 4) writes: "In other words I shall assume that a narrative has a central subject and that the task of the narrator is, at the very least, to tell us what has been true of that central subject at different times in a coherent way." As White indicates (pp. 13–18), such "truth" may be conceived as something essentially so about the situation described or a vision that pragmatically facilitates additional acts.

5. See, e.g., Boukous 1977; Charhadi 1964; Drouin 1975; K. Dwyer 1982; a Berber epic poem entitled "La Harka des Enfants," in Duquaire 1943, 178–212; Waterbury 1972.

titled "Work in Town," a young man from the Sous region south of Marrakech recounts, in Berber and Arabic, his attempts to find employment in the city. Throughout, the narrator indicates, by a constant use of dialogue, what the young man and his interlocutors did and said, rather than what he or anyone he encountered may have thought or felt. When asked by a friend why he wants to go to the city, he quotes himself saying: "I argue all the time with my father, my mother, and the village headman . . . ; in town there is work; here every man who is unemployed becomes a thief." At no time does he say what he or anyone else thinks or feels: the dialogue he recounts focuses instead on what men say, what they do, and what social consequences result. As in other such narratives, the vocabulary of inner states is almost entirely absent.

There follows a long series of vignettes in which the young man encounters a variety of other people in town. Each is a compact unit of dialogue. There is an encounter with another unemployed man in which the two exchange comments about work possibilities, followed by a dialogue centering around the purchase of goods by the narrator with his limited funds. This conversation is followed by another with someone from whom he seeks a meal and who in turn accuses him of stealing. The story concludes, after a dozen more such brief episodes, by the narrator trying to arrange food and a bed for himself one night. The conversational segments are all quite brief and their temporal arrangement is not indicated: indeed, there is strong internal evidence to suggest that the order of events is not recounted with any eye toward temporality. Like snapshots scattered on the table, the young man is made known to us by his situated encounters, each revealing an aspect of the type of individual—a Soussi migrant who is a bit of a rube come to town—and the personality that defines the narrator as a man. Events are not causally connected; rather they offer a synopsis of the person at the center by showing his many sides as revealed by a variety of encounters.

Throughout, the narrative is posed as a series of quoted utterances. Often in Moroccan narrative accounts, the narrator will say "So-and-so has said that" or "So-and-so told me that," thereby establishing the credibility of the account by tracing it to some reliable witness. In this particular account, believability is sought by constant quotation by the narrator of his and others' actual words. It is as if to say: "Here is what I said and what each of them said; I am not telling you *about* what happened; I am actually recounting it all to you as it occurred." At no time does the narrator in this particular account relate what he did not see or hear (though when this is done in many other Moroccan narratives some indication of the source from whom the narrator has obtained his information will be included). Through page after page, encounter after encounter, and dialogue after dialogue a picture of a young man seeking work is built up that makes virtually no use of statements about his inner self, the order of events, or their causal connection, but the picture is made recognizable and believable to the Moroccan hearer by its stress on context, action, and demonstrated validation.

The features present in this and similar accounts are wholly consonant with the way in which the person as a social entity is constructed in a number of domains of Moroccan life. In our discussion of the attribution of intentionality we have already seen that a person's inner state is largely irrelevant to an account of events in the world: since motive and intent are discernible in words and deeds, there is no felt need to discuss a person's interior state directly. The representation of an individual in such accounts is similar, in some respects, to the style of Homer. In Homeric narrative style, as Auerbach argued, everything is in the foreground, nothing is in the background: people's actions are what they appear to be, little being left to the influence of the unexpressed; the meanings of acts and words are unmistakable, there being no need to sort through a multiplicity of possible interpretations; all events are given much the same emphasis with only a few elements brought into sharp relief while most others are left comparatively obscure (Auerbach 1953, 23).[6] The identity between a man and his actions is very close, and there is little that is relevant to understanding an occurrence or what it means that is not rather uniformly illuminated on the surface. One could almost imagine a Moroccan poet saying of a Moroccan migrant worker as Homer said of Odysseus: "He saw the cities of many men and knew their mind."

Narratives such as that of the young man in town also try to tell us something about what is true about the characters, the events, or the forces at work in the world. The authority of the account must, as in other domains of Moroccan life, be brought into the realm of the true if it is to be regarded as true, and for this the role of the narrator himself must be authenticated. No Moroccan narrator can claim the omniscience granted narrators in other traditions, nor can any account be put forth without some form of validation. The process is very much like that we have described for validating utterances in other contexts: validation by reliable witness. The person relating the account refers to specific people who are themselves regarded—or by this reference are being touted—as reliable witnesses to the events. The method often bears similarities to the process by which the traditions of the Prophet (ḥadith) were authenticated: a chain of relators is traced back to the one who reliably saw or

---

6. Fränkel (1973, 79), says of Homeric man: "If what man wills and is, is straightway and without hindrance transformed into action, then every human trait and every character passes unchecked into outward expression and achievement; and the society of the *Iliad* is so organized that it affords broad scope for the noble character. So a man and his actions become identical, and he makes himself completely and adequately comprehended in them; he has no hidden depths. This situation justifies the epic in its traditional form. In its factual report of what men do and say everything that men are is expressed, because they are no more than what they do and say and suffer. They are not insulated from the outside world but their nature pours forth into the world with their deeds and their fortunes."

heard what the actor—or, in the case of the hadith, the Prophet—said or did.[7] It is a style of recounting events that became common in medieval Arabic literature when, as Gerhardt points out in her study of the *Thousand and One Nights,* the convention developed of the "witnessing system," in which each story that was meant to be taken seriously was attributed to a particular, highly personalized individual (Gerhardt 1963, 378–83). In these tales, as in modern Moroccan accounts, where no specific witness can be called forth, reference may instead be made to some unnamed other. "It has been said," "it is told that," etc. are doubtless relatively weak forms of authorization: they may even be used to weaken an account depending on the teller's tone and manner. But they also lend some authority to an account by indicating that what is told is publicly known or at least that the narrator is willing to offer his good services as an intermediary in relating what others have said to what his listeners are now asked to evaluate.[8]

Accounts of another's actions—and hence of that person's character and mind—also possess distinct stylistic features. In the presentation of dialogue, for example, each person is quoted directly, no emphasis being added to their purported statements. Assertions are often put in strongly affirmative and negative pairings. This feature of contrariety is central to the way Moroccans grapple with an understanding and representation of others. S. D. Goitein's argument that in Arabic narratives of the early Islamic era "characterization aimed at an understanding of men through their *contradictions*" is broadly applicable to Moroccan narratives as well (Goitein 1977, 7).[9] The alternative sides of a characteristic will be addressed not so much by direct explication as by revealing them in different contexts and by means of words that convey contrary meanings. Thus in accounts like that of the young man in town, an

---

7. Assessment of the testimony offered by such accounts therefore consists less of an acceptance of the "facts" than acceptance of the narrator (see Juynboll 1961b, 117–18). This emphasis on reliable witnesses becomes the basis for the response of an eighth-century humorist who, upon being challenged to tell a serious hadith (i.e., one attributable to two reliable witnesses), replied that the Prophet had distinguished two qualities that would assure one salvation, but that, alas, another man of great credibility had forgotten what one of these qualities was and he had forgotten the other (Lewis 1974, 270)!

8. On the narrator as intermediary, see Drouin 1975, 162. It is also common for Moroccans to assess the truth of an account by comparing the versions of independent witnesses. If the accounts are identical, the story of each is more believable. Thus during the 1967 Arab-Israeli War I was frequently asked to translate the reports of British and French broadcasts because my informants insisted that if all the broadcasters were saying the same thing, it must be true. The technique was similar to that used in Islamic law where two groups of witnesses may be interviewed one by one in front of two 'adul (notaries, "reliable witnesses"), and if their stories conform, a document will be issued that carries great weight in the legal proceeding. On this form of fact-finding, see Rosen 1980–81, 224.

9. The revelation of character through contradiction can also be seen in the Moroccan trickster figure, Juha (see Waterbury 1972, 92–96).

individual will be represented in one situation as generous and pious only to be portrayed in a coupled instance as violent and venal. Elsewhere, his acts may be characterized by a term like *jabara,* which means both "kindness" and "tyranny," an example of that class of Arabic terms that embraces contradictory qualities in a single word.[10]

The sense that people's acts embrace opposed elements whose different aspects cannot remain hidden if enough is known of the situations in which they must act and speak, gives added impetus to a narrative style intended to reveal, with the greatest plausibility, the "state" or "condition" of people and their contexts. The context-dependent nature of a person's character and actions is also given stylistic emphasis through the use of repetition. Repetition plays a key role in Muslim conceptions of how circumstance may shape and change an individual. Moroccans seem to agree with Ibn Khaldun that repetition creates habit, which in turn alters one's "state." Like the steady drip of one substance into another, a point can be reached where a fundamental shift occurs, a transposition into a new context of characteristics and actions. By repeating the same act or event, one separates it as a unit from what comes before or after and heightens its immediacy and its creative force. This may be true in the reiteration of Quranic passages or Sufic prayers; it may also be true when used as a stylistic device to indicate alteration in a person's qualities or situation.[11]

Narrative accounts—whether as conversational exposition, oral history, or popular storytelling—work on the assumption that no man acts without context; therefore to reveal a person in a variety of circumstances is to reveal him as a social person. Just as Moroccans seek in their ordinary lives to know how a man is connected to others and what he has said and done in a variety of situations, so, too, in the narrative it is important to see a person in different circumstances in order to understand his character and the import of his acts. In the account of the young man in town the subject is shown moving through a host of situations, each of which describes and defines the man.[12] The same focus on context is evident in other domains as well. When a judge allows or

10. On the ambivalent structure of many Arabic terms, see Berque and Charnay 1967.

11. On the relation of character revelation and the repetition of utterances or events three times—three being a number of great spiritual significance in Islam—see D. Dwyer 1978, 55–56. As an example of how "repetition, and not insistence, is the basis of persuasion" in the view of Tunisian Jews, Cohen (1975, 150) cites the saying: "A word in the morning, a word in the afternoon, you will transform a Muslim into a Jew" (Kelma f-ṣṣbaḥ u kelma f-l'ašīya, tredd l-mšelma yūdīya). Drouin (1975, 162) also notes the importance of repetition as a mnemonic or highlighting mechanism.

12. As the editor notes, the central character "parvient à 'camper' des personnages tranchés par leur psychologie et leur comportement en les plaçant dans les situations judicieusement choisies afin de révéler un aspect de leur personnalité en le mettre en lumière" (Boukous 1977, 311).

encourages litigants to confront one another directly, makes inquiries into their dealings in other situations, or sends an expert to observe a matter first-hand, his aim, to the limited extent that it is possible in a legal proceeding, is to let the statements of the parties stand forth in their original or replicated contexts (see Rosen 1980–81, 228–32). When assessing world leaders or events the thrust of inquiry is always toward evidence of their actions in other situations. A narrative account can, therefore, skip around in time: it is not temporal order that reveals the meaning and direction of another's acts but situated events. To the extent that individuals change, they do so in response to changing circumstances; consequently to see a person in a range of such conditions, irrespective of the temporal order in which they occur, affords the most comprehensible disclosure of the social and personal truth about him.

Character and circumstance are, therefore, intimately associated with the conception of time that informs Moroccan social life. Of course, time takes many different forms in the Islamic conceptual order: there is the idea of *dahr,* that eternal and undifferentiated duration, that "indefinite and inexorable un-dulation" which makes of time itself an ethical proposition, a test of humans against the timeless order of God; there is *mītāq,* that moment of creation, of "pure event," which, though set in no temporal order, bursts forth, a reaffir-mation of divine fiat, at moments of prophetic renewal; there is that fixed period (*ḥīn*), as brief as the clamorous instant when Allah announces his judg-ment yet expansive enough to fit an event to its proper season; there are historical divisions—an era named for its dominant figure, a time known for its central event—terms for the latter often partaking of that quality in Arabic verbs that gives stress not to the relation of act and agent but simply to the act itself; there are the intervals, closely marked yet unnamed, that take place between the formation of an obligation and its fulfillment, periods fraught with psychological, tactical, and ethical calculation; and there is the inter-twined array of calendars and astronomical sequences—lunar, agricultural, religious, European—by which the practical concerns of everyday life are given shape and order.[13] Yet through these manifold concepts of time—from the mystical expansion of the instant into the eternal to that businesslike divi-sion that constitutes, in the striking phrase of Foucault, a "materialism of the incorporeal"—there runs a common theme: a sense of time existing as a series of discontinuous instants, relatively self-contained units that encapsu-late and conform to the experience of those who partake of them.[14] This

13. The quoted phrases, as well as an examination of the theological and philosophical roots of many of these concepts, will be found in Hasnaoui 1977. See also Gardet 1976; Massignon 1952; Meziane 1976. On time intervals and reciprocal obligations, see Bourdieu 1977, 6–15.

14. Foucault's phrase, from his inaugural lecture, is quoted in Hasnaoui 1977, 73. The particular view of time as discontinuous packets of experience is generally associated with the concept of atomism as put forth by the followers of the ninth-century (A.D.) theologian al-Ash'ari.

conception of time as an array of discrete instants is deeply inscribed in the ideas and terms employed in Islamic theology and historiography.

Louis Massignon, recognizing that Quranic teaching had brought with it a vision of the pre-Islamic "Age of Ignorance" (*jāhilīyah*) as one that was ruptured by moments of divine and prophetic action, wrote that: "For the Muslim theologian, time is not a continuous 'duration,' but a constellation, a 'milky way' of instants" (Massignon 1952, 141). To early theologians, the points of contact between the mundane and the Almighty, though capable of sequential ordering, gain meaning not through their temporal placement but through that creative act that exists irrespective of time and space. As Gardet put it: "Time is less the measurement of movement than an indisputable sign of the impermanence of things" (Gardet 1976, 205).[15] Unlike the prophet in Judeo-Christian thought who prefigures the future in the present, the prophet in Islam cuts into time to repeat and reaffirm the instantaneousness of God's creative power and His age-free compact with man (Gardet 1977, 203–4; see also Bravmann 1971). History, for many Islamic thinkers, consisted of periods of chaos (fitna) broken by prophetic appearance.[16] For them time follows no clear sequence, whether cyclical, rhythmic, or linear. Indeed, as several commentators have pointed out, were events to be replicated by a predetermined principle there would be no need for the testimony provided by reliable witnesses to actual occurrences (Hasnaoui 1977, 33–34, citing Sinaceur 1972; Gardet 1976, 212). Instead, history can be presented as a "discontinuous succession of experiential 'moments,'" which, by centering on the acts of particular individuals, reflects the cultural assumption that character and circumstance, not temporal causality, explain each encapsulated time.[17]

The theme of time as discontinuous packets of experience that may be

---

Although, as Smith and Haddad (1981, 4) note, this view of time was intended less as an actual description of duration than of Allah's unlimited power, and notwithstanding the assertion of Hasnaoui (1977, 74) that Islamic concepts of time are highly diverse, the emphasis on time as discontinuous units clearly forms a central, though not all-embracing, aspect of the contemporary Moroccan concept of time.

15. The present description is much indebted to Gardet's work.

16. This was not, however, the view of history held by all Arab historians (see Hasnaoui 1977, 73). On Ibn Khaldun's spiral vision of time, for example, see Mahdi 1957, 133–59; Talbi 1967, 138.

17. The internal quotation is from Gardet 1976, 212. Noting how highly personalized each prophet is in Islam, Gardet (1976, 212) states: "In broad terms, it would be correct to say that, in the specifically Moslem view of the world, there are 'histories' but there is no such thing as 'history.'" And Goitein (1977, 16), writing about medieval Islam, says: "The purpose of Islamic biography, like that of pre-Islamic narrative, was information. . . . There was also a theological aspect to the matter. The Muslims did not have much use for the idea of causality. God creates our deeds as well as our thoughts. Things being so, there was not much purpose or inducement to explain a man's character out of the circumstances of his life, or his deeds out of his character." For a gross distortion of such ideas as applied to contemporary Arab modes of thought, see Patai 1976, 71–72.

discerned in the chronicles and theology of the classical Islamic period clearly possesses analogues in contemporary Moroccan usage and conceptions. Indeed it may be argued that for Moroccans, the actual content of time units— the feature that bounds and unifies a chosen unit—is the web of relationships, the networks of obligation that characterize that moment. Each unit of time is, therefore, a living instant, a moment when people, tied to one another by mutual indebtedness, affect each other's existence. This feature comes out quite clearly in the semantic range of certain terms. One of these terms, *zamān*, is usually translated as "time," but it conveys more exactly the sense of a relatively self-contained quantum of time which occurred at some point in the past. When one speaks of such times, however, one is not speaking about them predominantly in the sense of their connection to what comes before or after but of the relationships that held among people in that time and thus characterized both it and them.[18] A particular time-section is known— whether factually or mythically—for the bonds of obligation, the distribution of haqq, that held people together. It reveals what is true about its subject by revealing that which, to Moroccans, is always the most true, the most real thing there is: the bonds, the covenants, the obligations by which people, through their ties to one another and the supernatural, are formed into coherent communities.

As each time section centers around its constitutive social ties, it is not surprising that the sections themselves often form around a particularly significant event or person with reference to which other's relations tended to be set. In Sefrou, for example, such significant contexts include "the year of the ration ticket" (*'am l-bun;* 1945—a year in which everyone had to have ration tickets to obtain various commodities, an occurrence that clearly disrupted existing obligations and focused such ties on the symbol through which they were reconstituted); "the year Caid Omar al-Yusi died" (1905, an event that gave people the opportunity to rearrange many ties); and "the period of disorder (*siba*) after the death of Sultan Moulay Hassan" (1894—during which time there was considerable chaos and looting and a search for new, stabilizing relationships). Each such moment remains significant in the minds of the Sefrou people, not only because it is a focal point of past sets of relationships but because the very quality of these changeable and uncertain moments holds currency for their present concerns. The importance, however, lies not in their connectedness to what happens subsequently but in their representativeness of relational concerns, the usefulness of the information they provide about individual character and interpersonal relations.

As each unit of time recedes into the past, its relations to others often loses any connection to strict temporal ordering. The sequence of occurrences to which people may refer varies quite widely, not because memory or knowl-

18. For a discussion of *zamān* and the sayings cited see Gardet 1976, 22–24.

edge varies but because temporal sequence is not terribly important. As Dale Eickelman has demonstrated, conceptions of time and of temporal order vary a good deal in Morocco with level of education, social background, and degree of modernization. Yet as he also demonstrates, rural or more traditional people often relate events to one another in atemporal fashion, loosely referring to any time section whose full social context is unknown or no longer accounts for the full range of contemporary relationships as having happened in some unclearly specified "early" time (*bekri*) (Eickelman 1977, 50–53).[19] Unless clearly indicated, one cannot assume that events are related according to any lineal sequence. Fragments of time may, therefore, be temporally rearranged or made to seem close to periods that are not temporally contiguous with them but that seem close because they share certain features in common. Thus people will often link what happened in each of the three moments in Sefrou history mentioned above because the moments share a quality of disrupted social bonds and reveal aspects of people's relationships under such circumstances. Within a particular family or community, time may similarly focus on central events—births, deaths, weddings, etc.—rather than on time as a continuous process. For contemporary Moroccans, as Franz Rosenthal has said of the chroniclers of the medieval period, "history is biography" (quoted in Goitein 1977, 17).

This episodic, almost stochastic, view of time thus shows great relevance to the conception of individual identity and character. Whereas Westerners will speak of time and change in terms of metaphors like "growth" or "development," Moroccans speak of passage through disparate batches of time with a metaphor of travelling.[20] One finds in narrative and common description the constant use of *ja* and *mša*, "he came" and "he went." One says of a man who has died that he has "gone" (*mša*). Growth and development are inappropriate simply because people do not, in the Moroccan view, change from within anymore than they can create a view of the moral order from within. Rather, people change their contexts, their hal, their environment, their situated networks of obligation. To see an individual in many contexts is to see

19. Eickelman states (1977:50, 52): "For most tribemen, the term *bekri* refers to a temporal category in which events occur that affect the social order but whose full social context is not known. . . . Another feature of *bekri* is that it is constituted by events not clearly ordered in relation to each other. Within the horizon of the present, what is important are the salient points of personal power or events that significantly shape the social order. As events become less meaningful for current social action, they lose their temporal order and are considered to have occurred 'early.'" However, just because an event is considered bekri does not, I believe, render it less meaningful for current events; indeed, such a designation, as Eickelman himself recognizes, may serve to legitimize current acts by merging them with noteworthy precursors.

20. The terms for "before" (*qbel*) and "after" (*men b'ad*) are, of course, present but tend to be used where specific sequence is crucial. Compare the Moroccan situation in this regard, and their narrative style generally, with Errington 1979, 234. On the Western metaphor of growth and development, see Nisbet 1969.

what he is. "Men reveal themselves in journeys," says the proverb, not only because of the intimacy of constant companionship but because changing circumstances reveal situated characteristics. To go to another place is to put oneself into a new context with all that implies for those traits and ties that cumulate in the individual as a matter of his surround. It is not time that shows us what others are, but their placement in the social worlds through which they move. It is not their intrinsic qualities, their unrevealed selves, that make individuals what they are but the words and actions they create and display in the situations through which they move.

Indeed, the emphasis on time and context as frameworks for the interaction of individuals recalls our earlier discussion of consociation. Moroccans, it was argued, see those whom they have not encountered personally and those with whom they have direct contact as bound together in a chain of consociation, a set of links that join stranger and acquaintance as if they were engaged in actual or potential face-to-face associations. To see experience as packets of consociational bonds is to see time as units whose most essential ingredient is not their durational quality but their enclosure of a set of relational dynamics. Yet this conception—that others are significant to the extent that they can be engaged in face-to-face negotiation and obligation—influences the view not only of contemporaries as consociates but of predecessors and successors as well. For those who come before and after, to the extent they are out of the realm of direct negotiation—that is, to the extent they are nonconsociates— are simply nonpersons. Consider for example the role of the dead. In Islamic thought, death stands as a natural part of the continuum of existence: it is another context, however incomparable, in which a person, linked to others and to Allah, will come to be situated. Yet death breaks the possibility for face-to-face dealings. This is why, no doubt, it is said that saints are, in fact, alive in their tombs, for only with the living can a debt of obligation be created. Each man knows, too, that on the third day after his death—his properties divided, his power diffused—people will cease to mourn him and will say that he simply no longer exists.[21] It is not surprising, therefore, that a well-known Arabic saying should declare that "men resemble their times more than they do their fathers."

Similarly for those who will succeed us, it is not that they come after us that matters but that dealings with them cannot occur face-to-face. Thus all the categories of persons who can exist in time and space—contemporaries, consociates, predecessors, and successors—become grouped, in the logic of Mo-

---

21. It is true that some Berbers in the Sefrou region believe, for example, that on *lilat al-qader*—the twenty-seventh night of the month of fasting that commemorates the revelation of the Quran—the dead come back to help their kinsmen such that eating a meal in the graveyard becomes a form of commensality with the dead. But the orthodox Sunni view—and the thrust, if not the uniformly accepted orientation—is toward a vision of the dead as nonconsociates.

roccan culture, into two encompassing categories—consociates and nonconsociates—both of which are defined by the feature of actual or possible face-to-face relations. It is the individual, situated and understood in contexts defined not by duration but by relationships, linked to others by bonds of obligation that place and reveal his character, who is central to the cultural illumination, to borrow a phrase, of person, time, and conduct in Morocco.[22]

It is in this sense, too, that, as we noted earlier, a person's inner state—the realm of intent, niya—is something that exists in the world of the senses rather than in some private domain of the mind. For Moroccans, it can be argued, nothing is "real" until it comes into the world of obligation, until it takes a place within the scheme of human social life. Thus even the intent of prayer, to say nothing of prayer itself, must be externalized by word or by sign. And from the context of its manifestation a person's intent may be discerned. This is not to deny that there may be unspoken thoughts or hidden views, only that they mean nothing to others until they are exteriorized, brought into the world, connected to a context.

Human beings have often been characterized by philosophers and scientists for a single feature that is said to distinguish us from other creatures: as speech possessing (*homo loquens*) or tool making (*homo fabricans*), discerning (*homo sapiens*) or playful (*homo ludens*). From the point of view of a cultural anthropologist there is a temptation to think of Moroccans, whatever their other traits, as *homo contextus,* for our word "context," which comes from the Latin term meaning "to weave together, especially out of words," seems particularly apt to a view of the individual as one whose distinctive attributes and bonds are constructed out of a skein of words. Speech, both as utterance and as act, enters the public sphere where, like all other aspects of human interaction, it takes its shape as the bargains struck in its terms take shape. All the qualities that can be ascribed to a man and all the contractual ties he can form with others are thought to be subject to his endeavor, though it is often noted that it is in their nature for men to credit themselves with great accomplishment when in fact achievement is generally the result of being disciplined to the limits set down by God.[23] It is not by internal betterment that a man can achieve greater accord with the moral order of God but by placing himself in favorable contexts of interaction. Descendants of the Prophet, saints, respected teachers, and politically astute big men constitute points of attachment with and around whom multiple worlds of relationship are formed, contexts within which the man of reason can acquire the sought-for stability of ties and dependencies. Knowledge ('arf) is knowledge of these moral and

22. The phrase, and much of the stimulus for this discussion, comes from C. Geertz 1973, 360–411.

23. This attitude is expressed, for example, by the Berber merchant depicted in Waterbury 1972.

social contexts. Truth and reality are the fabric of such relations. "Man," says an Algerian proverb readily understood by Moroccans, "is man through men; God alone is God through Himself" (cited in Bourdieu 1966, 211).

A person's character is, therefore, a function of these social contexts, and though one's character does not, in our sense, develop from within, it is certainly possible that a change of context may profoundly alter the person. Thus, if one reads Arab plays or novels, whether written by Moroccans or by others in the Arab East, one is constantly struck by the unaltering nature of the individual represented, unless some shift in circumstances literally tosses him into a new condition of being, a new context of relationships.[24] Change for such characters comes not by gradual accretion but, if at all, as an almost cataclysmic jump-shift to a new circumstance, a new set of obligations. Similarly, a man who comes to live with a new rural group can become identified with them and meld his prior ascriptions into those made of him in his new situation. The same may be true for a Berber living in town, or even a Jew who has become extremely Europeanized. Confronting someone accused of a crime, clever judges are said to have disguised themselves and entrapped the accused in a similar situation, their object being to discern not whether a man actually did what he is charged with but whether, under a given set of conditions, he is the kind of man who would so act. Courts still probe for character, as evinced by actions in various contexts, as much as for the "facts" relating to a particular event (see Rosen 1980–81, 231–32). As we noted earlier, Moroccans also use that form of argument, the *trajectio ad absurdum,* in which one demonstrates the truth of a proposition by showing how it applies, even though other features would seem to argue against its plausibility (Lewis 1970, 19–20). Thus, to say that "*even* a woman can understand the Quran" or "*even* a black man can be learned" is to recognize that in the right context—education, good companions, just times—even those whose intrinsic nature is against them may succeed to attributes consonant with their situation.

The image of the self that emerges from an analysis of narrative style, concepts of time, and illustrations of personal alteration is not, therefore, one of a personally fashioned entity—an individual who has by whatever spiritual or psychological means created an inner self distinctive from all others. Nor is it a concept of the self as *persona,* a mask presented to others that conceals the deeper domain of one's true self. Rather, the Moroccan concept of the person

---

24. I am indebted to Roy P. Mottahedeh for this insight. An excellent example is provided by the novels of the contemporary Egyptian novelist Najib Mahfuz. See Somekh 1973, especially pp. 5, 16, 33, 60, 62, 74, and 161. Gardet (1976, 208) also notes the use of discontinuous time in Egyptian novels.

is one in which the individual is always a situated actor—an individual who maneuvers within the realm of relationships, circumstance, and human qualities to cumulate a set of publicly seen and worldly consequent traits and ties. It is a world—and hence a self—in which people are known by their situated obligations and by the impact their actions have on the entire chain of obligations by which they and their society are known. Human beings do not create themselves, but they do place themselves in those contexts—with teachers, partners, kinsmen, and strangers—through which their bargained-for relationships will yield an identity of their own. As *homo contextus,* the world of Moroccan men and women, spun out of a "web of words," gives evidence of both social regularity and creative articulation.

The world of social relations is, moreover, one whose style and logic is consonant with that of many other domains of Moroccan and more broadly Middle Eastern culture. As Katherine Gittes has shown, the style of Arab narrative is one in which the outer framework is open-ended and unfinished: as in the story of the young man in town, the focus is not on a central theme that informs the work from within but on a series of tales attached to a particular individual and not subject to the governance of a rigid structural form (Gittes 1983, 237–44). This quality of open-endedness is found in a host of other domains of classical Arab culture: in mathematics, where the development of the zero as a place holder and the emphasis on units linked into infinite chains underscores the orientation toward observation of the individual component; in poetry, where the pre-Islamic ode (*qaṣīda*) forms a loose framework around a series of episodes through which the poet moves and to which he personally attests; in the Quran, which appears to be a disconnected set of incidents yet achieves unity by attachment to the character and circumstances of the central figure; in music, where harmony is seen not as a closed and vertical chord but as a horizontal progression; in architecture, where buildings are envisioned not in terms of an overarching design that dictates the form of internal elements but as a series of discrete parts built up over the course of space and time. As Gittes puts it:

> The stress on the individual part in Arabic literature, architecture, and music results in a loose, malleable overall frame or structure that has an organizing rather than a governing function. . . . The concept of organization . . . emphasizes the individual unit and does not allow the open-ended and inconclusive overall framing structure to determine the nature or construction of a work's parts. (Gittes 1983, 243–44)

It is this style—of loosely structured relationships and constant attention to the individual as the locus of traits revealed by the contexts through which he moves—that is so characteristic of Moroccan perceptions of other persons. And it is to the process by which these features achieve common recognition and enactment that we shall, in conclusion, turn our attention.

The Negotiation of Reality

All life . . . comes back to the question of our speech, the medium through which we communicate with each other; for all life comes back to the question of our relations with each other. These relations are made possible, are registered, are verily constituted, by our speech, and are successful . . . in proportion as our speech is worthy of its great human and social function; is developed, delicate, flexible, rich—an adequate accomplished fact. The more it suggests and expresses the more we live by it—the more it promotes and enhances life. Its quality, its authenticity, its security, are hence supremely important for the general multifold opportunity, for the dignity and integrity, of our existence.

Henry James, *The Question of Our Speech* (1905, 10)

It has become almost commonplace to say of a people's language that it is by and through the categories of experience it embraces that a language provides, for those who trust to its representations, an instrument through which a world, acceptable as real, may be envisioned and composed. Yet such an assertion—that language helps to create what shall be regarded as real—must not be allowed to conceal a vital distinction between the capacity of a language to perform this function because it responds to a set of internal regularities subject to rational discernment and the view that language does its work no less effectively for being an "unsystematic and polymorphous array of working conventions [used] for a large and not simply classifiable range of human purposes."[25] For if we can treat language and the relationships it conceives as comprised of regularities of sharp distinction and precise design, it would seem most appropriate to analyze them with tools and ideas equal to the strict nature of the task. But if the subject itself is more like a shifting alignment of intrinsically malleable forms, then clearly our form of description and perhaps even the goal of our enterprise must be no less exact for being appropriately supple. If language does not reflect the world but is integral to its constitution, and if that constituted world is one in which the image of a handclasp is more fitting than of a crystal, a familiarity than a proof, an understanding than a certainty, we may be called upon to foreswear a quest for structural constants, however transmuted, in favor of an exploration of interpretive process, however contested, through which individuals engage in the inexact construction of their social ties.[26]

Such an approach has especial merit in the case of Sefrou. For although the process of constructing a world through speech may result, at one end of the spectrum, in a society in which, at a given moment, the conventions are

25. This phrase is borrowed from the characterization of Wittgenstein's approach in the *Philosophical Investigations* offered by Quinton 1966, 9.

26. The image of the handclasp and the crystal is taken from the discussion of meaning in Black 1968, 209. On the hermeneutic approach implied here, see Rorty 1979, 313–94.

sufficiently settled to give the appearance of stasis and uniform assent, Sefrou, at the time of this study, is, as I suspect it has long been, a society nearer the other end of the continuum, one in which people assess and gauge one another in a context of received possibilities by means of a set of relational guidelines that take shape only as a working arrangement for their use is achieved. It is not too much to say, therefore, that the cultural artifacts by which the people of Sefrou construct and even replicate their lives are themselves dependent on their own acts of interpretation and negotiation and that our appreciation of this kind of social formation must be responsive to the process it embodies.

Throughout this study, particular stress has been given to the element of negotiation in Moroccan life—the covenantal basis of religious ideology, the contractual bonds between pairs of individuals, the multifarious concepts through which alliances, partnerships, and networks can be imagined and deployed. But negotiation is an ongoing process, not an unyielding artifact, and therefore an analysis of it must be solicitous of the living quality of the subject. Accordingly, it will be necessary, first, to consider how such negotiation works—what presuppositions it requires, to what extent the concepts involved must be shared, and the role of substantive guidelines in the actual course of negotiation—and secondly, to show the relationship between the process and resultant social patterns, the coherence and scope of the social conception of reality, and the relations between convention and creation in the culture of the Sefrou region. In pursuing this analysis it may appear that what is being developed is a series of rules for negotiation and social relations, rules that are constitutive in that they not only regulate behavior but create or define new kinds of behavior, just as the rules of chess make its play both possible and regular (see Searle 1969, 33; Taylor 1971, 46). But this is true of the present case only up to—or, more precisely, only after—a certain point. For while it will be desirable to show that there are indeed regularized ways that inform the process of negotiation and make it negotiation and not something else, it will also appear that these constitutive rules are formed, as it were, on a substratum that is more variable, more subject to being extended in different directions under circumstances that are themselves not limited— qualities of the use of language in this society that add an element of the indeterminate to that of the systematic and that cannot be reduced to a simple set of epistimological propositions. This quality asserts itself most forcefully as one tries to work through the presuppositions to the process of negotiation.

If people are to bargain out their relationships with each other, they must begin with a broadly shared recognition that the situation in which they are placed is indeed one in which negotiation is appropriate, possible, or necessary.[27] Although, as we shall see, the question of how much the elements of

---

27. See Scheff 1968, 15–16, which has had a considerable influence on this section. For additional examples of the process described here, see Berger and Kellner 1964; Emerson 1969.

negotiation must actually be shared remains vexed, it is clear that, notwithstanding errors of judgment and approach, some joint awareness must exist
that the situation is indeed one calling for negotiation. As at other points in the
process, the relative control over vital resources, the differential power of the
parties, affects this recognition. A person who has the wealth, the connections, the rhetorical skills, and the personal forcefulness to succeed in imposing his or her definition of the situation may obviate a negotiation where
others must engage in it. The more evenly balanced these resources, the more
likely not only that negotiation will proceed but, ironically, the greater the
likelihood that the less-favored party will be able to control the situation's
definition, simply because the other is now dependent on the less-favored
party's agreement to go forward (Scheff 1968, 16). In Sefrou, this situation
may take the form, as we saw earlier, of a woman or a poorer man being able
to get his or her approach accepted even when others have the lion's share of
the relevant resources at their disposal. Sometimes this amounts to control by
the less favored, a power of weakness; at other times it is impossible to garner
sufficient support even to create a negotiating context. In general, though, it
may be argued that in the Sefrou region, anything that bears on the establishment or servicing of human relationships is regarded as subject to negotiation.
Differences of power, as we shall see, are more significant to the course of
negotiation than to the possibility of its existence.

Once negotiation is applicable, a series of presuppositions about its basic
character come into play. In parts of the Western world, for example, it can be
argued that negotiation is based on the assumption that the parties involved
are distinct and autonomous individuals, that their actions are subject to their
own will and decision, that they recognize when and how they are entering
and leaving the negotiating process, and, until otherwise shown, that everyone will bargain rationally and in good faith. But as Charles Taylor (from
whom these points are drawn) has noted, although negotiators may bring their
own attitudes and goals into the matter, the practices that define and guide the
nature of bargaining are themselves composed of publicly acknowledged and
broadly shared assumptions about other persons and the nature of their actions
(Taylor 1971, 24–26). Bearing in mind that we are only concerned here with
those instances in which social ties are being defined and enacted, we can
include, at a minimum, the following intersubjective assumptions among
those that form the basis for the negotiation of relations in the Sefrou region.

The negotiator is always a situated actor. Although people in the Sefrou
area comprehend the idea of an autonomous individual and demonstrate their
clear belief that people are responsible for their actions, they see individual
actors as always existing in contexts; to speak of a person as somehow "de-
contextualized" would be to speak of someone with whom negotiation is not
really possible. The inquiries into origins, family, knowledge, and rela-

tionships are, as we have seen, attempts to place the other in context and thus to bring that person within the realm of those with whom negotiation is possible. To confront another person in a negotiation is not to confront either a disembodied role or one who is subject only to his or her own reason or desire, but a social being, someone who is defined by enacted traits and personally inscribed relationships. A person's freedom of action, within the bargaining process, will be shaped and colored by these contexts, and though efforts to adduce and evaluate information about them may affect the course of negotiation, the assumption that it is only a situated person who can engage in the process is integral to the existence of the process itself.

Intent is discernible through action and consequence.   When bargaining out their relationships the Sefrou people work with certain presuppositions to guide their comprehension of the meaning of another person's utterances. Characteristically, Moroccans are not greatly concerned with trying to determine what another's goals will be as they enter into the negotiation or what it is that prompts the other to act as he or she does. Purpose will become evident, if at all, through the course of events; motive through a knowledge of social background and relationships. Both of these features are separate from and largely irrelevant to the more immediate concern—the comprehension or interpretation of what the person means when he says something. What is at issue is not the dictionary definition of the terms used or the importance they have for the listener, but the need to be relatively sure that what it is the other seeks to convey is not taken to mean something quite different than what the speaker meant to be understood. Here, conventionalized understandings come into play. Most significant, in terms of the presuppositions of negotiation, is the convention that there is indeed a direct relationship between utterance and intent, that as much as one needs to know about another's state of mind is directly available in the things a person says, the way they are said, and what one does by the very act of saying them. If, for instance, one man seeks to engage another in the validation of his claim of an obligation due him, the convention governing validation by, say, Socratic dialogue and agreement indicates what it is the other intends by this maneuver. Moreover, as one witnesses in oneself and others the consequences of another's statements, one can draw on the underlying assumption that the person must have meant for a certain train of events to have occurred. Such presumptions thus allow negotiation to go forward on the understanding that mutual comprehension is not only possible but that there will be no substantial gap between what each says or does and what the other would comprehend by it.[28] Nor do such presumptions either predetermine the course of negotiation or limit the open-endedness of the relational concepts employed.

28. See, in this regard, the discussion of meaning and intent in Skinner 1972.

Every act affects the balance of obligations.   In our discussion of the concept of haqq we saw that all acts imply the idea of reciprocation and that every act contributes, however subtly, to the shift in what has been appropriately called "the calculus of mutual liability" (Mottahedeh 1980, 74).[29] Moreover, given the highly negotiable network of relationships one may form, it is not clear what one's actual ties may count for until some situation calls for their manifestation. Prior to entering into the negotiation of one's own ties to another it is assumed that the successful conclusion of the matter will undoubtedly affect one another's networks, and even the failure to strike a relationship may have a significant social impact. This knowledge contributes to the seriousness of the process and, indeed, to the eliciting of signs—the exchange of meals, gifts, "favors," etc.—that one is pursuing the matter in full recognition of its potential import. Furthermore, to engage in the negotiation may require, by that very act, the precipitation of some of one's existing ties—seeking contributions to a festive meal, drawing on others' resources to ingratiate oneself to another—which, in turn, tests the existence, scope, and intensity of these ties and creates new ones. It is a precondition to all such instances in which people bargain out the definition of their situation and their bonds to one another that such actions have the general and unavoidable consequence of affecting, to whatever degree, the existing balance of obligations.

Statements about relationships are not subject to evaluation as true or false until validated.   Until some form of validation takes place, the Sefrou people understand that utterances that have a bearing on the formation of relationships cannot be judged against the standards of truth. In our own society statements like "we are friends," "we are members of the same group," or "you have an obligation to me" describe a situation and can be evaluated as true or false. By comparison, statements like "I apologize" or "Open the door!" are usually referred to as performatives and are not subject to evaluation as true or false. In Morocco, some statements that we would regard as truth-bearing are treated as solely performative. Thus, in Morocco to say "we are friends" is not a description about our relationship subject to assessment as true or false; rather, such an utterance is itself the performance of an act, in this case the act of signalling that a negotiation over the applicability of this concept is in order. Only when some form of validation occurs—an oath, a verbal agreement, an act of reliance, a demonstration of personal reliability— does such a statement become transformed into a proposition that possesses some truth value. Until this occurs negotiators simply assume that truth is not a factor in the consideration of another's meaning about the asserted rela-

29. The author uses this phrase to characterize the relation of ruler and subject in the medieval context.

tionship. For the Sefrou people the meaning of an unvalidated utterance lies in its contribution to the enactment of a negotiating situation.

The concepts that bear on human relationships are essentially negotiable concepts.   There remains a feature that is not only a key presupposition to the process of negotiation but an aspect of Moroccan language and culture that is central to our entire study. For at the very heart of the concepts Moroccans use to comprehend and order their relationships lies a quality that, building on the seminal argument of W. B. Gallie, may be referred to as essential negotiability (Gallie 1968, 157–91). Gallie noted that there exists a class of concepts—what he called "essentially contested concepts"—for each of which there is no single use that can be designated as uniformly accepted and hence standard or correct. Thus, in our own culture, concepts like "art," "democracy," or a "good Christian" are concepts over whose applications people not only disagree but whose very existence depends on the dispute that pervades their every use. Gallie characterizes an essentially contested concept by the following features: (1) the concept involves an appraisal or evaluation in that it signifies or accredits a norm of excellence or achievement; it points to something held up as exemplary and serves to assess it; (2) the achievement has an internally complex character, being comprised of a series of related concepts yet treated by disputants as a whole; (3) a number of rival descriptions of these features and their relationship to the whole exist simultaneously such that initially at least there may be a number of incompatible descriptions as to why the achievement is so highly valued; (4) the achievement itself must have an open quality in that it must be amenable to modifications that cannot be prescribed or predicted in advance; and (5) each of the parties must recognize that its own use is contested by others and must have some appreciation of the criteria others are using when they claim an application for the concept; each will then maintain his or her use, aggressively or defensively, toward the other. Thus Gallie can argue, for example, that the concept "democracy" possesses the characteristics of an essentially contested concept in that it is evaluative; composed of a number of complex elements—such as majority rule, equality, and citizen participation—whose arrangement and priority are subject to dispute; open-ended in that the practices that may be characterized as "democratic" often change in unpredictable ways; and used both as a sword and a shield as people contend with one another over its use. By characterizing a concept as essentially contested, Gallie therefore seeks to capture this disputing quality that is central to the concept's living uses. Moreover, Gallie sees such concepts as intimately related to their historical sources in two key respects—that there exists an original exemplar whose authority all contestants acknowledge and that the authority of this original exemplar will itself be best sustained by the simple fact that various parties continue to enter competing claims to its proper use.

If we take Gallie's notion of essentially contested concepts and apply it to the Moroccan situation, we can see that, with certain additions and deletions, we can gain an insight not only into one of the fundamental presuppositions of the process of negotiating relationships but grasp a fundamental feature of Moroccan society and culture. For it can be argued that the concepts employed in the bargaining over relationships possess a quality we may refer to as essential negotiability. The concepts in question are, for example, those of haqq ("obligation"), various terms of extended kinship ("tribe," "fraction," etc.), and asel ("origins") that we have previously discussed as central relational concepts subject to varied implementation. The notion of essential negotiability, however, allows us to specify their qualities more precisely. Thus, using Gallie as a base we can say that essentially negotiable concepts possess the first five features noted by Gallie—they are appraisive, internally complex, variably describable, open to modification, and may be used aggressively and defensively. To this list we must add two elements: First, there is no original exemplar that disputants support simply by contending for the concept's use. As Ernest Gellner has argued, the idea of an original exemplar assumes that present circumstances may only be understood against the background of their progenitors, whereas in fact a concept may function quite independently of its source of origin (Gellner 1974, 95–112). However, in the Moroccan context—though not necessarily as a universal rule—it may be said that while no *original* exemplar exists, there is an *archetypal* exemplar with which an essentially negotiable concept is usually involved. Thus, the idea of "tribal" unity may call forth images of a time or place when such attachments were believed to have existed in more or less pristine form, or the concept of "family" may be attached to a model that incorporates its ideal features. The Quran, traditions, myths, and so on may supply reference points for the concept, but there is generally some rather concrete example that stands as a paragon and around which the dispute may, in significant part, be couched. However, Gallie's condition that the disputants are fighting for this particular exemplary instance appears inapplicable in the Moroccan context since it is too much to say that the optimum goal is to capture this prototype for one's own use, although in some circumstances (nationalist or religious symbols) this may occur. More crucial to our definition of essential negotiability is a feature that must be added to Gallie's account: that only through dispute over a concept's use is it possible to achieve enough of a working agreement about the concept's applicability for further action by the parties to be possible and capable of interpretation. The need for such a negotiated agreement, covenant, or compact is indispensable to the way the concept itself may be employed.[30]

---

30. I am here rejecting Kekes' (1977) idea of rational resolution. I do, however, accept his criterion of voluntary and directed acts within the more distinctively Moroccan version of the situated actor set forth earlier.

We can now characterize an essentially negotiable concept as one whose proper use inevitably involves ongoing dispute and discussion on the part of its users, without which a working agreement constitutive of further action and interpretation is not possible.[31] It is the open-endedness of the concepts and the fact that their application must be accomplished that contributes to the flexibility of the relationships created by and through them. Although Gallie's historical requirement is not essential to an understanding of the contemporary operation of such concepts, it is not difficult to imagine the historical and functional implications of their existence. Living in a world conceived as chaotic and in which relationships are crystallized only as contexts demand, the essential negotiability of the concepts affecting relationships can help maintain the multiplicity of resources available for forming relationships, the flexibility that aids in the formation of various ties, and the dispersion of one's obligations in a society of shifting political alliances and mobile populations. The process of negotiating one's obligations—of negotiating those mutual dependencies that count for what is true and real—through concepts that inscribe this very quality in their heart is a vital aspect of what generates and characterizes the culture of Sefrou.

All of the presuppositions of negotiated relations we have been analyzing incorporate a feature that must, however, be given more direct attention in its own right. For negotiation to work, for presuppositions to exist, it seems obvious that the participants must hold in common a number of concepts and orientations. Indeed, it has become a virtual axiom of the contemporary definition of a culture that its members share in the use and appreciation of the symbols that help to define their world and offer them direction within it. But anthropologists have not always been sufficiently attentive to the question of how much and in what ways it is necessary that people share these concepts in order to be regarded as members of the same culture. The problem has particular importance for Sefrou society where men and women, Muslims and Jews, rural and urban dwellers would appear to possess, on one level, different orientations to concepts that they may be said, on another level, to share. Analyses of this cultural characteristic have, for the most part, fallen into two distinct types, usually referred to as the normative and the interpretive.[32] Proponents of the former approach see the order of society as based on a system of shared symbols which define the roles, values, and institutions that individuals internalize and enact. The social actor who cannot be expected to engage in strategic choices at every turn thus acquires a set of normative needs, attitudes, sentiments, and orientations which account, in rulelike fashion, for his behavior. "Deviance," both beneficial and harmful, may occur,

---

31. This contrasts to "concepts the proper use of which inevitably involves endless disputes about their proper uses on the part of their users" as formulated by Gallie 1968, 158.

32. See, for example, the discussion in T. Wilson 1970 and the sources cited therein. For an interesting exploration of this distinction in a specific ethnographic context, see Bilmes 1976.

but such actions tug at the crucial regularities that hold society together. By contrast, the interpretive approach sees the applicable principles as themselves problematic: individuals orient their actions toward one another, not as a function of internalized rules but by constantly reading others' actions against a series of contexts which are themselves subject to reformulation as the parties' relationships alter. The interpretive view of social order thus acknowledges standards by which social assessments are made but sees, in the very diversity by which people define and redefine their experience, principles of organization that are themselves given substance by the act of publicly espousing, analyzing, and applying ideas and beliefs that cannot be deduced from a series of preexisting rules.

The present study obviously lies closer to the interpretive than the normative orientation. Without asserting it as a universal proposition, it seems reasonable, in the context of Sefrou society, to suggest that for purposes of negotiating the social arrangements that form such a central element of their social reality, what the Sefrou people predominantly share is a repertoire of possible relations and a recognition of certain procedures by which any particular result may be precipitated. In particular, it is the common recognition of the range of possible meanings and applications associated with various relationships and the recognition of their essential negotiability that the Sefrou people share. It is not that each person can, as G. H. Mead suggested, place himself in the other's roles and hence assume his intent or that, as Schelling posited, he can tacitly guess what the other thinks he is thinking (Mead 1956, 209–16; Schelling 1956). For although Moroccans focus their attention on the single individual as the supreme and irreducible unit of social interaction, it is as the composition of culturally regularized and articulated traits and ties that the individual is conceived. Men, for example, may see the proportions of women's nature as different from their own while continuing to share in the concepts that comprise an evaluation of all human nature and the implications that accompany its attribution. Muslims and Jews may be unable or unwilling to engage in full reciprocity, but both share in a recognition of how such ties are formed, by means of which institutions and customs their interdependence is channelled, and the procedures by which their particular bonds may be formed. Whether it is in the election to a local office, the contrivance of a network of economic dependents, or the composition of a dispute over the marriage of one's dependent, what the people of Sefrou share, however constrained or expansive the repertoire of relations open to them, are the concepts and procedures by which relationships may themselves be negotiated. It is in this process, more than in the arrangement of its resultant forms, that we must seek the regularity and distinctiveness of Sefrou culture.

Nowhere are the central features of this negotiating process more deeply inscribed than in the composition and use of language by the Sefrou people. Language is, we have argued, a critical resource in the construction of the

Sefrawi's world: the ability to define a situation, to capture the terms of discourse, to render one's own or another's assets critical or irrelevant by the way an issue is characterized places language at the forefront of interpersonal arrangements. Deeply embedded in those linguistic terms that embrace the concepts of relationship and form the very tools through which they are shaped is that particular kind of ambiguity, of open texture, that imparts energy to, even as it derives discrete resolutions from, the continual process of negotiation. That such terms as "haqq" or "tribe," "family" or "group feeling" should be subject to variant connotation and application in no way detracts from the regularity, indeed, the stability, of the overall system in which they exist. If, to borrow Jacques Berque's phrase, the "mode of classification" of Moroccan social groupings is "interchangeable" (Berque 1955, 449), if the disagreement over viewing a situation as a favor or an obligation fails to achieve consistent resolution, and if the same concept may yield different effects in similar circumstances, it is not only the recognition that such is the nature of these concepts but that their deployment is part of a broader set of bounding procedures. Thus the people of Sefrou can seek in the concept of consociation a framework within which they can apprehend the contingent but not disorderly basis for interpersonal negotiation. They can turn to the working assumption that consequence is directly linked to intent and that what another says or does can be influenced by the characterization of the context involved. Or they can seek comprehension through that code of cultural entailment that suggests that gender implies motivation; motivation, knowledge; knowledge, social position; position, network; and network, repercussions. Just as in music where a particular passage becomes unambiguous only in the light of its context and implications, so, too, in the orchestration of Moroccan social relations "the unambiguous meaning of the whole may be a product of the ambiguity of the part."[33] But where a musical composition may achieve closure and clarity within its own framework, the play of language and relations in Sefrou finds order in the very process of its continual emergence.

So vital and malleable a resource as language owes much of its character to the individuals who work it, and thus the overall design of the social system of Sefrou gives emphasis at every point to the personal. The leader is a man whose qualities must be acknowledged, even as the discussion over the nature and ascription of such features proceeds. The saint must demonstrate that he actually possesses the traits he claims, while those who would seek to be his clients shape the very terms by which his localized force will be acknowledged and purveyed. Partners and enemies, neighbors and foreigners are individuals, poised in their own webs of relatedness, concrete embodiments of features that only make sense when mixed to form a person one can face and

---

33. The image of musical composition, as well as the quoted phrase, are from Meyer 1956, 52.

bargain with. Groups coalesce as individuals mold personal networks from relational possibilities, and until they are actually put to the test their very existence remains contingent and problematic. For the Moroccan, as Michael Meeker has so suggestively posited for the North Arabian Bedouin, the world is not formless or chaotic for being comprised of uncertain relationships: rather "the person, as a political actor and speaker, emerges as a central conception" and "the relations between groups [being] uncertain, political and social life cannot be extensively conventionalized (Meeker 1979:27, 28). But whereas for the Bedouin, in Meeker's view, the central problem was that of constructing a "personal voice"—a set of words and deeds, an eminence, an honor, a group of intimate companions in whom one's force of character might be evinced and reposed—for the Moroccan the uncertainty of ties leads not to an obsessive concern with paternal descent as a secure base in a world of problematic relationships, nor to the cultivation, at once refined and excited, of the memorable word or deed, the heightened attention to the symbols of personal honor. By contrast the Moroccan lives unashamedly embroiled in the details of alliance in which elaborate calculation of individual honor gives way to the concretization of bargains struck and attachments forged. It is not the styling of a self through detached oratory or rhetoric that counts: what matters is the effect of speech in the world. Moroccan social life thus gives support to Kluckhohn's general assertion that "the meaning of a word or phrase is not its dictionary equivalent but the difference its utterance brings about in a situation" (Kluckhohn 1949, 146–47). For the people of Sefrou the fact that speech and acts may always be treated as an "open work"—an occurrence that never closes off possibilities—reinforces the freedom to act on information even as it increases the highly personalistic quest for knowledge and association.[34]

Regularity and variation, which in other societies may exist at the level of social-group relations, the rituals of group dynamics, or the careful distribution of economic or ecological resources, resides, for the Sefrou people, in the shared modes of interpretation, the recognizable forms by which individual effort precipitates personal associations. Words, being tools, must inevitably be used in contradictory ways; judgments, both personal and legal, may arrive at different points notwithstanding common facts. It is in the shared process of negotiating meaning that the unifying element resides, an element that retains its tensive, dynamic quality by itself being open and malleable. The ability to bargain with and through the verbal repertoire is highly valued. Indeed, it may be argued, this is one reason why poets are so important in the societies of the Middle East. For it is the poet, the master of words, who probes the bounds of

---

34. On action as "open work," see Ricoeur 1971. See also the discussion of Wittgenstein's approach to this issue in Pitkin 1972, 85–93, and the discussion of Arab personalism and language in Lahbabi 1964.

meaning, who tries to make the meaning of a word carry relational implications that no one has previously or so effectively attached to them. It is he who can use a word in such a way that others may conceive relationships in its terms. The capacity to capture a word's meaning is not restricted to poets. It is often noted by Arabs who grew up in Egypt in the days of Nasser that he would use words in such a way that no one could use them again without invoking the connotations he attached to them—rather like, for an American of the times, being unable to hear the *William Tell* Overture without conjuring up visions of the Lone Ranger. Each person, in probing the limits of words, can be a poet of reality—a creator of the meanings, the impact on relationships, that such concepts effect. Whether it is the old Haj bargaining with the mother over the meaning of terms applicable to the marriage proposed for her daughter or my friend negotiating over the meaning of haqq versus fabor as applied to the countryman's invitation for tea, the issue is the same: individuals may probe the limits of language not for its own sake but for its very pragmatic importance to relationships that may be conceived in its terms.

Yet if negotiation of relationships, and hence of their view of reality, is indeed so central for the Sefrou people, are there no limits to what may be negotiated? Do people actually create their relationships anew at each moment, or, in fact, do they not usually accept the circumstances and attachments presented them in routine fashion? To these questions the answer must surely be that convention and creation are by no means mutually exclusive and that in the particular case of Sefrou the broad range of negotiable leeway is itself an integral part of the effective implementation of routinized affiliation. This is not to say that one's freedom to negotiate is without religious or institutional constraint. The outer boundary is divinely established. "These are the limits of God" the Quran repeatedly asserts, and the prescribed limits, the haqq of Allah, is clearly defined. Within these limits, however, lie the haqq of man—the stipulations, conditions, provisions, and terms that people are free, through discourse and tactic, to forge for themselves. One could imagine, therefore, that the Moroccan who had become enamored of Wittgensteinian philosophy might very well maintain that the limits of *God's* language are the limits of *my* world.[35] And whereas in some other societies the exercise of choice—picking a mate from one lineage or another, engaging in the range of social options each individual is afforded, in Sefrou the consequence of any decision is not to place one in a particular slot in that society—

35. The reference, of course, is to Wittgenstein's statement (1958, para. 5.6) that "*the limits of my language* mean the limits of my world." As Martland (1975, 20) explains: "To assert that the limits of my language mean the limits of my world is to assert that language is not a coat or map which we make to fit some previously established limit but that it is an activity which is bound up with the development of these limits themselves." Perhaps in this sense it may be said that it is through the interaction of the "limits of God" and the "rights of man" that the Muslim achieves his own limits.

a role or status that subsequently orders one's relationships—but to add yet one more personalistic feature that will enable, rather than reduce, yet more negotiated ties. The multiplicity of names by which men and women may be known proclaims this malleability; the concept of humanity as situated in discrete units of time and circumstance sustains this flexibility. What may appear, therefore, as the simple replication of the acts and ties of another person, another generation, or another group are, at base, acts of creation that are as contingent on the conventions from which they are cast up as they are constitutive of the acts that give social regularity its life.

Faced, as each person is, by a world threatened by chaos yet ordered by the customs through which relationships may be formed, the Sefrawi must acquire knowledge not of rules but of cases, a synoptic view, an overview, of the range of combinations in which person, situation, background, and nature may cohere into discrete instances. In Sefrou society one cannot know if a grouping will be precipitated until it actually is; one cannot expect an attachment to maintain itself without the constant attention of those for whom it forms an element of personal identity. Intent and consequence may be incomprehensible without the conventions that surround and suffuse them, but security and certainty, beyond that which God delimits, remain as elusive for those whose lives are ordered by these concepts as for those who seek to comprehend them. One is confronted in Sefrou society with a kind of indeterminacy in which social forms take shape from a process of negotiation whose own terms acquire meaning only as the relationships formed through them are bargained out. To contain this process in a set of rule-like propositions is not, then, the pursuit of unpalatable formalism: it is a radical misapprehension of the nature of the subject. For just as in mathematics where various limitative proofs have shown that no set of rules can be constructed to account for the actual range of mathematical and logical possibilities, so, too, in Sefrou society a driving force of the culture, the negotiation of relations, is illimitable and indeterminable. Like the people of Sefrou itself, the world we study is not disordered for being open, nor incomprehensible for being free.

There is, of course, no one feature of a culture that can adequately represent the whole. Yet if a single image can suggest the range and vitality of Moroccan social life, it might be found in that archetypal Moorish form, the arabesque. Simple in concept yet elaborate in design, its draped arcades, hedged round by divine oration, describe a model of regularity and certitude, and, at the same time, a template for contingency and contrariety. For those who partake of it, it is a labyrinthian world and an exacting one. And if, like those for whom this world is manifestly real, we are sensitive enough to glimpse its general shape and clever enough to contrive the outline of its course, we ourselves may not remain unchanged simply for having tried to embrace and understand it.

References

Abdel-Massih, Ernest J. 1970. *A course in Moroccan Arabic*. Ann Arbor: University of Michigan, Center for Near Eastern and North African Studies.

Abitol, Amor ben Solomon. 1950. *Minhat ha-ʿomer*. Ed. David Obadia. Djerba, Tunisia: Bouâz Haddad Imprimerie Librairie.

Abu-Lughod, Janet L. 1980. *Rabat: Urban apartheid in Morocco*. Princeton: Princeton University Press.

Adam, André. 1949–50. Le "Bidonville" de Ben M'sik à Casablanca. *Annales de l'Institut d'études orientales* 8:61–198.

———. 1972. *Casablanca*. 2 vols. Paris: Editions du Centre National de la Recherche Scientifique.

Al Amin, Ahmed. 1968. L'évolution de la femme et le problème du mariage au Maroc. *Présence africaine* 68:32–51.

Arberry, Arthur J. 1964. *The Koran interpreted*. London: Oxford University Press.

Aubin, Eugène. 1908. *Le Maroc d'aujourd'hui*. Paris: Librairie Armand Colin.

Auerbach, Erich. 1953. *Mimesis: The representation of reality in Western Literature*. Princeton: Princeton University Press.

Austin, J. L. 1961. Other minds. In *Philosophical papers, 44–48. Oxford: Oxford University Press.*

———. 1965. *How to do things with words*. New York: Oxford University Press.

———. 1971. Performative-constative. In *The philosophy of language*, ed. J. R. Searle, 13–22. Oxford: Oxford University Press.

Barrett, William. 1979. *The illusion of technique*. New York: Anchor Press.

Bell, Daniel. 1966. Sociodicy: A guide to modern usage. *American Scholar* 35:696–714.

Benhalima, Hassan. 1977a. L'Artisanat traditionnel sefrioui: Son agonie et les limites de sa renovation. *Révue de géographie du Maroc*, no. 1:41–51.

———. 1977b. Sefrou: De la tradition du dir à l'integration economique moderne. 2 vols. Thèse Doctoral de 3ème Cycle, Université Paul Valery–Montpelier III.

Berger, Peter, and Hansfried Kellner. 1964. Marriage and the construction of reality. *Diogenes* 46:1–24.

Berger, Peter L., and Thomas Luckmann. 1966. *The social construction of reality.* New York: Doubleday & Co.

Bernstein, Basil. 1964. Elaborated and restricted codes: Their social origins and some consequences. *American Anthropologist* 66 (no. 6, pt. 2):55–69.

———. 1965. A socio-linguistic approach to social learning. In *Penguin survey of the social sciences, 1965.* Baltimore: Penguin Books.

Berque, Jacques. 1955. *Structures sociales du Haut-Atlas.* Paris: Presses Universitaires de France.

———. 1958. *Al-Yousi: Problèmes de la culture marocaine au XVIIème siècle.* The Hague: Mouton & Co.

———. 1974. *Maghreb, histoire, et sociétés.* Gembloux, Belgium: J. Duculot; Algiers: S.N.E.D.

———. 1978. *Cultural expression in Arab society today.* Austin: University of Texas Press.

Berque, Jacques, and Jean-Paul Charnay. 1967. *L'Ambivalence dans la culture arabe.* Paris: Editions Anthropos.

Biarnay, S. 1924. *Notes d'ethnographie et de linguistique nord-africaines.* Paris: Editions Ernest Leroux.

Bilmes, Jack. 1976. Rules and rhetoric: Negotiating the social order in a Thai village. *Journal of Anthropological Research* 32:44–57.

Black, Max. 1968. *The labyrinth of language.* New York: New American Library.

Blum, Allan F., and Peter McHugh. 1971. The social ascription of motives. *Sociological Review* 36:98–109.

Bok, Sissela. 1978. *Lying: Moral choice in public and private life.* New York: Random House.

Bouanani, Ahmed. 1966. Introduction à la poésie populaire marocaine. *Souffles,* no. 3:3–9.

Boudjedra, Rachid. 1969. *La répudiation.* Paris: Denoël.

Boukous, Ahmed. 1977. *Langage et cultures populaires au Maroc.* Casablanca: Imprimeries Dar El-Kitab.

Bourdieu, Pierre. 1962. *The Algerians.* Boston: Beacon Press.

———. 1966. The sentiment of honour in Kabyle society. In *Honour and shame: The values of Mediterranean society,* ed. J. G. Peristiany, 193–241. Chicago: University of Chicago Press.

———. 1977. *Outline of a theory of practice.* Cambridge: Cambridge University Press.

Bourgeois, Paul. 1959–60. *L'Univers de l'écolier marocain.* Fasicles 1–5. Rabat: Ministère de l'education national de la jeunesse et des sports, Faculté des lettres et des sciences sociales.

Bowie, Leland. 1970. *The impact of the protegé system in Morocco, 1880–1912.* Papers in International Studies, African Series No. 11. Athens, Ohio: Ohio University Center for International Studies.

———. 1976. An aspect of Muslim-Jewish relations in late nineteenth century Morocco: A European diplomatic view. *International Journal of Middle East Studies* 7:3–19.

Bowles, Paul. 1963. *Their heads are green and their hands are blue.* New York: Random House.

―――. 1982. *The spider's house.* Santa Barbara: Black Sparrow Press.

Bravmann, M. M. 1971. The expression of instantaneousness in Arabic. *Le Muséon* (Louvain):449–523.

―――. 1972. *The spiritual background of early Islam.* Leiden: E. J. Brill.

Breton, Hubert. 1963. Elections professionnelles et locales marocaines. In *Annuaire de l'Afrique du Nord II, 1963,* 107–18. Paris: Centre Nationale de la Recherche Scientifique.

Broms, Henri. 1972. *How does the Middle Eastern literary taste differ from the European?* Edidit Societas Orientalis Fennica 44. Helsinki: Studia Orientalia.

Brown, Kenneth L. 1976. *People of Salé: Tradition and change in a Moroccan city, 1830–1930.* Cambridge: Harvard University Press.

―――. 1977. Changing forms of patronage in a Moroccan city. In *Patrons and Clients in Mediterranean Societies,* ed. Ernest Gellner and John Waterbury, 307–28. London: Duckworth.

―――. 1980. Une ville et son mellah: Salé (1880–1930). In *Juifs du Maroc,* 187–99. Colloque international sur la communauté juive marocaine: vie culturelle, histoire sociale et évolution. Paris: Editions La Pensée Sauvage.

―――. 1982. The "Curse" of Westermarck. In *Edward Westermarck: Essays on his life and works,* ed. Timothy Stroup, 34:219–59. Helsinki: Acta Philosophica Fennica.

Brown, Leon Carl, ed. 1966. *State and society in independent North Africa.* Washington: Middle East Institute.

Brunot, Louis. 1918. Cultes naturistes à Sefrou. *Archives berbères* 3:137–43.

―――. 1931. *Textes arabes de Rabat.* Vol. 1, *Textes, transcripts, et traduction annotée.* Paris: Librairie Orientaliste Paul Geuthner.

―――. 1952. *Textes arabes de Rabat.* Vol. 2, *Glossaire.* Paris: Librairie Orientaliste Paul Geuthner.

Brunschvig, Robert. 1960. Le système de la preuve en droit musulman. *Recueil de la Société Jean Bodin pour l'histoire comparative des institutions* 18:169–86.

Burke, Edmund. 1972. The image of the Moroccan state in French ethnological literature: A new look at the origin of Lyautey's Berber policy. In *Arabs and Berbers: From tribe to nation in North Africa,* ed. Ernest Gellner and Charles Micaud, 175–200. Boston: D. C. Heath.

Burke, Kenneth. 1945. *A grammar of motives.* Berkeley: University of California Press.

―――. 1957. *The philosophy of literary form.* New York: Vintage Books.

―――. 1965. *Permanence and change.* Indianapolis: Bobbs-Merrill.

Caix, Robert de. 1913. La population du Maroc. *L'Afrique française* 23:179–82.

Calverley, E. E. 1943. Doctrines of the soul (*nafs* and *rūḥ*) in Islam. *Moslem World* 33:254–64.

―――. 1965. Ḥaḳḳ. In *Encyclopedia of Islam* 3:82–83. New ed. Leiden: E. J. Brill.

Centre National de la Recherche Scientifique. 1980. *Les relations entre juifs et musulmans en Afrique du Nord, XIXe–XXe siecles.* Paris: Editions du Centre National de la Recherche Scientifique.

Cerych. Ladislaw. 1964. *Européens et marocains, 1930–1956: Sociologie d'une décolonisation*. Bruges: De Tempel.

Chaoui, Mohamed. 1978. Sefrou: De la tradition à l'integration, ce qu'est un petit centre d'aujourd'hui. *Lamalif*, no. 99:32–39.

Charhadi, Driss ben Hamed. 1964. *A life full of holes*. Trans. by Paul Bowles. New York: Grove Press.

Chelhod, Joseph. 1955. *Le sacrifice chez les arabes*. Paris: Presses Universitaires de France.

Chenier, Louis Saveur de. 1788. *The present state of the empire of Morocco*. London: G. G. J. and J. Robinson.

Chiapuris, John. 1979. *The Ait Ayash of the High Moulouya Plain: Rural social organization in Morocco*. Museum of Anthropology Anthropological Papers, no. 69. Ann Arbor: University of Michigan.

Chouraqui, André N. 1950. *La condition juridique de l'israélite marocain*. Paris: Presses du Livre Français.

———. 1965. *Les juifs d'Afrique du Nord entre l'Orient et l'Occident*. Series G, Etudes Maghrebines no. 5. Paris: Fondation Nationale des Sciences Politiques.

———. 1968. *Between East and West: A history of the Jews of North Africa*. Philadelphia: Jewish Publication Society of America.

Cohen, David. 1975. *Le parler arabe des juifs de Tunis*. Vol. 2. *Etude linguistique*. The Hague and Paris: Mouton.

Colin, Georges S. 1920. Notes sur le parler arabe du nord de la région de Taza. *Bulletin de l'Institut français d'archéologie orientale* 18:33–119.

Comaroff, John L., and Simon Roberts. 1981. *Rules and processes: The cultural logic of dispute in an African context*. Chicago: University of Chicago Press.

Corcos, David. 1976. *Studies in the history of the Jews of Morocco*. Jerusalem: Rubin Mass.

Cragg, Kenneth. 1965. *Counsels in contemporary Islam*. Edinburgh: Edinburgh University Press.

Crapanzano, Vincent. 1973. *The Hamadsha: A study in Moroccan ethnopsychiatry*. Berkeley: University of California Press.

———. 1980. *Tuhami: Portrait of a Moroecan*. Chicago: University of Chicago Press.

Cuisenier, Jean. 1962. Endogamie et exogamie dans le mariage arabe. *L'Homme* 2:80–105.

Deshen, Shlomo, and Walter P. Zenner, eds. 1982. *Jewish societies in the Middle East*. Washington, D.C.: University Press of America.

Dewey, John. 1924. Logical method and law. *Cornell Law Quarterly* 10:17–27.

Dominguez, Virginia R. 1977. Social classification in Creole Louisiana. *American Ethnologist* 4:589–602.

Donaldson, D. M. 1943. Truth and falsehood in Islam. *Moslem World* 33:276–85.

Doutté, Edouard. 1901. Une mission d'études au Maroc: Rapport sommaire d'ensemble. *Renseignements coloniaux, supplement au bulletin du comité de l'Afrique française* 8:161–78.

Drouin, Jeannine. 1975. *Un cycle oral hagiographique dans le Moyen-Atlas marocain*. Paris: Publications de la Sorbonne, Imprimerie Nationale.

Duquaire, Henri. 1943. *Anthologie de la littérature marocaine*. Casablanca: Plon.

Dwyer, Daisy Hilse. 1978. *Images and self-images: Male and female in Morocco.* New York: Columbia University Press.

Dwyer, Kevin. 1982. *Moroccan dialogues: Anthropology in question.* Baltimore: Johns Hopkins University Press.

Eickelman, Dale F. 1976. *Moroccan Islam.* Austin: University of Texas Press.

———. 1977. Time in a complex society: A Moroccan example. *Ethnology* 16:39–55.

———. 1978. The art of memory: Islamic education and its social reproduction. *Comparative Studies in Society and History* 20:485–516.

Les élections communales du 21/11/76. 1977. In *Annuaire de l'Afrique du Nord XV, 1976,* 870–79. Paris: Editions du Centre National de la Recherche Scientifique.

Emerson, Joan. 1969. Negotiating the serious import of humor. *Sociometry* 32:169–81.

Errington, Shelly. 1979. Some comments on style in the meanings of the past. *Journal of Asian Studies* 38:231–44.

Ezorsky, Gertrude. 1967. Pragmatic theory of truth. In *The encyclopedia of philosophy,* ed. Paul Edwards, 6:427–30. New York: Macmillan.

Fallers, Lloyd A. 1969. *Law without precedent.* Chicago: University of Chicago Press.

Fingarette, Herbert. 1967. Performatives. *American Philosophical Quarterly* 4:39–48.

Fish, Stanley. 1980. *Is there a text in this class?* Cambridge: Harvard University Press.

Forbes, Rosita. 1924. *El Raisuni: The sultan of the mountains.* London: Thornton Butterworth.

Foster, George M. 1961. The dyadic contract: A model for the social structure of a Mexican peasant village. *American Anthropologist* 63:1173–92.

———. 1963. The dyadic contract in Tzintzuntzan, II: Patron-client relationship. *American Anthropologist* 65:1280–94.

Foucauld, Charles de. 1888. *Reconnaissance au Maroc, 1883–1884.* Paris: Challamel.

Fränkel, Hermann F. 1973. *Early Greek poetry and philosophy.* New York: Harcourt Brace Jovanovich.

Gallagher, Charles F. 1966. Language and identity. In *State and society in independent North Africa,* ed. Leon Carl Brown, 73–96. Washington, D.C.: Middle East Institute.

Gallie, W. B. 1968. *Philosophy and the historical understanding.* New York: Schocken Books.

Gardet, Louis. 1967. *Dieu et la destinée de l'homme.* Paris: Librairie Philosophique J. Vrin.

———. 1976. Moslem views of time and history. In *Cultures and time,* ed. L. Gardet et al., 197–227. Paris: Unesco Press.

———. 1977. The Prophet. In *Time and the philosophies,* ed. H. Aguessy, 197–209. Paris: Unesco Press.

Geach, P. T. 1967. Ascriptivism. In *The linguistic turn,* ed. Richard Rorty, 224–26. Chicago: University of Chicago Press.

Geertz, Clifford. 1968. *Islam observed.* New Haven: Yale University Press.

———. 1973. *The interpretation of cultures.* New York: Basic Books.

———. 1976. "From the native's point of view": On the nature of anthropological understanding. In *Meaning in anthropology*, ed. Keith Basso and Henry A. Selby, 221–37. Albuquerque: University of New Mexico Press.

———. 1979. Suq: The bazaar economy of Sefrou. In *Meaning and order in Moroccan society*, 123–313. *See* Geertz, Geertz, and Rosen 1979.

———. 1983. *Local knowledge*. New York: Basic Books.

Geertz, Clifford, Hildred Geertz, and Lawrence Rosen. 1979. *Meaning and order in Moroccan society*. New York: Cambridge University Press.

Geertz, Hildred. 1979a. The meaning of family ties. In *Meaning and order in Moroccan society*, 315–91. *See* Geertz, Geertz, and Rosen 1979.

———. 1979b. A statistical profile of the population of the town of Sefrou in 1960. In *Meaning and Order in Moroccan Society*, 393–506. *See* Geertz, Geertz, and Rosen 1979.

Gellner, Ernest. 1969. *Saints of the atlas*. Chicago: University of Chicago Press.

———. 1974. *Contemporary thought and politics*. London: Routledge & Kegan Paul.

———. 1981. *Muslim society*. Cambridge: Cambridge University Press.

Gerber, Jane S. 1980. *Jewish society in Fez, 1450–1700: Studies in communal and economic life*. Leiden: E. J. Brill.

Gerhardt, Mia I. 1963. *The art of story-telling: A literary study of the "Thousand and One Nights."* Leiden: E. J. Brill.

Ghallab, Said. 1965. Les juifs vont en enfer. *Les temps modernes*, no. 229:2247–55.

Gibb, H. A. R., and J. H. Kramers, eds. 1961. *Shorter encyclopaedia of Islam*. Leiden: E. J. Brill.

Gilsenan, Michael. 1976. Lying, honor, and contradiction. In *Transaction and meaning*, ed. Bruce Kapferer, 191–219. Philadelphia: Institute for the Study of Human Issues.

———. 1982. *Recognizing Islam: Religion and society in the modern Arab world*. New York: Pantheon Books.

Gittes, Katherine Slater. 1983. The *Canterbury Tales* and the Arabic frame tradition. *PMLA* (Publications of the Modern Language Association) 98:237–51,

Gluckman, Max. 1965. *The ideas in Barotse jurisprudence*. New Haven: Yale University Press.

Goitein, S. D. 1955. *Jews and Arabs*. New York: Schocken Books.

———. 1967–78. *A Mediterranean society*. 3 vols. Berkeley: University of California Press.

———. 1977. Individualism and conformity in classical Islam. In *Individualism and conformity in classical Islam*, ed. Amin Banani and Speros Vryonis, 3–18. Wiesbaden: Otto Harrassowitz.

Goldberg, Harvey E., ed. 1980. *The book of Mordechai: A study of the Jews of Libya. Selections from the "Highid Mordekhai" of Mordechai Hakohen*. Philadelphia: Institute for the Study of Human Issues.

Grice, H. Paul. 1957. Meaning. *Philosophical Review* 66:337–88.

———. 1975. Logic and Conversation. In *Syntax and semantics*, vol. 3, *Speech acts*, ed. Peter Cole and Jerry L. Morgan, 41–58. New York: Academic Press.

———. 1978. Further notes on logic and conversation. In *Syntax and semantics*, vol. 9, *Pragmatics*, ed. Peter Cole, 113–28. New York: Academic Press.

Grunebaum, Gustave E. von. 1953. *Medieval Islam*. Chicago: University of Chicago Press.

Halstead, John P. 1967. *Rebirth of a nation: The origins and rise of Moroccan nationalism, 1912–1944*. Middle East Monograph Series. Cambridge: Harvard Middle East Center.

Harrell, Richard S. 1962. *A short reference grammar of Moroccan Arabic*. Washington, D.C.: Georgetown University Press.

———. 1965. *A basic course in Moroccan Arabic*. Washington, D.C.: Georgetown University Press.

———. 1966. *A dictionary of Moroccan Arabic: Moroccan-English*. Washington, D.C.: Georgetown University Press.

Hart, David Montgomery. 1976. *The Aith Waryaghar of the Moroccan Rif*. Tucson: University of Arizona Press.

———. 1981. *Dadda ʿAtta and his forty grandsons: The socio-political organisation of the Ait ʿAtta of southern Morocco*. Cambridge: Middle East and North African Studies Press.

Hartnack, Justus. 1967. Performative utterances. In *Encyclopedia of philosophy*, ed. Paul Edwards, 6:90–92. New York: Macmillan.

Hasnaoui, Ahmed. 1977. Certain notions of time in Arab-Muslim philosophy. In *Time and the philosophies*, ed. H. Aguessy, 49–79. Paris: Unesco Press.

Hassan II. 1965. Proclamation de l'état d'exception. In *Annuaire de l'Afrique du Nord, IV, 1965*, 695–698. Paris: Editions du Centre National de la Recherche Scientifique.

Heffening, W. 1961. S̲h̲ahid. In *Shorter encyclopaedia of Islam*, 517–18. *See* Gibb and Kramers 1961.

Hertzberg, Arthur. 1970. *The French enlightenment and the Jews*. New York: Schocken Books.

Hirschberg, H. Z. 1963. The problem of the Judaized Berbers. *Journal of African History* 4:313–39.

———. 1981. *A history of the Jews in North Africa*. Vol. 2. *From the Ottoman conquests to the present time*. Leiden: E. J. Brill.

Houston, J. 1970. Truth valuation of explicit performatives. *Philosophical Quarterly* 20:139–49.

Hungerland, Isabel C. 1960. Contextual implication. *Inquiry* 3:211–58.

Institut des hautes etudes marocaines. 1945. *Initiation au Maroc*. Paris: Vanoest.

Izutsu, Toshihiko. 1964. *God and man in the Koran*. Tokyo: Keio Institute of Cultural and Linguistic Studies.

———. 1966. *Ethico-religious concepts of the Qurʾān*. Montreal: McGill University Press.

Jacobsen, Klaus H. 1971. How to make the distinction between constative and performative utterances. *Philosophical Quarterly* 21:357–60.

James, Henry. 1905. *The question of our speech*. Boston: Houghton Mifflin.

Jamous, Raymond. 1981. *Honneur et baraka: Les structures sociales traditionnelles dans le Rif*. Cambridge/Paris: Cambridge University Press/Editions de la Maison des Sciences de l'Homme.

Juynboll, T. W. 1961a. ʿAd̲h̲āb. In *Shorter encyclopaedia of Islam*, 15–16. *See* Gibb and Kramers 1961.

————. 1961b. Ḥadīth. In *Shorter encyclopaedia of Islam,* 116–21. *See* Gibb and Kramers 1961.

Keddie, Nikki. 1963. Sincerity and symbol in Islam. *Studia Islamica* 19:27–63.

Kekes, John. 1977. Essentially contested concepts: A reconsideration. *Philosophy and Rhetoric* 10:71–89.

Khatibi, Abdelkebir. 1976. Jacques Berque ou la saveur orientale. *Les Temps modernes* 31 (no. 359):2158–81.

Khuri, Fuad I. 1970. Parallel cousin marriage reconsidered. *Man* 5:597–618.

Kister, M. J. 1965. "God will never disgrace thee": The interpretation of an early Ḥadīth. *Journal of the Royal Asiatic Society of Great Britain and Ireland,* series 3, pts. 1 and 2:27–32.

Kluckhohn, Clyde. 1949. *Mirror for man.* New York: McGraw Hill.

Lacouture, Jean, and Simonne Lacouture. 1958. *Le Maroc à l'épreuve.* Paris: Editions du Seuil.

Lahbabi, Mohamed Aziz. 1964. *Le personalisme musulman.* Paris: Presses Universitaires de France.

Lamghili, Ahmed el Kohen. 1976. La "Boulitique" d'une élection. *Lamalif,* no. 84:32–35.

Lanigan, Richard L. 1977. *Speech act phenomenology.* The Hague: Martinus Nijhoff.

Lapanne-Joinville, J. 1957. Etudes de droit musulman malékite: Les présomptions. *Révue algerienne, tunisienne, et marocaine de legislation et de jurisprudence* 73 (no. 4):99–113.

Laroui, Abdallah. 1977. *The history of the Maghrib.* Princeton: Princeton University Press.

Laskier, Michael M. 1983. *The Alliance Israélite Universelle and the Jewish Communities of Morocco, 1862–1980.* Albany: State University of New York Press.

Lehman, F. K. 1967. Ethnic categories in Burma and the theory of social systems. In *Southeast Asian tribes, minorities, and nations* 1:93–124. Princeton: Princeton University Press.

Lesne, Marcel. 1959. Histoire d'un groupement berbère, les Zemmour. Thèse complémentaire pour le doctorat ès lettres présentée à la Faculté des Lettres et Sciences Humaines de Paris.

Levy, Reuben. 1962. *The social structure of Islam.* Cambridge: Cambridge University Press.

Lévy-Corcos, Joël. 1968. Y a-t-il un problème juif au Maroc? *Lamalif,* no. 21:10–18.

Lewis, Bernard. 1970. *Race and color in Islam.* New York: Harper & Row.

————. 1974. *Islam.* Vol. 2. *Religion and society.* New York: Harper & Row.

————. 1980. Translating from Arabic. *Proceedings of the American Philosophical Society* 124:41–47.

Liebesny, Herbert J. 1975. *The law of the Near and Middle East.* Albany: State University of New York Press.

Llewellyn, Karl N., and E. Adamson Hoebel. 1941. *The Cheyenne way: Conflict and case law in primitive jurisprudence.* Norman: University of Oklahoma Press.

Loubignac, Victorien. 1952. *Textes arabes des Zaër.* Paris: Librairie Orientale et Américaine Max Besson.

Macdonald, D. B. 1961a. Ḥaḳḳ. In *Shorter encyclopaedia of Islam*, 126–27. *See* Gibb and Kramers 1961.

———. 1961b. Ḥāl. In *Shorter encyclopaedia of Islam*, 127. *See* Gibb and Kramers 1961.

McHugh, Peter. 1968. *Defining the situation: The organization of meaning in social interaction*. Indianapolis: Bobbs-Merrill.

Mahdi, Muhsin. 1957. *Ibn Khaldûn's philosophy of history*. Chicago: University of Chicago Press.

Maher, Vanessa. 1974. *Women and property in Morocco*. Cambridge: Cambridge University Press.

———. 1978. Women and social change in Morocco. In *Women in the Muslim world*, ed. Lois Beck and Nikki Keddie, 100–123. Cambridge: Harvard University Press.

Malka, Victor. 1978. *La mémoire brisée des juifs du Maroc*. Paris: Editions Entente.

Marçais, Ph. 1977. *Esquisse grammaticale de l'arabe maghrébin*. Paris: Librairie d'Amérique et d'Orient.

Marçais, W. 1911. *Textes arabes de Tanger*. Paris: Imprimerie Nationale.

Martland, T. R. 1975. On "The limits of my language mean the limits of my world." *Review of Metaphysics* 29:19–26.

Mas, Marie. 1959–62. La petite enfance à Fès et à Rabat: Etude de sociologie citadine. *Annales de l'Institut d'etudes orientales* 17:1–144; 18–19:167–275; 20:277–400.

Massignon, Louis. 1952. Le temps dans la pensée islamique. In *Eranos-Jahrbuch, 1951*, 20:141–48. Zurich: Rhein-Verlag.

———. 1968. *Essai sur les origines du lexique technique de la mystique musulmane*. 3d ed. Paris: Librairie Philosophique J. Vrin.

Mayer, Philip. 1950. Privileged obstruction of marriage among the Gusii. *Africa* 20:113–25.

Mead, George Herbert. 1956. *On social psychology: Selected papers*. Chicago: University of Chicago Press.

Meeker, Michael E. 1979. *Literature and violence in North Arabia*. Cambridge: Cambridge University Press.

Meredith, George. 1956. *An essay on comedy*. New York: Doubleday.

Mernissi, Fatima. 1975. *Beyond the veil: Male-Female dynamics in a modern Muslim society*. New York: John Wiley and Sons.

Meyer, Leonard B. 1956. *Emotion and meaning in music*. Chicago: University of Chicago Press.

———. 1967. *Music, the arts, and ideas*. Chicago: University of Chicago Press.

Meyers, Allen R. 1982. Patronage and protection: The status of Jews in precolonial Morocco. In *Jewish societies in the Middle East*, ed. Shlomo Deshen and Walter P. Zenner, 85–104. Washington, D.C.: University Press of America.

Meziane, Abdelmajid. 1976. The empirical apperception of time among the peoples of the Maghreb. In *Cultures and time*, ed. L. Gardet, 214–27. Paris: Unesco Press.

Michon, Jean-Louis. 1973. *Le soufi marocain Aḥmad Ibn ʿAjība et son miʿrāj: Glossaire de la mystique musulmane*. Paris: Librairie Philosophique J. Vrin.

Milliot, Louis. 1953. *Introduction à l'étude du droit musulman*. Paris: Sirey.

Mills, C. Wright. 1940. Situated actions and vocabularies of motive. *American Sociological Review* 5:904–13.

Milson, Menahem. 1967. Tāhā Ḥusayn's "The Tree of Misery": A literary expression of cultural change. *Asian and African Studies* 3:69–99.

Monteil, Vincent. 1964. *Morocco*. London: Vista Books.

Moore, Sally Falk. 1978. *Law as process: An anthropological approach*. London: Routledge & Kegan Paul.

Mottahedeh, Roy P. 1980. *Loyalty and leadership in an early Islamic society*. Princeton: Princeton University Press.

Mounir, Samira. 1971. Le recensement de 1971. *Lamalif*, no. 51:12–13.

Murphy, Robert F., and Leonard Kasdan. 1959. The structure of parallel cousin marriage. *American Anthropologist* 61:17–29.

Nisbet, Robert A. 1969. *Social change and history: Aspects of the Western theory of development*. Oxford: Oxford University Press.

Noin, Daniel. 1970. *La population rurale du Maroc*. 2 vols. Paris: Presses Universitaires de France.

Noy, Dov. 1966. *Moroccan Jewish folktales*. New York: Herzl Press.

O'Shaughnessy, Thomas J. 1971. Creation with wisdom and with the word in the Qur'ān. *Journal of the American Oriental Society* 91:208–21.

Patai, Raphael. 1976. *The Arab mind*. New York: Charles Scribner's.

Pedersen, J. 1961. Ḳasam. In *Shorter encyclopaedia of Islam*, 224–26. *See* Gibb and Kramers 1961.

Pellat, Charles. 1955. *Textes berbères dans le parler des Ait Seghrouchen de la Moulouya*. Paris: Larose.

———. 1970. ʿĀr. In *Encyclopedia of Islam: New Edition, Supplement*, 78–80. Leiden: E. J. Brill.

Percy, Walker. 1976. *The message in the bottle*. New York: Farrar, Strauss, and Giroux.

Périgny, Maurice. 1917. *Au Maroc: Fès, la capital du nord*. Paris: P. Roger et Cie.

Pitkin, Hanna Fenichel. 1972. *Wittgenstein and justice*. Berkeley: University of California Press.

Quinton, A. M. 1966. Contemporary British philosophy. In *Wittgenstein: The philosophical investigations*. New York: Anchor Books.

Raban, Jonathan. 1979. *Arabia: Journey through the labyrinth*. New York: Simon and Schuster.

Rabinow, Paul. 1975. *Symbolic domination: Cultural form and historical change in Morocco*. Chicago: University of Chicago Press.

———. 1977. *Reflections on fieldwork in Morocco*. Berkeley: University of California Press.

Radi, Abdelwahad. 1969. Processus de socialisation de l'enfant marocain. *Etudes philosophiques et litteraires*, no. 4:37–51.

Ricoeur, Paul. 1971. The model of the text: Meaningful action considered as a text. *Social Research* 38:529–62.

———. 1981. Narrative time. In *On narrative*, ed. W. J. T. Mitchell, 165–86. Chicago: University of Chicago Press.

Rorty, Richard. 1979. *Philosophy and the mirror of nature*. Princeton: Princeton University Press.

Rosen, Lawrence. 1968a. A Moroccan Jewish community during the Middle East crisis. *American Scholar* 37:435–51.

———. 1968b. The structure of social groups in a Moroccan city. Ph.D. diss., University of Chicago.

———. 1970. "I divorce thee": Moroccan marriage and the law. *Trans-action* 7:34–37.

———. 1972a. Muslim-Jewish relations in a Moroccan city. *International Journal of Middle East Studies* 3:435–49.

———. 1972b. Rural political process and national political structure in Morocco. In *Rural politics and social change in the Middle East*, ed. Richard T. Antoun and Iliya Harik, 214–36. Bloomington: Indiana University Press.

———. 1973. The social and conceptual framework of Arab-Berber relations in central Morocco. In *Arabs and Berbers: From tribe to nation in North Africa*, ed. Ernest Gellner and Charles Micaud, 155–73. London: Gerald Duckworth.

———. 1978. The negotiation of reality: Male-Female relations in Sefrou, Morocco. In *Women in the Muslim World*, 561–84. *See* Maher 1978.

———. 1979. Social identity and points of attachment: Approaches to social organization. In *Meaning and order in Moroccan society*, 19–122. *See* Geertz, Geertz, and Rosen 1979.

———. 1980–81. Equity and discretion in a modern Islamic legal system. *Law and Society Review* 15:217–45.

———. 1985. Intentionality and the concept of the person. In *The theory of criminal justice*, NOMOS 27, ed. J. R. Pennock and J. Chapman. New York: New York University Press.

Rosenthal, Franz. 1966. Muslim definitions of knowledge. In *The conflict of traditionalism and modernism in the Muslim Middle East*, ed. Carl Leiden, 117–33. Austin: University of Texas.

———. 1970. *Knowledge triumphant: The concept of knowledge in medieval Islam.* Leiden: E. J. Brill.

Royaume du Maroc. Secrétariat d'Etat au Plan et au Développement Régional. 1971a. *Population legale du Maroc.* Rabat: Direction de la Statistique.

———. 1971b. *Population rurale, region du centre nord.* Rabat: Direction de la Statistique.

———. 1973. *La consommation et les depenses des ménages au Maroc, avril 1970–1971.* Vol. 1, *Premiers resultats à l'echelon national.* Rabat: Direction de la Statistique.

———. 1977. *Recensement general de la population et de l'habitat de 1971: Données communales.* Rabat: Direction de la Statistique.

Ryle, Gilbert. 1949. *The concept of mind.* New York: Barnes & Noble.

Sandler, R. 1976. The changing concept of the individual. In *Introduction to Islamic civilisation*, ed. R. M. Savory, 137–45. Cambridge: Cambridge University Press.

Santucci, J.-C. 1978. Les elections législatives marocaines de juin 1977. In *Annuaire de l'Afrique du Nord, XVI, 1977*, 215–42. Paris: Editions du Centre National de la Recherche Scientifique.

Schacht, Joseph. 1961a. Ḳatl. In *Shorter encyclopaedia of Islam*, 227–31. *See* Gibb and Kramers 1961.

————. 1961b. Khata'. In *Shorter encyclopaedia of Islam,* 249–50. *See* Gibb and Kramers 1961.

————. 1961c. Ḳiṣāṣ. In *Shorter encyclopaedia of Islam,* 261–63. *See* Gibb and Kramers 1961.

————. 1961d. Sharīʿa. In *Shorter encyclopaedia of Islam,* 524–29. *See* Gibb and Kramers 1961.

————. 1964. *An introduction to Islamic law.* Oxford: Clarendon Press.

Scham, Alan. 1970. *Lyautey in Morocco.* Berkeley: University of California Press.

Scheff, Thomas J. 1968. Negotiating reality: Notes on power in the assessment of responsibility. *Social Problems* 16:3–17.

Schelling, Thomas C. 1956. An essay on bargaining. *American Economic Review* 46:281–306.

Schutz, Alfred. 1964. *Collected papers.* Vol. 2. *Studies in social theory.* The Hague: Martinus Nijhoff.

————. 1967a. *Collected papers.* Vol. 1, *The problem of social reality.* The Hague: Martinus Nijhoff.

————. 1967b. *The phenomenology of the social world.* Evanston, Ill.: Northwestern University Press.

Searle, John. 1969. *Speech acts.* Cambridge: Cambridge University Press.

————. 1979. *Expression and meaning: Studies in the theory of speech acts.* Cambridge: Cambridge University Press.

Serfaty, A. 1969. Le judaïsme marocain et le sionisme. *Souffles,* no. 15:24–37.

Sesonake, Alexander. 1965. Performatives. *Journal of Philosophy* 62:459–68.

Shokeid, Moshe. 1980. Jewish existence in a Berber environment. In *Les relations entre juifs et musulmans en Afrique du Nord, XIXe–XXe Siècles,* ed. Centre National de la Recherche Scientifique, 62–71. Paris: Editions du C.N.R.S.

Shokeid, Moshe, and Shlomo Deshen. 1982. *Distant relations: Ethnicity and politics among Arabs and North African Jews in Israel.* New York: Praeger.

Siegel, James. 1969. *The rope of God.* Berkeley: University of California Press.

Simmel, Georg. 1921. The sociological significance of the "Stranger." In *Introduction to the science of sociology,* ed. Ernest W. Burgess, 322–27. Chicago: University of Chicago Press.

Sinaceur, M. A. 1972. Connaissance des Arabes. *Critique* 28:254–73.

Skinner, Quentin. 1970. Conventions and the understanding of speech acts. *Philosophical Quarterly* 20:118–38.

————. 1971. On performing and explaining linguistic actions. *Philosophical Quarterly* 21:1–21.

————. 1972. Motives, intentions, and interpretation of texts. *New Literary History* 3:393–408.

Smith, Jane I. 1979. The understanding of *nafs* and *rūḥ* in contemporary Muslim considerations of the nature of sleep and death. *Muslim World* 69:151–62.

Smith, Jane Idleman, and Yvonne Yazbeck Haddad. 1981. *The Islamic understanding of death and resurrection.* Albany: State University of New York Press.

Smith, W. Robertson. 1903. *Kinship and marriage in early Arabia.* Boston: Beacon Press.

Smith, Wilfred Cantwell. 1969. Orientation and truth. Lecture in honor of T. Cuyler Young, Program in Near Eastern Studies, Princeton University.

————. 1971. A human view of truth. *Studies in Religion* 1:6–24.

Somekh, Sasson. 1973. *The changing rhythm: A study of Najīb Mahfūz's novels.* Leiden: E. J. Brill.

Stetkevych, Jaroslav. 1970. *The modern Arabic literary language.* Chicago: University of Chicago Press.

Stewart, Charles F. 1964. *The economy of Morocco, 1912–1962.* Cambridge: Harvard University Center for Middle Eastern Studies.

Stillman, Norman A. 1973. Sefrou remnant. *Jewish Social Studies* 35:255–63.

————. 1975a. Muslims and Jews in Morocco: Perceptions, images, stereotypes. In *Proceedings of the seminar on Muslim-Jewish relations in North Africa,* 13–39. New York: World Jewish Congress.

————. 1975b. New attitudes toward the Jew in the Arab world. *Jewish Social Studies* 37:197–204.

————. 1979. *The Jews of Arab lands: A history and source book.* Philadelphia: Jewish Publication Society of America.

————. 1980. L'Experience judéo-marocaine: Un point de vue révisioniste. In *Judaïsme d'Afrique du Nord aux XIXe–XXe Siècles,* ed. Michael Abitbol, 5–36. Jerusalem: Institut Ben-Zvi.

Sudnow, David, ed. 1972. *Studies in social interaction.* New York: Free Press.

Talbi, Mohammed. 1967. Ibn Haldūn et le sense de l'histoire. *Studia Islamica* 26:73–148.

Taylor, Charles. 1971. Interpretation and the sciences of man. *Review of Metaphysics* 25:3–51.

Tessler, Mark A. 1981. Ethnic change and nonassimilating minority status: Jews in Tunisia and Morocco and Arabs in Israel. In *Ethnic Change,* ed. Charles Keyes, 155–97. Seattle: University of Washington Press.

Tritton, A. S. 1971. Man, *nafs, rūh, ʿaql. Bulletin of the School of Oriental and African Studies* 34:491–95.

Tyan, Emile. 1960. *Histoire de l'Organisation judiciaire en pays d'Islam.* 2d ed. Leiden: E. J. Brill.

Vadet, Jean-Claude. 1969. Quelques remarques sur la racine FTN dans le coran et la plus ancienne littérature musulmane. *Revue des études islamiques* (1969):81–101.

Vincent, Joan. 1969. Anthropology and political development. In *Politics and Change,* ed. Colin Leys, 35–63. Cambridge: Cambridge University Press.

Vinogradov, Amal Rassam. 1973. Man's world, woman's place: The politics of sex in North Africa. Typescript.

————. 1974a. *The Ait Ndhir of Morocco: A study of the social transformation of a Berber tribe.* Museum of Anthropology, Anthropological Papers, no. 55. Ann Arbor: University of Michigan.

————. 1974b. French colonialism as reflected in the male-female interaction in Morocco. *Transactions of the New York Academy of Sciences,* series 2, 36:192–99.

Voinot, L. 1948. *Pèlerinages judéo-musulmans du Maroc.* Paris: Editions Larose.

Waismann, Friedrich. 1960. Verifiability. In *Logic and language,* ed. Anthony Flew, 1st ser., 117–44. Oxford: Basil Blackwell.

Waterbury, John. 1972. *North for the trade: The life and times of a Berber merchant.* Berkeley: University of California Press.

Wehr, Hans. 1976. *Arabic-English dictionary*. Ed. J. Milton Cowan. Ithaca, N.Y.: Cornell University Press.

Weir, T. H. 1961. Diya. In *Shorter encyclopaedia of Islam*, 78. *See* Gibb and Kramers 1961.

Wensinck, A. J. 1961. Nīya. In *Shorter encyclopaedia of Islam*, 449–50. *See* Gibb and Kramers 1961.

Westermarck, Edward Alexander. 1926. *Ritual and belief in Morocco*. 2 vols. London: Macmillan.

_____. 1930. *Wit and wisdom in Morocco*. London: George Routledge & Sons.

White, Hayden. 1981. The value of narrativity in the representation of reality. In *On narrative*, ed. W. J. T. Mitchell, 1–23. Chicago: University of Chicago Press.

White, Morton. 1963. The logic of historical narration. In *Philosophy and history*, ed. Sidney Hook, 3–31. New York: New York University Press.

Wilson, Edmund. 1956. *Red, black, blond, and olive*. New York: Oxford University Press.

Wilson, Thomas P. 1970. Conceptions of interaction and forms of sociological explanation. *American Sociological Review* 35:697–710.

Wittgenstein, Ludwig. 1958. *Philosophical investigations*. New York: Macmillan.

Zakya, Daoud. 1976. Analyse des résultats électoraux. *Lamalif*, no. 84:22–29.

Zenner, Walter P. 1980. Censorship and syncretism: Some social anthropological approaches to the study of Middle Eastern Jews. In *Studies in Jewish Folklore*, ed. Frank Talmadge, 377–94. Cambridge, Mass.: Association for Jewish Studies.

Zenner, Walter P., and Shlomo Deshen. 1982. Introduction: The historical ethnology of Middle Eastern Jews. In *Jewish Societies in the Middle East*, ed. Shlomo Deshen and Walter P. Zenner, 1–34. Washington, D.C.: University Press of America.

Index

Note: The boldface number following each foreign term refers to the most complete definition of that term in the text.